LOVE LINDISFARNE

Escape to Northumberland and
lose yourself amongst the stars...

Kimberley Adams

Shy Bairns Publishing

To my mam Miranda, and my nana Millie,
Two of the brightest northern stars
ever to have shone.

CHAPTER 1

I drained the glass of champagne almost before it was poured.

'Whoa there Ellie Nellie, we've got all night!'

'Fill her up Tara.' I grinned, eagerly shoving my glass in front of her.

We were at our office Christmas party, always held in the same charmless, corporate hotel on the North Circular, with more cheese in the songs than you'd ever find in the mini quiches. My dear friend and work colleague looked at me intently, her left eyebrow twitching. I knew this to be a sign that she was tense about something, and I felt my insides squeeze into an even tighter band of anxiety. Had she guessed what I was about to do? I hadn't told a soul, not even my best friend and flatmate Sophie. Somehow, I had actually managed to keep this a secret. I grabbed the bottle from her and necked it like it was lemonade, hoping it would deter the self-doubt. Tara threw her arms around me.

'Ellie, you know I'll always be here for you, don't you?'

'Tara, you're scaring me. You sound all serious.

Is there something you're not telling me?' But before she could answer, her boyfriend Toby strolled across, clumsily crashing into the table because his glasses were steamed up.

'You're late, as usual.' Tara smiled turning to Toby. She'd gently removed his spectacles, polishing them carefully on her best dress, before replacing them on his nose and planting a big kiss on his flushed cheek. I'd been momentarily swept away by the tiny but loving gesture which said so much. Could I imagine my boyfriend Matt doing the same for me and polishing my glasses on his designer shirt? No, I couldn't, not in a million years, but then I didn't wear glasses, so everything was okay – wasn't it? Matt and I had been together for three years and in all that time, I couldn't honestly recall him being big on romantic gestures of any kind.

I left Tara and Toby to it, and made my way to the bar, hastily downing various themed cocktails for Dutch courage, then glancing at my watch went to find Matt who, it would appear, had sampled his way through the Christmas cocktail list too. I dragged him for a drunken dance, neither of us capable of doing anything more adventurous than a shuffle.

On the stroke of the hour, the music had gone quiet as pre-arranged, and a spotlight fell on Matt and I propping each other up on the dance floor. I'd sank down on to bended knee. Matt tried to haul me back up, clearly thinking I had fallen, but like Bambi on ice, his legs splayed, and he promptly ended up next to me on the floor in a drunken heap. This was not going according to plan. Ignoring the sea of faces staring at me like I was certifiable, I pulled out a small red box and flipped it open, its contents shining like the Christmas Star reflecting the light from the glitterball above. Considering it was a ten quid special from Peckham market, purely as a holding token of course, it looked, to my tipsy eyes, pretty bloody impressive. I stared into Matt's glazed eyes, noticing traces of lipstick all over his cheeks, and it wasn't the Santa Baby red that I was wearing. His shirt was crumpled and sticking to his sweaty body, his hair all over the place - and Matt was usually so groomed he put Rylan to shame. Maybe I should have stopped right there, but my alcohol induced psyche wasn't exactly working properly, so I blithely carried on with my plan.

'Matthew James Morton, you are the Yang to my Yin, the star to my sun, er I mean moon, the erm... fish to my chips!' I blurted out the most unromantic of comparisons, unable to remember the other things on my list. By this point I had expected a few gasps from the crowd, the odd tear of joy or sign of a hankie to protect the party mascara, but as I looked around the faces, they continued to stare at us agog, with mouths flapping open like swing bin lids. I caught sight of Tara, who was slowly shaking her head, a horrified expression on her face, and I could see that Toby was holding her back. It almost looked like he was stopping her from rushing across to me.

'Matt,' I continued, 'it's about bloody time we got married.' Hardly the romantic proposal I'd planned, but a) I couldn't remember my speech and b) I needed to hurry this along before one, or both of us, passed out.

Matt looked around at the crowd and fixated on Karen the Cougar, whose eyes were boring holes into us like lasers.

'Erm, I suppose so,' he slurred, and I waited for the cheer to go up from the crowd before I moved on. There was nothing but stony silence, the atmosphere in the room nosediving quicker than Tom Daley at his Olympic best.

'Yes! Yes! Yes!' I shouted, filling the void, somewhat reminiscent of Meg Ryan, except without her sex appeal and with a copious amount of alcohol on board.

'No! No! No!' shrieked Karen the Cougar, rushing onto the dance floor, dropping onto her knees next to us, and tightly wrapping her arms around 'my' fiancé.

At that, a gasp of significant proportions did emerge from the crowd, who continued to focus on us intently. They'd be getting the popcorn out soon.

'He's not marrying you, Ellie. He's already secretly engaged, to me, and at least now we can make it official,' she sneered, turning to Matt. 'Matthew darling, will you marry me?'

Matt's head swivelled from me to her like he was watching a centre court match at Wimbledon, before dropping it into the neutral position and suddenly taking a great interest in his feet.

'Err I do... I mean, I will...' he mumbled, not moving his head nor looking at either of us.

At that, Karen snatched the ring out of my hand and jammed it onto Matt's finger before I knew what was happening. I was having trouble taking everything in, and a quick glance at the faces of the now thinning crowd, all buzzing with conversation, confirmed that they probably knew about this already. It was hardly surprising as we worked together, and you couldn't eat a sly Snickers in Randy Parrot Public Relations without someone knowing about it. Except naïve, gullible me it would appear.

Suddenly Tara and Toby appeared, took an elbow each and hauled me to my feet.

'Engaged? You utter cow!' she spat at Karen. 'I thought we agreed that you would keep your fat mouth shut until the *missing link* there,' she nodded her head towards Matt, 'did the honourable thing and told her himself.'

Tara knew. Toby knew. They all knew. Big hot tears rolled down my cheeks and I felt them splashing onto my toes through my new silver sandals, bought especially for my engagement.

'Come on Ellie Nellie, let's get you to your room,' said Tara gently. I glanced at Matt and Karen, the sanctimonious cow beaming at him like she was the archangel flipping Gabriel, and I couldn't help it, I grabbed the nearest drink and threw it over the pair of them before I allowed myself to be led away from them, preserving what little dignity I had left.

We got back to the room. Tara sat me in a chair and immediately sprang into action.

'Toby, get every last thing belonging to that tosser into his case and take it to that cow's room, or better still, just lob it out of the window.'

She gave me a big glass of water, kneeled in front of me and gently wiped away my tears with a towel, and looked directly into my eyes.

'Ellie darling, I'm so, so sorry. I swear that I've only known about whatever those two have been up to for a few days. I overheard Anna and Natalie talking about them in the loo at work, and it was obvious that they had only just found out too. I demanded to meet the pair of them and told the prize prick in no uncertain terms to be upfront and to tell you straight away. I told her to keep quiet until he had done the decent thing for once, the snake that he is. He said he didn't want to spoil Christmas for you, and the holiday you have almost had to sell a kidney to pay for. Bloody coward was just delaying the inevitable, but I went with that. Had I any idea what you were about to do tonight, I would have stopped it, I promise. We love you Ellie Nellie and all I was trying to do was cause you the least pain possible.'

'Tara's telling you the truth Ellie,' said Toby, patting me on the shoulder like I was a Labrador. 'She came in from work on Wednesday and I thought that she might have a stroke she was so angry. We both knew that you were looking forward to Christmas and had the trip to the Maldives planned, and we thought that you may as well enjoy the holiday of a lifetime before the, err, you know what, hit the fan.'

I couldn't help a wry smile. Toby was just so proper and the idea of saying a profanity was alien to him.

'Did you tell Sophie? I sniffed.

'No, no-one, I promise. Are we good Ellie? I'd hate for that pair of brainless imbeciles to come between us.'

I reached out and hugged her.

'Tara, you and Toby are two of my best friends, part of our inner circle, and we are more than good, and

I'm going to need my friends. How could he do this to me? Maybe he thought I was serious with the cheap ring?' I wailed.

'Ellie, you're in shock. We can talk about this now, but I think it would be better if you sobered up a little bit and got some sleep, then you might be able to think straight. Toby, make Ellie a cup of strong coffee and I'll help her get sorted for bed. We'll all help you get through this Ellie. We love you loads, remember that.'

They left me tucked up in bed with a toilet roll on the pillow next to me to dry my eyes. Not exactly the bed companion I had imagined on my engagement night, and I'd already cried every last iota of moisture out of my body, so much so that I was in danger of becoming a dried-out husk.

I switched off the light, cuddled the toilet roll, somehow managed to squeeze out a few more tears, and hoped that sleep would swallow me up into a big, black, dreamless hole.

CHAPTER 2

Of course, I couldn't sleep. My mind was whirring round like a washing machine on full spin. I switched on the bedside lamp and looked at the time on my phone, not even midnight. Maybe one more teensy little drink might help knock me out. All I needed right now was a quick sleigh ride into oblivion, so I looked through the mini bar, chose a small bottle of brandy – it is known to be good for shock after all – and downed it in one. But the longed-for oblivion didn't happen, so I went on to Plan B. Distraction therapy. I lay on the bed and looked at my phone, ready to vent my spleen on social media, but a picture of a sad little dog wearing a Santa hat caught my eye. A cute whiskery face and big brown eyes beseeched me to read the advert next to it. I squinted to focus, reading the words which were doing the rhumba on the screen.

'Email Santa Paws and tell him what you want for Christmas. A £2 donation per email will go to 'Dogs are for Life' which will help me and my furry friends throughout the year, and not just at Christmas. Thank you and Happy Christmas, love Nacho x'

I clicked the pay button and drunkenly began to type with my one remaining steady finger, already appreciating that this may not be the best time to be sending messages to anyone, never mind Santa! However, I blithely carried on...

To: santapaws@dogsareforlife.com
From: ellienellie@fastermail.com

Dear Santa Paws,
I'd like a giant bottle of gin and a new life please.
Yours, Ellie.

***

The next morning, I woke up to my head banging and my email pinging. Where was I and who let that Mariachi band in? I hauled myself up and looked at my surroundings, which gave away no clues, as it could have been any bland, boring room in any budget hotel anywhere in the world. Then, like a huge wave rolling in, it all came crashing back: the party, Matt and Karen, the emails and the very cute little dog. I stretched around looking for my phone and through one eye, squinted tentatively at the message flashing in front of me, expecting it to be from Matt begging my forgiveness, but it wasn't.

To: ellienellie@fastermail.com
From: santapaws@dogsareforlife.com

Dear Ellie,

There may be some difficulty with your request for gin. Firstly, most of my customers are too young, there's not much call for it. Secondly, if I had it in stock, the elves would no doubt help themselves and run amok at our busiest time of the year. The new life might also prove problematic. I may have to watch some videos on how to gift wrap such an item.

Thanks for supporting Dogs are For Life.

Santa Paws.

I felt a hot flush of embarrassment wash over me as I recalled the previous night; my poorly timed and, quite frankly, mega-stupid proposal (hindsight is indeed a marvellous thing.) I recalled throwing a *Sleigh Bellini* all over Matt and Karen and calling them 'elfish bastards before Tara and Toby propelled me to my room. And as for the dodgy emails to Santa Paws – opening my heart to a total stranger – oh my God, what was I thinking? I buried my head under the covers, wishing it would all just go away. It wouldn't. So, I decided I could at least put the email situation right.

To: santapaws@dogsareforlife.com
From: ellienellie@fastermail.com

Dear Santa Paws,

Thank you very much for your reply and I'm sorry about the many embarrassing messages I sent you. I know you must be terribly busy and have lots of little people to email instead of pandering to a big kid like me! In my defence, I'd had the worst night of my entire life. I'm now off gin completely – in fact, all alcohol – so perhaps a nice gift box of tea and sympathy?!

Yours, Ellie.

From: santapaws@dogsareforlife.com
To: ellienellie@fastermail.com

Dear Ellie,

Please don't worry about your messages. Santa Paws has a strict code of discretion. I keep millions of secrets about gifts every year! As you are my most generous customer (your considerable number of donations add up to enough to help Nacho and his furry friends have a fantastic Christmas), I'd like to invite you to our doggy Christmas party where you can meet Nacho. You seem to have taken a real shine to him. You never know, you may like us enough to become a volunteer and start that new life you asked for. Then I would also feel like I have

fulfilled my brief at giving everyone the Christmas gift they want.

Yours, Santa Paws.

To: santapaws@dogsareforlife.com
From: ellienellie@fastermail.com

Thanks so much, I would like that and want to support the fantastic work you do. Please send me the details and I will do my best to be there.

Yours, Ellie.

To: ellienellie@fastermail.com
From: santapaws@dogsareforlife.com

Wonderful. It's a little earlier than usual this year due to other commitments. I hope it's not too short notice for you. It's this afternoon at 2.30 p.m. Our address and full details of our charity, so you can check our validity, can be found on our website. I look forward to meeting you Ellie, and just to let you know, we have a fantastic raffle, so do bring some change!
Yours, Santa Paws.

Today? Maybe the timing wasn't great, but then I felt like I needed to keep focused. It had just gone 8 a.m. so there was plenty of time to sneak out of the hotel without having to face anyone, go home, and have a cry on my best friend Sophie's shoulder. Then it would be time to get ready to go and meet Santa Paws, who in my imagination had morphed into some gorgeous hero straight out of the pages of a romcom. Distraction therapy indeed; however, he could turn out to be a Hollywood A lister and I wouldn't be interested. Unless he had a cold nose and a waggy tail, he was out of luck!

***

I stepped into the flat, dropped my bag, and wiped away yet another tear that trickled down my cheek. Those bad boys just kept on rolling.

'Soph?' I tapped gently at her door. 'Are you awake?'

Her boyfriend Jake's head stuck out from behind the bedroom door.

'She's having a lie in, exhausted you know, wink, wink!' He grinned.

I did know but could hardly muster a smile.

'Hey Ellie girl, you look like death warmed up. What's wrong? Hang on, you go and put the kettle on, and I'll be through in a minute.'

Jake reappeared wearing Sophie's Christmas onesie. It fit where it touched as it was far too small for him, but that would never worry Jake. He was ultra-confident in his own skin. I handed him a mug of coffee and he sat down at the kitchen table.

'Ellie, your eyes look like you've gone ten rounds with Tyson Fury. What's happened, or would you rather we wake Sophie up?'

'I'm short of time, anyway, so just let her sleep. I'll explain, then you can tell her and ask her to try and be home this evening so we can catch up. It's probably safer if I tell you first anyway. You know how volatile Sophie can be!'

I told Jake the whole sorry tale.

'Tosser,' he growled, after I'd told him the full shebang. 'I never warmed to him Ellie. You know that already as I've been upfront about it in the past. He never struck me as the Homer to your Marge if you get my drift girl.'

'Or the Mr Darcy to my Miss Bennet.' I sniffed, suddenly remembering my script from last night. Thinking about it now, was he ever my Mr Darcy?

Matt and I had first met in the kitchen area

of Randy Parrot Public Relations Agency. It had to be the stupidest name of any PR agency ever, but Randy Parrot (The Third, which brings into question the sanity of his lineage) was indeed the real name of our American CEO. He insisted on the name, citing that once heard, never forgotten, and it appeared he was right – and it hadn't seemed to dent their reputation as a leader in the field. Saying, 'Good Morning, Randy Parrot,' was never easy however, even on the best of days, and I really took exception to some of the straplines – '*Always on the job*' being a prime example. It was my first proper role, and Matt was already established as an Account Executive. We had both reached out for the last remaining *Jaffa Cake* (which he got to first) and it was full-moon, half-moon and total eclipse before the day was out, when I found the little circle of orangey delight on my desk, with a post-it asking me out on a date.

'So, what are you up to today, Jake?' I asked, desperately trying to move the subject away from a painful trip down Memory Lane.

He drained the last of his coffee, stood up and headed towards the door.

'Need to get a wriggle on and get back home to collect my gear. Playing squash at midday with Sebastian the Snout, right posh boy wheeler dealer. He's always good for a few financial tips. That giant conk of his could sniff out a turd in a perfume factory. Got to be up and on it, Ellie – in it to win it girl! Now you listen to me. You are a babe, you deserve far better than that cheating bar steward, so you get up and back on that 'orse girl, and I'll see you soon.'

I went to get ready for my trip to the dog sanctuary, glancing out of the window at the busy street below. Sophie and I lived in Peckham, above a barber shop. It was affordable (just), spacious, and even had a small garden. The place was in need of an overhaul, but it was home, and we had both grown to love the vibrancy of the area. Aside from the Del Boy jokes about us living in *Nelson Mandela House* and drinking in the *Nag's Head*, it had suited us well over the last seven years, but change was coming. Sophie had been staying with Jake more often and they had told me a couple of weeks ago that they were moving in together after Christmas. I was so happy for them, and stupidly assumed that maybe Matt would move in here with me. I couldn't even contemplate what was going to happen now.

It took me ages to try and disguise the dark circles under my eyes and I eventually gave up, giving my blonde hair a quick brush and applying a slick of lip-gloss. My hangover needed coffee, like really needed it, so en route to the bus stop, I went to see Stanislaw and ordered a double strength Americano from his converted yellow three-wheeler coffee cart. He parked outside of *Boycie's Bargains*, a second-hand shop that Sophie and I had almost furnished our entire flat from when we first arrived. Stanislaw was drop dead gorgeous and had the sexiest of accents you could literally melt to, but then his boyfriend Aleksy wasn't too shabby either.

They were part of our inner circle, the gang of eight: Sophie and Jake, Tara and Toby, Stan and Alek and me and… I gulped, the realisation that we were now a seven hitting me like an express train.

'Wowzer Ellie, you look like sheeeet this morning!' Stan peered at me whilst steaming the dark aromatic liquid into the cup.

'Just say it how it is, Stan,' I mumbled, before yet another fat tear dripped down my nose and on to my chin.

'Oh, my gorgeous girl, what is wrong?'

He put down the cup and enveloped me in a big bear hug, his 6' 2" muscular frame cuddling me as gently as if I was a china doll.

'It's Matt,' I wailed. 'He's been cheating on me, and he's engaged to Karen the Cougar now.'

'Karen the who? Ellie, you are making no sense, how can he be engaged to someone else so quickly?'

'I don't know how long it's been going on. I haven't got much time now as I've got to catch the bus to a charity event, so I'll tell you all about it later.'

'Of course,' he said, lowering me to the pavement and handing me the cup. I offered him the money.

'Absolutely not. I won't take money off my heartbroken friend. Please, take some advice from me, which also comes free. You are one of the kindest and most genuine people I know, and worth far more than that snake.' Yet another of the Matt fan club, it would seem. 'One more thing Ellie, when you are on the bus, put some blusher on your cheeks – you are the colour of a custard cream!'

As I took my seat, the phone began to ring. It was Sophie. I really didn't want to give my broken heart an airing on the packed bus, so sent her a text.

Soph, on the bus and it's rammed so can't really speak. Call you soon, love you. Xx

Ellie, I have a particular skill set. I will look for him and I will kill him, you do understand that don't you? X

Hey Liam Neeson, do you need any help? Xx

No need, the pleasure will be all mine. Now why are you on the bus and where are you going? Jake mentioned some charity thing? X

I'm off to see a man in a red coat about a dog. It's a long story xx

A dog? Ellie, I've spoken to Tara. She said you were very drunk and upset, which is understandable. Are you sure you're okay babe? This seems a strange thing for you to be doing, quite out of character? x

I'm sort of okay Soph, just numb, but I wanted to keep occupied. I'm going to a Christmas charity thing at a dog sanctuary. Like I said, long story. Xx

Dogs? Ellie babe, you don't know a Dachshund from a Doberman. Please don't tell me you are going to replace that two-legged mongrel for one with four legs?

No, well maybe, that's not such a bad idea, although we can't keep dogs at the flat. You know I've always loved animals of any kind xx

You can tell all later. Inner circle support group here tonight, curry from Dehlicattesen and all the love you can shake a waggy tail at! Call me anytime, you hear me? Love you x

There was also a text from Tara.

Morning Ellie. Hope you are okay. Reception gave me your message about going home early. Toby and I are still at the hotel, but at least that pair of vile specimens have had the decency to disappear – Timbuktu wouldn't be far enough. Give me a ring as soon as you want to talk, otherwise see you tonight. Tara xx

There was nothing from Matt. Deep down, I hadn't really expected there to be, and I didn't know whether to be sad or glad about that. This was all unchartered territory for me and until the numbness had thawed, I couldn't even begin to decide how I should be feeling.

CHAPTER 3

Tentatively, I pushed open the door in the foyer of the dog sanctuary. A very smiley girl wearing a spotty dog suit greeted me warmly. She led me through several locked doors before we arrived at a large room, full of people in various festive costumes and Christmas jumpers. The room had been dressed in dog related decorations. A big tree stood in the corner with dog biscuits attached instead of baubles, and I felt my foot tapping along to Who Let The Dogs Out – the background music was all dog related tunes. It looked like some of the adopters had returned with their dogs as there was an eclectic mix of pooches – most in fancy dress – and a hum of happy chatter jostled with the playlist. It was difficult to feel miserable in this environment.

A man about my dad's age, wearing a bone shaped bow tie, smiled at me, and I noticed his name badge – *Jerry, Centre Manager.*

'Hi Jerry,' I said, holding out my hand to shake his. 'I'm Ellie. Santa Paws and Nacho invited me.'

'Ah yes, our leading email donor. Santa Paws told me all about you—'

I could feel my cheeks burning, wondering

just how much Santa Paws had told him. I had read all the emails and, it was fair to say, I hadn't held back from giving it chapter and verse. I blamed it on the cocktails... and the champagne... and Matt. I would never otherwise have entered into an online confessional with a stranger, but he was just *so* nice.

'I'm so pleased you could come. Let me get you a drink – no alcohol I'm afraid!'

'Suits me fine.' I smiled. 'Although it was alcohol that got me here in a roundabout way, I'm never drinking again – ever!'

He grinned, handing me an orange juice.

'So, you like dogs Ellie?'

'Yes, love them, although I haven't ever had one of my own, or any other animal come to that. Unless you count two weeks over Christmas once, when my mother relented and said I could look after Buzz, the class guinea pig, but that ended in disaster.'

He raised a quizzical eyebrow at me.

'It got out of its cage and escaped,' I explained. 'Chewed through the cable on the oven, which was cooking the turkey. There was a bang, and then no guinea pig... or turkey come to that. Mum blamed me for leaving the cage open, but I blamed Dad for not getting round to sorting the electrics. We had just moved into the house, and he knew they were suspect. No-one else was hurt by the way. Only in the sense that we ended up with sandwiches for the first Christmas lunch in our new home, and I cried all the way through *The Polar Express*.'

'Buzz went out with a bang then,' said Jerry,

his mouth twitching, desperately trying not to laugh. Regaining his composure as befitting of a man who spent his life rescuing animals not frying them, he smiled kindly. 'I'm sure it was no-one's fault really. Moving house is such a stressful time. What happened when you got back to school?'

'The whole class hated me for about a week, until Priscilla arrived. She was a longhaired guinea pig and far more attractive than poor old Buzz, who was as goofy as his namesake, Buzz Lightyear. Anyway, that's my experience of caring for animals, but I still love all of them. I hope I would do a better job these days if I ever got the chance. I'd love a dog when the time is right. I fell for Nacho the minute I saw his gorgeous little face.'

'Follow me Ellie, let me introduce you to Santa Paws and Nacho. I believe they are looking forward to meeting you.'

I trotted behind Jerry, who pointed towards Santa Paws, who was sitting on a huge throne, surrounded by bags of gifts. And there, by his side, resplendent on a stool, atop a red velvet cushion, was Nacho, dressed as a tiny little reindeer. I felt yet more tears, but of a different kind, welling up as I looked at his big brown eyes peeping out from beneath the padded antlers that were wobbling about on his spikey golden-brown head. There was no doubt about it, I was well and truly smitten. I peered across towards Santa Paws. It was difficult to tell under all of the facial fluff, but I didn't think he was quite the romcom idol I had half imagined.

'Santa Paws is our patron, Lord Bamburgh, and since the email initiative began a few years ago, he insists that he deals with all the messages himself.'

'So that's who I sent all my messages to?' I stuttered with shame.

'Yes, every single one. But don't worry Ellie, Lord Bamburgh is a model of discretion, so anything you said to Santa Paws stays with Santa Paws! Come on, let me introduce you.'

We approached the throne, and a pair of bright blue eyes peeped out from behind a mass of white fluff.

'Ellie, I presume?' he enquired in a cut glass accent.

'The one and only,' I squeaked in return, my cheeks the colour of his robe.

He carefully lifted Nacho off the stool and gestured for me to sit down. As soon as I was settled, he placed the tiny dog on my lap. Nacho looked up at me with bright enquiring eyes, then stood up on his spindly back legs and, with one tiny paw on each of my shoulders, shoved his tiny fuzzy face in front of mine, and looked deep into my eyes as if he was searching for my very soul. Clearly satisfied with what he saw, he gave my nose a delicate lick, lay down on my lap and sighed contentedly.

'I think you have a fan, Ellie,' said Santa Paws.

'Same goes for him. He truly is the cutest little dog I've ever seen. I feel like it's kismet, you know, fate bringing us together,' I said sincerely. 'Problem is, I'm not in a position to keep him at the moment. It wouldn't be fair.' I sniffed, and then, unable to stop myself, burst into floods of tears again.

Santa Paws handed me a silk handkerchief.

'Clean as a whistle.' He smiled. 'Don't be afraid to use it. I have so many of those – the perils of being regarded as the man who has everything, I'm afraid – but they have their uses! Feeling better?' he asked, after I had calmed down.

'Yes thanks. I've been feeling all at sea today thanks to the hangover, and erm, my break-up. I can't begin to tell you how sorry I'm for sending those emails. It was the alcohol talking. I read them all back and I'm mortified,' I said, staring at Nacho to avoid eye contact with Lord Bamburgh. 'Offloading to a total stranger online is completely out of character for me and to say I'm embarrassed is an understatement.'

'Ellie, what I read were the musings of a young woman. Okay, maybe more like ramblings at times,' he said, smiling. 'It was unforgiveable what that young man did to you and hardly any wonder you are feeling delicate.'

'It puzzles me what I ever saw in someone who could be so callous. When I think back, there were the odd occasions where he had been very selfish, and I had forgiven him and swept it under the carpet.'

'Well Ellie, it sounds to me like you could do with a break away from it all. I was going to suggest you coming here to the centre to volunteer, but after talking with you, I think I have a new plan. Let's have a little Christmas cheer now – I have the gift you asked for. Then perhaps we can meet after I have fulfilled my Santa Paws duties and I can explain in more detail.'

'Do I open this now or on Christmas Day?' I asked, taking the gift from him.

'You have Santa Paws' permission to open it now,' he said gravely.

Nacho, on hearing the rustle of the paper, jumped off my knee and helped me unwrap the parcel, his tiny teeth nipping the ribbon. Inside was a hamper of beautiful teas from *Fortnum and Mason.*

'You asked for tea and sympathy, so here is your tea. As for sympathy, I come from a long line of Bamburghs, and our family motto is *Vi et Virtute* – By Strength and Valour. I was indoctrinated from an early age to face problems head on. However, as a father and grandfather myself, I have learned there is always a place for sympathy and kindness when the need arises. Whilst you are waiting for me,' he said, scooping Nacho into his arms and passing him to me, 'I'm sure this little chap could do with a walk around the exercise area. If you see Becky over there – she's the one dressed as a Dalmatian – she will show you the ropes.'

I took Nacho from him and clutched his warm little body, which was quivering with delight, his feathery tail wagging furiously, and we went off in search of a spotty dog.

CHAPTER 4

It was gone 7 p.m. by the time I got back to the flat. As soon as I got through the door, I was met by the enticing aroma of one of Mrs Kapoor's finest curries drifting from the kitchen.

'Hi, I'm back,' I yelled, pulling off my coat and scarf, throwing down my bag and carefully placing my tea hamper on the hall table.

'In here!' Sophie yelled back from the living room.

'What's all this?' I asked, as I entered the room, gazing around at my best friends, all staring back at me with concerned expressions on their faces. There was a bottle of Champagne in an ice bucket, tealights dotted around, and Sophie had even tidied up – and she *never* tidied anything *ever*.

'Just wanted to make it nice for you. We all chipped in for the bottles of bubbly, to either commiserate with you, or celebrate...' she tailed off.

'Err, I've given up alcohol,' I said primly, ignoring her comment, and thinking it was still less than twenty-four hours since I'd got seriously drunk and vowed never to do it again.

'Well, this can be your final indulgence.

Anyway, it's only a few glasses of fizz, it doesn't count.' She laughed.

'How are you, Ellie?' asked Tara. 'I thought you might have rung me today, but Sophie said you had gone to some dog thing?'

'Well, at least she hasn't brought one back, unless it's hiding in her bag!' quipped Sophie, handing me a glass of bubbly.

'Ellie, we are all here for you. Do you want to talk about it, or we just get drunk and call him all the bad names you teach Stan and me?' Aleksky smiled.

'Let's just eat. I'm starving, and I can tell you all about my day out.'

'Err Ellie, you seem surprisingly chipper for someone who has just been right royally dumped,' said Sophie raising an eyebrow.

'I'm not, believe me, but on the bus back, I decided that this is a new beginning and to start it positively and not let that pair of... of... well, you know, cause me more pain than they have done already.'

'That's the spirit,' piped Toby. 'Be a Boudica!'

Toby was a historian and one of those people who know a lot about everything. He and Tara were chalk and cheese, but it just worked.

I told them the whole sorry story of the emails to Santa Paws leading to my visit to *Dogs Are For Life*.

'After reading my emails, Santa Paws was going to suggest I join the charity as a volunteer, walking the dogs and the like, which was a great idea, but after talking, he came up with something else entirely. He said maybe I needed to get away from my job – and Matt and Karen – for a while, get some fresh air and recharge the batteries. Turns out some people he knows are going to New York. I'm not sure who, because it was all quite surreal, and I didn't really take it all in, but their daughter has just had her first baby. There are a number of animals that they have rescued over time, and he said they would appreciate some help looking after them whilst they are away.'

'What kind of animals? Please God, no guinea pigs!' guffawed Sophie.

'Not sure what animals,' I admitted. 'But what really clinched it was he said I could take Nacho with me – that's the little dog I saw online – and when I come back to London, he would stay with the family, but I'm not planning on coming back. I'm packing in my job, and I'm going next Saturday, when they have had time to check me out.'

'You are what?' spluttered Sophie.

Six pairs of eyes bored into me, and I was in danger of turning into a colander.

'I met with Santa Paws, Lord Bamburgh, after he had finished dishing out the gifts. He's a lovely chap.'

'I bet he is,' muttered Jake under his breath.

'Santa Paws – I mean Lord Bamburgh – is married with three grown up kids, and he's a grandad.'

'Ellie, don't you think you are being a little hasty? What do you know about animals? You've had a nasty shock and should really consider this carefully when you're thinking straight. Maybe go for the few weeks on offer if you must, like an extended holiday, but is there really any need to give up your job and the flat?'

'Yes, there is. Sophie, we've talked about the flat for the last month. I know you and Jake are moving in together and this whole Matt thing has probably made things easier, in that we can give up the lease straight away.'

'Jake and I told you we would help with the rent until you got yourself a new flatmate, one that we could choose together. I'm not having anyone taking my place as your bestie.'

'I know, and I appreciate it Soph, but whatever happens, I won't be going back to Randy flipping Parrot, so I probably won't need to be in central London.'

I looked around the room and they all stared back at me expectantly, waiting for me to continue.

'I thought about things on the way home. I've clung on to familiarity like a Z lister clings on to fame. My job, which I really don't like and that's aside from Matt and Karen both working there. This flat, which you have tried to encourage us to move from for yonks Soph. Let's face it, it's really rather tired around the edges, but I resisted. And of course, Matt, who after about the first few months of our relationship, was not someone I should have stayed with all this time. It's time to call a halt and break out.' I took a deep breath.

'If you're really sure, it's your choice babe, and you know you can come and stay with Jake and me if you need to – anytime.'

'So, where do these people live? You said he was posh, so presumably they are too. Surrey or the Cotswolds maybe?' asked Tara, her left eyebrow twitching frantically.

'Somewhere called Northumberland.'

'Where? Never heard of it. Is it in Scotland?' gasped Sophie.

'Not sure, not heard of it either. It's north somewhere… obviously.'

'Like York? Remember, we went there to Georgia's hen do, lovely place, although in the back of bloody beyond. Took ages on the train I recall.'

'Soph, it was only two hours, but I do believe it's the furthest north we have ever been.'

'It's the last county of England, one stop short of falling right off the top of the country if Scotland wasn't there to catch it,' said Toby. 'Fantastic place, so much history, the Romans, the Vikings…'

'Okay Toby, we get it,' said Tara, cutting him off before we got chapter and verse.

'Oh my God,' squealed Sophie, looking at a map on her tablet. 'That's millions of miles away. Look, there's Newcastle.'

'*Geordie Shore!*' we both shouted excitedly.

'Ant and Dec,' threw in Tara.

'Alan Shearer,' said Jake.

'Who?' asked Stanislaw and Aleksy in unison.

'All those hunky Geordies,' giggled Sophie.

'Furthest thing from my mind right now Soph.'

'If I may be so bold Ellie, it's precisely what you need – a right good seeing to from a sexy Viking, all flowing blonde locks and muscles. Someone like that will sweep you off your feet and drag you off to see his longboat and take you to Valhalla.'

'I hope not! I think that's when you're dead. Wait a minute,' I said, pointing to the screen, 'Newcastle isn't even in Northumberland. It's in a place called Tyne and Wear.'

'The orange splodge which is Northumberland is huge. How do you know which bit you are going to?' asked Jake.

'I don't, but Santa Paws is really called Lord Bamburgh, so let's google him and see if we can find him. He did say where I was going wasn't too far from where he lives.' I typed in Lord Bamburgh, which it turned out, was spelt nothing like it was pronounced.

'Oh. My. God!' shouted Sophie, peering at the screen. 'That is Santa Paw's house... or should I say, castle?' Seven pairs of eyes stared at the screen. My first glimpse of Northumberland and it was mind blowing. Bamburgh Castle was perched precariously on top of a large hill, totally dominating the landscape, and overlooking the coast below. It was huge, with towers that reached endlessly up towards the bright turquoise sky, which was dotted with fluffy clusters of white clouds. The castle had a wall around it, no doubt to protect it from invaders in bygone ages, and looked foreboding, yet at the same time managed to look stunningly beautiful. This was no Disney fairy-tale castle; it was a grey fortress of substantial proportions, yet tinged in pink as caught by the light, and looked like it might topple into the aquamarine sea at any minute. A silver sand beach reflected the light and stretched away from the castle in both directions and, most surprisingly, was almost deserted. The whole scene looked like a film set, somehow unreal.

'Wow, just wow, it's utterly amazing,' said Sophie.

'Don't get carried away. That's not where I'm going,' I said. 'Probably to some nearby cottage which will be tiny without any mains electricity or running water.'

'Well, at least we now know you are probably going to be as far north as it's nearly possible to be in England,' said Tara, phone in hand, looking up facts about Northumberland as I gazed dreamily at the photograph of the castle. 'It says here that it's fifty miles between Bamburgh and Newcastle. Apparently, Northumberland has seventy castles. It's got fewer people than any other county, the darkest skies where you can see the brightest stars, a massive wall built by some Roman soldiers, and Hogwarts is there. Maybe it's not such a bad place to go for a break away from it all.'

'It sounds like one big empty space to me,' muttered Sophie.

'Not to me,' said Toby. 'It's a historian's dream

and hopefully we can come and visit.'

'Not a bad place at all.' I nodded, already mesmerised by the beauty in the one photo I had looked at, and sounding far more confident than I felt, and certainly not about to let them see how trepidatious I felt about going somewhere so remote and far away on my own.

CHAPTER 5

'Right Ellie Nellie, there's only us here now. Tell me how you really are?' said Sophie as she closed the door on our friends.

We slumped in our respective seats – Sophie her full length of 5'2" on the two-seater sofa, me and my 5'7 legs outstretched on the overstuffed armchair we found in a skip when we first moved in – we both sighed.

'Suppose I'm still numb Sophie. I had no idea what was going on, nor for how long, but I know that things have been very rocky between Matt and me for a long time. I'm not sure he ever really loved me, you know.'

'And did you really love him?'

'Good question. I think I did at the beginning but it's back to the familiarity thing. I just couldn't let go. I think it might have something to do with the time my dad left my mum for that tennis instructor. It affected me really badly at the time, and whilst it wasn't for long and he was soon back, I've always been prone to cling on as change is so scary.'

'Ellie, I hope you're not hoping that because your dad came back, Matt might do the same? That's not to say he won't, but would it be right? It was different back in your parents' day. For one thing, no social media shoving stuff you would otherwise be blissfully unaware of in your face. By the way, have you seen your socials today?'

'Not had time... scared to look... why?'

She came and perched on the edge of my chair, phone in hand.

'Are you sure you want to see?'

'Yes, like you say, there's no hiding these days, so I may as well get it over with.'

There on Karen's feed was a photo of her and Matt, outside of an expensive Jewellery shop. They must have gone straight there from the hotel. The caption read: 'Whoop! Whoop! He said yes and thought I deserved a 'proper' ring!'

'So sorry babe, that's just twisting the knife.'

'Just seals it for me Sophie, that is beyond cruel, she's having a swipe at my joke ring, isn't she? What a cow. So, in answer to your previous question, no! I'm not hoping Matt comes back, they're welcome to each other. Incidentally, did any of you actually like him, Soph?' I whispered, kind of knowing the answer already.

'Honestly Ellie, I think it was easier for us on the outside looking in to see that he wasn't right for you, especially lately. He'd always been on the periphery, never fully got into our inner circle, never seemed to want to, even after all the time you were together. He was so penny-pinching as well, nearly always leaving it to you to foot the bill, and Jake especially can't tolerate that. That's not being sexist Ellie, it's about sharing, and we knew Matt was paid more than you. We all agreed though that he was your choice, you'd been together years, and we had the utmost confidence that things would either swing round for the better, or you would eventually see the Matt we saw and dump him. I don't think any of us thought he would stoop as low as what he has though, and never thought for a minute that you would propose to him. Tell me babe, what on earth was going through your head?'

I looked at her, my eyes welling up.

'Things have been very difficult lately. Matt had become increasingly distant, and I stupidly thought it was because he was feeling guilty because he couldn't afford to buy me an engagement ring. We had discussed getting engaged a while back, but it never happened, so I thought I would take the bull by the horns, with a joke ring. I thought he would be happy, and everything would work out from then on.'

'Oh Ellie.' She gave me a big hug. 'And what about the all-singing first-class holiday to the Maldives?'

I shuddered. I'd almost forgotten about that amid all of the drama. We were supposed to be going in under a week.

'Was that another of your attempts to salvage things?'

'Yes, it was,' I admitted, my face flaring in embarrassment. 'I don't suppose we'll get any of our money back now.'

What I didn't tell Sophie was that I had paid for the entire cost of the holiday as Matt said he was maxed out. It had taken nearly every penny of what was left of my inheritance from Granny Joan, which was supposed to be towards a deposit on a house. Our house. The rest of my nest egg had been 'loaned' to Matt over time, who always had a sob story about not being able to afford something or other, and stupidly, I had never learned to say no. I now knew exactly why he had been so hard up recently. It was glinting right there, in front of my face, on Karen the Cougar's finger, and probably mainly paid for by me, and now I was broke. I knew if I divulged about the debt to Soph, she would firstly want to go and rip Matt's head off and demand he pay me back, then, she would do everything she could to persuade me to keep my job and stay until it was sorted out and I'd got the money back. Maybe she would be right, but knowing how long that would take, probably an eternity, it just wasn't going to happen. I had enough left to get me through until the new year without a salary coming in if I was careful, and hopefully Matt would eventually do the right thing – for once.

'I'm never going back to him Soph, so don't worry. In fact, the new Ellie isn't up for a long-term relationship with anyone. Quite frankly, I don't think I'll be interested in a serious relationship ever again! I've never played the field before, so maybe it's time to start, casual is the way forward – better late than never, eh?'

'Erm, Ellie babe, you don't strike me as the love 'em and leave 'em type! And incidentally, are you hoping to start this version of the new you in Northumberland? You'll be lucky to find anyone up there in the middle of nowhere, never mind a field full to choose between.'

'Hey, don't burst my bubble already, it's about time I had some fun! Anyway Miss Olatunji, let's not waste anymore breath talking about Matt the Pratt.'

'Twat more like,' she guffawed.

'We've been sitting in this exact position for seven years Soph. Obviously not all the time mind, which would be odd!'

'Yes, you on that flea-bitten chair and me on Ikea's finest, and even then, second-hand from *Boycie's Bargains*. Remember when we came here Ellie, not two pennies to rub together and full of dreams of taking London by storm?'

'I do, it seems just like it was yesterday. We were twenty years old Soph, ready to party hard and get discovered, you as a top florist and me as a... as a... I don't think I ever decided what I really wanted to be. I know now it's not working in PR!' I laughed.

'I should have stuck to Plan A. Flowers are far more fragrant than the smelly feet I deal with day in day out! We did good though girl, even if we didn't quite realise our dreams, although still time.' She smiled.

She filled up our glasses and we clinked.

'To us! You are my bestest friend, Ellie Nellie, my twin, my soul-girl. I never thought it would be me to meet *'the one'* first, you know. When you met Matt, I thought that was it, you were on your way to a life of Domestos bliss.'

'It's domestic you goof!'

'Is it? Well, I tell you what, I could bleach his testicles for the way he's treated you and seriously, you are *way* too good for him, and I think I would have kicked him to the kerb a long time ago. Prick. Anyhow, I love Jake. I really, truly, absolutely do.'

Her face adopted a shy smile of Diana-esque proportions.

'He is my one, and I even like his ginger pubes, so there.'

I burst out laughing, tears running down my cheeks for the umpteenth time that day.

'Too much information, Sophie,'

'It's going to be a wrench leaving you and our cosy flat, especially now when you need me the most. The timing stinks.'

'Shove over Soph,' I said, standing up, legs as wobbly as a newly born foal. I was drunk – again. I plonked on the sofa beside her, and we had a big hug.

'You look super-hot, you know,' she said, leaning back to stare at my face. 'Just like Snow White's red apple, all shiny and round.'

'An apple? You're comparing me to the most boring fruit in the bowl?' I said indignantly.

'Not just any old apple,' retorted Sophie. 'An irresistible temptress of an apple. If I'd said you looked like a Granny Smith, you'd really have something to complain about!'

'Let you off then. I can live with being an irresistible temptress! You look, well as per usual you look amazing, even if your eyes have taken on the appearance of a bloodshot panda. I'm delighted for you Sophie. I love Jake too, plat... plat... you know like that thing... he is your one, but I'm your soul sister, together forever.'

And before the leaky eyes could start all over again, we heaved ourselves off the sofa and staggered to bed.

'Night Ellie, missing you already,' she sniffed.

'Night Soph, sweet dreams.'

'You too babe, except sexy dreams for you, of a fit, muscular Viking with a very big longboat!'

First thing on Monday morning I rang my boss, Anna 'the Spanna' Jarvis, and told her I wouldn't be going back. I hadn't expected any sympathy, which was just as well, as she was as cold as usual, totally devoid of emotion. I got the 'it will be difficult to give you a reference' speech, and 'you will never work in London PR again' threats, but it was matter less, she could have offered me her job on double pay, and I wouldn't have accepted. If that's what a long-term career in Randy Parrot did to you – Anna was almost cryogenically frozen – then it was just another reason to get out now.

It was Tuesday before I heard from Matt. I could have predicted it and knew exactly what he wanted before he even asked. I had pre-empted it yesterday when I rang the holiday insurance company. It would appear that being dumped by a cheating bastard did not qualify me for a refund.

'Ellie, you know this holiday? It seems such a shame to waste it so I was wondering, well, err, I thought that maybe we could change the name of the ticket to erm, Karen...'

There wasn't a sorry, or a hint of remorse.

'If you make a BACS transfer for the entire amount, then I'll get it sorted,' I answered tersely.

'Erm, thing is, I've had a bit of expense lately Ellie. You know I'll come good though, I mean, it's not like you need a house now, is it?'

I could feel my blood pumping with anger fuelled adrenalin.

'Okay, of course I know you'll pay me eventually, so I'll text you the details,' I said through gritted teeth, quickly hanging up.

Sophie, having heard every word, was looking at me like I was certifiable, her jaw almost on the floor.

'Ellie, remember, this is the new you. Don't let him do this to you... again.'

'No intention Soph. Here, hold the phone, ring him on video call and point it at me.'

I grabbed the tickets and as Matt picked up, I waved them in front of the screen and slowly ripped them up, throwing them into the air in a theatrical gesture.

'I guess that's a no. Matt, I wouldn't give you the skin off my rice pudding. If you and grandma want a holiday, bloody well pay for it yourselves. I never want to see you again Matt, ever. I hope you and Karen have the life you both deserve, you heartless bastard.'

'Wow, way to go girl,' said Sophie, clicking off the phone, a shocked expression on her face. 'That was a very expensive gesture, it probably felt great though, did it?'

'I'm not that daft, Soph. They were the old tickets, and anyway, it's all online these days. I've got some new tickets though, I've had the names changed to you and Jake, and I don't want the money for it. Call it an early Christmas present. I'd rather someone used the holiday than lose all of the money, and who better than my bestie?'

'Ellie, you can't!'

'Oh yes I can, so don't argue,' I replied firmly.

'I don't know what to say, other than thank you. But there is one condition. We won't accept it for free, and we'll give you back your share of the cost in full. That cheating rat isn't getting one penny of his contribution though. Are you absolutely sure?'

'I'm sure. I can't go now I've committed to Northumberland. You two have the best time and send me back lots of photos so I can experience it vicariously through you!'

Now wasn't the time to tell her that Matt hadn't paid one penny towards his share of the trip.

***

The rest of the week went by in a blur, packing and helping Sophie decide what was happening to all our joint stuff, as she would be left to deal with it. What to skip, what to give to the charity shop and what we couldn't bear to part with. We were in the midst of trying to decide on our much-loved sofa, which neither of us wanted to part with, but Jake was adamant it wasn't going into their new flat, when my phone pinged.

To: ellienellie@fastermail.com
From: jerrybarclay@dogsareforlife.com

Hi Ellie,

So sorry it has taken me time to come back to you with the details. It's been a nightmare here. Did you see the news about the raid of the puppy farm in Bedfordshire? We've been taking in some of the dogs, and you can imagine the work that's been involved, especially so close to Christmas. Anyway, we have ascertained you are a suitable person (!) and hope you got your train ticket sorted for Saturday. The address is Courtyard Cottage, Lindisfarne, TD55 2XY. I do believe that Lancelot is bringing Nacho to you on Sunday. Don't hesitate to give me a ring if you need help with anything and good luck. Have a fantastic adventure Ellie, and Happy Christmas when it arrives. Jerry.

Lancelot! That must be Lord Bamburgh – my knight in shining armour. I put my phone down and got straight back to business, a newfound decisiveness surging through me.

'Let's just put the sofa in the skip, no clinging on, remember? This is a new start for both of us!'

On Friday, I bit the bullet and caught the train

to Cambridge to tell my parents the news. I wasn't looking forward to it at all.

'Oh Ellie, whilst we're appalled at Matthew doing that to you, surely you can't be serious about giving up such a good job that you have worked hard for. Why not stay and look for something else with another agency?' Mum looked at me beseechingly and Dad mumbled something about my mother being right.

'My mind is made up Mum. I need a fresh start.'

We sat down to eat, and I thought Mum was going to choke on her casserole as she listened to me telling them the bits of the tale that I felt able to divulge.

'Looking after animals? You? What experience do you have?'

'I've only got to feed and walk them,' I retorted indignantly. 'They will be leaving full instructions,' I said, with far more confidence than I felt.

'And what kind of animals are they, and how many?'

'Oh, just dogs and maybe a couple of cats,' I replied, crossing my fingers under the table. Truth was, I still had no idea what type of animals were involved, but surely as it had been organised through *Dogs Are For Life,* it made sense they would most likely be canine companions.

'And where are you going?' enquired Dad, hastily changing the subject before me and Mum started to bicker – as was our usual mode.

'Northumberland,' I answered.

'Fantastic!' shouted Mum, immediately brightening. 'Fabulous place.'

'You've been? When? I can't remember that.' I raised a quizzical eyebrow at her.

'Well, no, not exactly, but I've watched every episode of *Vera*, at least twice! It's a stunning place, quite a few murders, but Vera is always on the case.' She laughed.

'*Vera*? Is she the one that wears the hat?' I'd heard of her of course but never watched the programme.

'Yes, that's her, lovely accent, *pet*,' she howled. 'And her Geordie sidekick is rather easy on the eye too!'

CHAPTER 6

It had just gone 8 p.m. by the time I got back to the flat, which was in darkness. Sophie must have gone out, and I couldn't help but feel a slight tinge of disappointment that I was going to be spending my last night in London on my own – until I pushed open the living room door.

'Surprise!'

The lights flashed on, and there were my closest friends, cheering and smiling and all wearing fancy dress.

'You didn't think we were just going to let you go without a party, did you?' said Sophie. 'We're having a Geordie night to celebrate your trip up north!'

I looked around the room at my friends and laughed. Sophie was dressed as one of the *Geordie Shore* girls; it was impossible to tell which one she had modelled her look on. She was wearing a bright blonde wig which tumbled down her back, false eyelashes so long and heavy that they could double up as hammocks, faux leather leggings which looked like they had been sprayed on, and a fluorescent pink tee shirt with PURE MORTAL written across the front; although the writing was somewhat out of alignment due to the fact that she had suddenly developed huge boobs.

'What on earth?' I said, pulling up her tee shirt to reveal two giant Jaffa oranges suspended in one of *my* best bras, the cheeky minx!

'I didn't know citrus fruit could be such a turn on,' said Jake's voice, coming from underneath a furry black and yellow bee outfit, complete with wings and antennae.

'And what's the Geordie relevance of your costume, Jake?' I laughed.

'Sting! Genius, eh? He's from Newcastle. Best I could do at short notice Ellie girl.'

'Well, you look buzzing,' I said, trying to get my arms around his rotund bee belly to give him a hug.

Tara was sitting on the sofa. She was wearing a long brown mac, a fishing hat and blue vinyl gloves.

'*Vera!*' I howled.

Toby came and gave me a peck on the cheek.

'And you Toby? What have you come as?' I asked, puzzled.

Toby was wearing a home-made costume consisting of a giant tee shirt which had masses of tea bags stuck all over it. He was omitting a pungent, perfumed aroma which smelled remarkably familiar.

'I'm Earl Grey.'

'Oh, like the tea?' The penny dropped as to the

smell.

'Precisely like the tea. Except of course they didn't have tea bags in his day. It would have been exceedingly difficult to adhere proper tea leaves to this shirt,' he said seriously. 'Earl Grey was from Howick in Northumberland,' he explained. 'He was the British Prime Minister from 1830 to 1834. His notable political achievements include the Reform Act of 1832 and the Slavery Abolition Act of 1833, but even back then, like the celebrity culture of today, sometimes people became famous for something far less important, and in his case, it was Earl Grey tea. Did you kn—'

Tara gave him a poke in the ribs which stopped him mid-flow.

'Let's get you another drink,' she said, dragging Toby towards the table. 'Have you seen the cocktails yet Ellie?'

'See you've pushed the boat out on the linen,' I said, nodding to the newspapers that were spread all over the table.

'Black and White! Jake came up with that one.'

'We have *Stephenson's Rocket Fuel*,' said Tara, gesturing to what looked like a new washing up bowl filled to the brim with liquid, a strong smell of alcohol drifting up from it.

'I named that one,' said Toby. 'One of Northumberland's most famous sons, known as the Father of Railways—'

'Toby, all Ellie needs to know is to avoid it and leave it to the rest of you drunks. We've made a mocktail for me and you, Ellie, I'm not drinking alcohol tonight either,' she said, pointing to a smaller bowl. 'I named that one the *Ant and Decorum*,' she hooted. 'Alcohol free sparkling wine and more fruit than you can pick from Carmen Miranda's headgear.' She topped up Toby's glass to the rim with *Rocket Fuel*. 'Once he's had a few of these,' she whispered, 'I promise you, history will be consigned to history.'

There was a knock at the door.

'That'll be Stan and Aleksy,' shouted Sophie, who shot off to answer.

In marched Stanislaw dressed as a Roman soldier, resplendent in a silver pleated mini tunic, his muscular legs clad in leather gladiator sandals, and a plumed red feather helmet on top of his closely cropped dark hair. Aleksy was seriously just... well, he just had this golden glow about him, from tip to toe. He was wearing a very skimpy white cotton toga tied with a gold chain, and laurel leaves were wrapped around his blonde, tousled hair.

'Factually speaking,' began Toby, 'a Legionnaire found on Hadrian's Wall wouldn't—'

Tara and I looked at each other and at the same time shouted, 'Time for a top up, Toby?'

Stan handed me a big bag of coffee.

'Your favourite blend to take with you, Ellie. I don't suppose you will find good coffee in the north place you are going.'

'You could be right,' I said, breathing in the rich aroma. 'I will think of you both every time I have a cup.'

'Sorry to interrupt, but you need to go and get changed into this,' said Sophie, handing me a black and white bundle. 'Go and put it on, and we can really get this party started.' I headed towards my room feeling so blessed. My friends were amazing, the best. I opened the costume and got changed.

'What on earth is this?' I shouted at Sophie, as I waddled back into the living room, flapping my arms as I went.

'It's a penguin,' she responded indignantly. 'I will have you know I did my research and there are several bird sanctuaries just off the coast of Northumberland where you will find thousands of them.'

'Erm, if you don't mind me correcting you Sophie,' slurred Toby, 'I think you are getting confused with puffins. You won't find any penguins off the Northeast coast.'

The room erupted into laughter.

'Penguins, puffins, same thing really, both black and white birds with funny looking beaks.'

'Yeh, that's right babe,' said Jake, backing her up. 'Same 'orse, different jockey, as the old man says!'

'Anyway Ellie,' said Sophie, grinning at me, 'you look like a right numpty, so job done. Now get that Geordie playlist going Jake, and let's get ready to rumble.'

***

I was up early the next morning feeling as

fresh as a daisy. I'd gone to bed at about 1.30 a.m. and the party had still been in full flow. As I moved around the flat getting ready, it became apparent that none of them had actually made it home. Stanislaw and Aleksy were sprawled out comatose on the rug in front of the fireplace, bits of fruit from the mocktail splattered over Stan, and the floor around him. Tara was curled into a ball on the tiny settee and buried beneath a throw, and Toby – where was Toby? I crept around and there he was, out cold in the bath, Aleksy's laurel leaves around his neck, Stan's plastic sword lying across his chest, and someone had written *history is a mystery* on his forehead! Not one of them returned to the living world before it was time for me to leave for the train, so I scribbled a quick note.

Love you all, you soft southern lightweights. Message when I get there xxxxx

And so, exactly one week to the day after the hotel debacle, I set off for Kings Cross to start my new life.

***

The journey passed uneventfully, and about three hours after getting onto the train, the announcer informed us that we were about to arrive at Newcastle Central Station. As the train slowed down and crawled over the river, I looked out across the most amazing view of bridge after bridge, spanning across the Tyne. The couple opposite were giving me an extremely useful travelogue about how the bridges link Gateshead to Newcastle. They were of various heights, styles and eras – it really was an impressive sight. On the south side of the river was the most amazing glass building. It was huge and looked like a giant snail. On the north side there was a wide quayside. I could see lots of bars and restaurants and people strolling along towards the final foot bridge, which looked like a big, silver eye. Newcastle was nothing like I had imagined; it looked fabulous, and I knew that before my time here was over, I had to visit and do some serious sightseeing.

The train sped on after leaving the city and we were soon out in open countryside. I was beginning to see glimpses of the sea. Suddenly the train slowed and ground to a halt. The tannoy system crackled into life, the guard informing us that there was another train ahead which had broken down and was awaiting parts, asking us to please be patient and bear with them. Easier said than done I reckoned, glancing around at my fellow passengers in various stages of agitation. I concentrated on the scene outside of the carriage window, which was enough to calm anyone's soul. Beyond the railway line, fields gave way to an estuary where sailing boats were moored, and on the far side there looked to be a row of pastel-coloured houses or cottages, which curved their way around the landscape towards the sea beyond. It was so pretty and inviting and reminded me a little of Tobermory. I had no idea if we were actually in Northumberland yet, but if we were, then it was already stealing its way into my heart.

I got off the train in Berwick upon Tweed. Thanks to getting stuck on the line, we were fifty minutes late. I stepped onto the platform and was at once struck by a blast of icy air. As people scurried about the station, I heard voices that had an almost Scottish lilt to them, and I wondered if Berwick was actually in Scotland. Perhaps once we had gone over that rather impressive viaduct into the town, we had crossed the border. I hurriedly made my way to the exit to look for the taxi rank, pleased to get out of the cold, and I began to question whether the clothes I had brought with me were going to be of any use.

'Hullo hen, where we aft tae?'

The taxi driver had a Scottish accent so thick it would toast beautifully. I didn't fully understand what he had said but guessed he was asking for directions, so I read out the postcode for him to put into his sat nav. He typed it in, then swung round in his seat and glowered at me, shaking his head in disbelief, a perplexed look on his face.

'Yer kidding me. This says Lindisfarne. Yer cutting it fine darlin' and I dinae ken if a'll get ye all the way there. It's a fixed fare of £40 wherever I drop ye mind.'

'Yes, that's right, it is Lindisfarne. Is there a problem?'

He muttered something under his breath, which, quite frankly, was said so quickly in his broad accent that I had no chance of deciphering it. A glance at the rank showed no other taxis waiting, and I hadn't any desire to get back into that cutting wind again.

'Fine,' I said, handing him the cash, thinking maybe he had another job to hurry back to or something – it wasn't my fault the train was late.

'It's very cold here in Scotland,' I said to the driver.

'Scotland? This is the Borders. You're still in England. Mind I'm frae Glasgae if that's what's confusing ye. This is no cold, trust me. It'll be freezing the balls off a brass monkey soon enough.'

The car took a sharp right and soon we crossed a bridge from where I got a magnificent view of the town, and the river that ran through to the open sea. I settled down in the back of the car. The driver didn't seem the chatty type, thankfully, and I was able to watch the passing landscape in silence as we made our way out of Berwick, and on to what was clearly the main road, signposted A1 South. What struck me as the miles rolled by, was that apart from the odd farm or cottage, there was little sign of development, just farmland and forestry. There were no villages at all along the roadside and, apart from a couple of caravan sites, it was just miles of open space. It didn't take too long before the taxi swung off to the left and onto a country road. Oddly, there was a lot of traffic passing us in the opposite direction. The driver shook his head, tutting.

'Did'nae think sae. A'll get ye as far as the causeway and then it's up to you. Cannae afford to get stuck.'

I was just about to ask him what he meant when we came to an abrupt halt. He jumped out of the car, retrieved my wheelie case from the boot, and held the door open for me.

'I hope your lift's waiting for ye, time is tight,' he said, pointing down the long, straight road which lay ahead. 'Good luck tae ye darlin'.

And before I could blink or ask him what he meant, he was swinging the car round and had vanished in a trail of dust and exhaust fumes.

CHAPTER 7

I peered anxiously down the road. The very idea of walking along it filled me with dread, and I could feel my anxiety levels rising, my newfound bravado quickly ebbing away. The weather was atrocious; a grey mist had descended, and I struggled to see very far ahead – it was absolutely nothing like the glorious weather in that photo of Bamburgh Castle, which was partially responsible for luring me here in the first place.

The tarmac road ahead was almost like a ground level bridge across an expanse of sea. On either side, there was a sandy, muddy shore with waves lapping beyond, but thankfully the water was not that near to the sides of the road. The sky was a peculiar shade of gunmetal and the sea reflected this; I couldn't really see a join between the two. The wind was fierce, whipping up sand which was swirling across the road. The words of the taxi-driver ringing in my ears, I decided to walk briskly. Lindisfarne couldn't be too far, surely. A few metres in and I regretted wearing the shoes that were meant to impress. The soles were so slippery that they had no grip on the wet road. I struggled along, head down, pulling my wheelie case. There was a constant stream of vehicles passing me in the opposite direction, each one spraying me with a coating of sand, salt and water. The ferocity of the wind had blown my hair into knots. I struggled to tuck it into the back of my coat, but to no avail; it kept escaping and blocking my vision as it stuck to my face in wet clumps. My eyes were streaming with the wind, and I could almost feel my mascara dripping down my cheeks.

I walked on, my pace slowing in the awful conditions. Momentarily, I wondered if I should open my case and search for anything that might help me keep warm, but, for once, sense prevailed; I had visions of my newly bought underwear blowing all the way to Norway, or whichever country lay on the other side of that angry sea. The landscape was eerie and surreal – the sky meeting the sea – and everything looked the same shade of dirge grey. There was an extensive line of tall, wooden poles embedded into the seabed to my right, looming up into the mist, and a little into the distance, I could make out what looked like some kind of shed on stilts at the side of the road.

This place was seriously odd, and I made an effort to speed up. In doing so, I slipped on some seaweed and fell forward onto my knees. Thankfully, I wasn't really hurt, but I now had two massive holes in my expensive designer tights. As I struggled to my feet, I noticed that the sea, which had been at quite a distance from the road when I set off, had somehow crept nearer to me. Suddenly things got profoundly serious, and I was scared witless, panic rising inside me. *What if that sea just keeps on coming?*

For the first time in a week, I wished my feckless ex-boyfriend was with me. However, that was a very fleeting moment as a) he'd probably save his own neck well ahead of me, and b) if the worst was to happen, I was not going to Davy Jones' Locker with my last earthly image of Matt the Twat imprinted on my brain! I decided to flag down a car on the opposite side of the road, but they all seemed to have disappeared, and nothing had passed on my side for ages. I was on my own, freezing, soaking and totally out of my depth. The sea seemed to have crept even nearer the road, and there was no getting away from the increasingly possible scenario of me being swallowed up by a giant wave, swept out to sea, and no one would even know where I was. I supposed Lord Bamburgh might miss me and raise the alarm... eventually. Now wasn't the time to prevaricate however, and my survival instinct kicked in. I had to at least try and get to somewhere safe.

I was just about to hurry on, trying to decide whether to head towards the funny shed, or try to go back, when the headlights of a vehicle came towards me. Oh, thank God, someone was coming and maybe I wasn't going to drown today after all. I wasn't being dramatic. I fully appreciated that the situation in which I found myself was very grave indeed. Adrenalin fused with relief, and I stood in the middle of the road waving frantically, and an old-style campervan ground to a halt right in front of me.

The driver, a man, jumped out, hurrying towards me.

'What the hell are you doing?' he yelled angrily, shouting above the noise of the waves which were thrashing towards us by the second.

I burst into tears, unable to answer him and stood stock still, in shock and unable to move. He grabbed my wheelie case and steered me towards the passenger door, literally bundling me into the warmth. He got in the driver's side and without another word, spun the vehicle around and set off in the direction I had been aiming for. I couldn't even look at him, I was that terrified. I was God knows where, in a vehicle with a total stranger – an angry one at that – and my entire body was shaking with fear and cold. There was an extraordinarily strong smell of coffee in the van for some reason, which helped calm my breathing, because it made me think of Stan, and the familiarity was reassuring, comforting even – almost.

I stared out of the window and thankfully, we seemed to have made it onto a proper road which had land to the side. He slowed down the van, pulled over and switched off the engine. My whole body continued to shake, my teeth still chattering, and I wished with all my heart that I was back in my nice cosy flat in Peckham with Sophie. I braced myself for more anger, or worse, from the man, but a calmer, and much gentler voice spoke to me.

'Look, I'm sorry for shouting at you. I can see how distressed you are, and I don't want you to worry any further. You're safe, but what you have just done was so extremely dangerous.'

I couldn't even string a sentence together to reply, and with my head still turned away from him, I eventually heard myself squeak.

'Where are we?'

'Where are we? Did you bang your head? We're on Holy Island.'

'Holy Island? Where's that? The taxi-driver was supposed to take me to a place called Lindisfarne.'

He laughed gently.

'Holy Island *is* Lindisfarne. Just you tourists tend to know it by that name.'

'An island? What do you mean island?' I could hear the hysteria in my own voice.

He opened his door, got out and came round to my side. He was tall, but that was about all I could deduce in the gloom; plus, he was wearing a beanie and a scarf which was covering up most of his face.

'Come and look,' he beckoned gently.

I stepped out of the camper, back into the howling wind, and he turned me around to face the direction we had travelled from. The road was gone, hidden beneath a vast expanse of grey sea crashing to the shore covering where it once lay. I turned to the man and, for the first time, noticed his eyes peeping out from between the hat and scarf. They were kind eyes, dark and brooding, yet filled with concern as he looked at me. Despite my distress, I suddenly felt safe, and it was like our eyes had locked together. I swear I heard the click as we gazed at each other in the gloom.

'Oh my God, thank you,' I stuttered, dragging my eyes from his and struggling to regain my composure. 'I think you may have just saved my life. And is it just me, or can you smell coffee?'

His eyes crinkled at the corners, so I guessed he was smiling, but he didn't reply, and we turned back towards the van and set off along an isolated road. After a short distance, there were streetlights and buildings – we had arrived in a village. I was still shaking and couldn't contemplate any small talk, but thankfully, the man remained silent. I clutched my phone, having thought about ringing for help a million times, but who was going to reach me? I wasn't even sure where I was. We passed through what looked to be the village centre, but it was dusk, and the weather was so gloomy that it was difficult to make anything out properly. I could see the tower of a church. He steered the van onto yet another long straight road, exiting the village and leaving the houses behind. It suddenly occurred to me that I hadn't told him the address of where I was going, and he hadn't asked, and once again, even though I had seen those genuinely concerned, kind eyes, I started to feel uneasy.

'I didn't tell you the address,' I said shakily.

'No need,' he said. 'You will soon learn that living on Lindisfarne is a bit like living in a goldfish bowl at times. Everyone knows everyone – and their business. Am I right in thinking you're the woman from London who has come to help Bert with James and Grace's menagerie?'

'Yes,' I said, astonished that apparently the whole village knew of my arrival. We didn't even know all the names of our immediate neighbours in Peckham.

'Who is Bert? There was no mention of anyone by that name, just James and Grace, and is the cottage not in the village?' I managed to ask.

'Did you not get all the details before you left London?' he asked incredulously.

'Erm no, not really,' I mumbled, realising how stupid that sounded. 'It was organised in a hurry and *Dogs Are for Life* were extremely busy taking in dogs from a puppy farm, so it was all hands-on deck.'

'Ah okay, you'll find out soon enough I suppose,' he replied non-committedly, and we continued along the road with the dark, brooding sea on the right and open pasture as far as I could see to the left.

Out of the gloom, at the end of the straight road, there was a rocky hill with an almost circular building on the top. The van began to climb up the steep craggy slope which curved around the structure, the land dropping off sharply to one side towards the coast and waves beneath. From what I could make out, it looked like a castle, albeit a much smaller one than Bamburgh. We swept around the side of the building and came to a stop in front of huge, studded wooden gates.

'Can't go any further than this,' he said. 'No vehicles allowed in the courtyard, so we'll have to make a dash for it.'

I followed him as he pressed a code into a pad and opened a small door, set within the gates, into a large, cobbled courtyard at the back of the ancient building. The rain was pouring down and it was difficult to see clearly, but I could just about make out what looked like stables and outhouses around the perimeter of the yard, and a small cottage nestled in the corner, lights glowing from its arched mullioned windows. The door to the cottage burst open and an older man hurried across the yard, clutching a large umbrella which he was battling to keep upright.

'Bit late for that Bert,' said the driver. 'She's already wetter than an otter's pocket!'

'Well don't just stand there lad,' said the older man, 'let's get her inside before she catches her death.'

CHAPTER 8

Bert took my arm and guided me into the cottage as the driver retrieved my soaking suitcase. The door led into a small porch full of wellingtons, coats and animal paraphernalia, an open door leading into a cosy open-plan kitchen living room. An older woman was standing at an Aga, stirring a pot of something that smelled delicious. She turned to look at me.

'Eeh lass, what on earth has happened to you?' she asked, her voice full of concern. She put down the spoon and came towards me. Taking me by the arms, she gently steered me to a spot right in front of the warm Aga.

I saw her look me up and down, and it wasn't difficult to understand her shock at my appearance. Not only was I drenched, but my hair was hanging like rats' tails and dripping down my camel coat, which was covered in a layer of dirt and salt. My tights were shredded and my shoes, well, my shoes were ruined. There was a mirror hanging on the wall and a quick glance left me in no doubt – I looked like a ghoul from Halloween. My mascara was all down my cheeks, and my face, as far as you could see under the layer of muddy splashes, was the colour of parchment. I looked ghastly.

'I found her halfway across the causeway, on foot and minutes away from high tide,' said my rescuer bluntly.

'Oh, my goodness. How on earth—' said the woman horrified, then stopped mid flow. 'No worries, you can tell us when we get you sorted my pet. I'm Meg by the way, and that there is Bert,' she said, pointing at the older man who had taken off his coat to reveal green overalls, a damp, tweed cap still on his head. 'And you are Ellie I presume? Unless you're a stray mermaid washed in by the tide.' She laughed warmly.

I couldn't help but smile. The pair of them exuded warmth.

'Well, lucky he found you lass,' said Bert. 'And as for you, Zen, whilst I'm pleased you found Ellie here, how many times have I warned you about crossing the causeway at the last minute? You've lived here nearly all your life Zen; you know more than most that the sea takes no prisoners and will always win.'

My rescuer had the grace to look as shamefaced as one who was shrouded in a hat and scarf could. He was much taller than the older man and I could see he had broad shoulders. Long dark curls were poking out from the sides of the beanie and his eyes were the colour of dark roasted coffee beans. Odd that, as from the minute I had met him, I had detected the aroma of coffee. I hoped that my gift from Stanislaw hadn't burst in my case.

'I needed to get to Alnwick to collect a delivery but had to wait until the last batch was ready first. Couldn't just leave it, health and safety and all of that,' he explained.

'Health and safety my arse,' echoed Bert. 'Haway man. You weren't thinking about health and safety whilst tide dashing now, were you? No excuses lad, none. Now heed this, in future, I don't want to hear that you've been cutting it fine – again. We leave that to the tourists. And whilst we islanders know the tides to the 'enth degree, it still isn't worth risking a surge. You know the score Zen, lad.'

'Hear you loud and clear Bert,' said Zen – an interesting name for a very intriguing character. It was clear that Bert and Meg knew him well. The relationship between them was like close family.

'You can cross tomorrow lad, nothing that can't wait, except babies and medical emergencies, as we islanders always say.'

'True,' he murmured. 'Okay, I'll be off. Hope you feel better soon, Ellie. I'm sure you will with Meg and Bert looking after you.'

'Night, Zen lad. By the way, have you seen Harriet lately?'

My ears immediately pricked up. *Who was Harriet?*

'Yes, I have, she's great. I'll call over tomorrow and give you the low-down.'

'Thanks again,' I said, looking into those

coffee bean eyes, the only part of his face still visible. I had a sudden urge to whip down the scarf and see if the rest of his face matched up to the promise of his gorgeous eyes, but all the while wondering who Harriet was. My rescuer gave Meg a bear hug, Bert a nod, and disappeared back out into the stormy night.

'Right lass,' said Meg, turning to me. 'First things first, a tot of medicinal brandy or a hot shower?'

'Shower please,' I said, noticing my teeth had finally stopped chattering, 'and then perhaps a cup of tea?'

'Eeh a lassie after my own heart. Nice cup of tea it is then pet, and then we'll have something to eat. I'm not taking you over the way tonight after you've had such a shock, so you'll have to make do with our tiny spare room.'

I had no idea where she meant by "over the way" and prayed it did not involve another trip across the causeway any time soon. I was just grateful for the warmth and care they were showing me. I followed her to a tiny room, with bunk beds along one wall, a desk and chair, and a small wardrobe.

'Bathroom's over there. I'll sort you out some towels and show you how the shower works, and by the time you come out, I'll have this bed made up for you. Bottom or top?' She laughed.

'Bottom thanks. Knowing my luck today, I'd end up falling off the top one!'

After a steaming hot shower, I wrapped myself in the soft lavender scented towels Meg had given me. True to her word, she had made up the bottom bunk with some pretty bedding and switched on the table lamp, which gave the tiny room a comforting glow. Meg had left me a hairdryer, a long cotton nightdress, and what seemed to be a new pink dressing gown, which was fluffy and warm. I wrapped myself into it – Meg, whilst shorter than me, was a couple of sizes bigger. On the floor was a pair of men's slippers, again new. I thought I was being honoured with previous gifts, so far unused, from birthdays or Christmas! There was no sign of my suitcase or the wet clothes I had left piled on the floor. I checked my phone signal, which was surprisingly good, and sent a text to my parents telling them I had arrived. Then, I messaged my friends on the group chat we set up so I could keep everyone up to date.

Long journey, even longer story, but got here eventually. I'm on an actual island!!! Haven't seen much of it as too dark and weather dreadful. Staying with a lovely couple called Meg and Bert in their cottage, so no diversion into the sex trade… yet. Nice that you all got up to see me off this morning. More tomorrow you bunch of drunks xxxxxx

No need to tell them of my rescue, or my rescuer more to the point – I wanted to keep him to myself for the moment. The replies pinged in.

Like Love Island? Hope you couple up quickly before they suss you out and kick you off! Missing you already babe, so let's do lots of vid chats.
Love Sophie x

Toby is Earl Grey Face today. He has become best friends with a bucket and says he is never drinking again. Keep in touch and don't get on any boats from that island, it could be a holding place before your dispatch to a life of crime and Bert and Meg are probs the gangmasters!
Love Tara x

OH MY GOD. WE IS BROKEN. Don't drink any northern cocktails. They are killers. Even my strongest brew hasn't shifted our hangovers and now we are both the colour of custard creams. I'm not sure we will even manage to watch Strictly tonight. If not, I will call for ambulance! Speak soon & take care.
Kochamy Cie, Stan & Alex xx

***

'Now that's better. What a bonnie lassie you are, Ellie, pink suits you.' Meg smiled as I went back in the room. 'Look Bert, she's just like a mermaid with that lovely long blonde hair.'

'Aye pet, she is that. It'll be all around the *Crab and Oyster* that we have a sea nymph staying with us,' said Bert, putting on his coat and heading for the door.

'Oh, my goodness, please don't tell me that it

will get out about my, erm, arrival? Everyone will think I'm so stupid, and they'd be right.'

'Listen pet, they won't hear it from me or Bert, and don't you worry about Zen. That young man would never put anyone in an embarrassing situation intentionally.'

Relieved, I gratefully accepted the mug of tea Meg handed to me.

'Well, you drink that, and we'll eat as soon as Bert gets back in. He's just popped out to see to the dogs.'

I was going to ask about the animals, but Meg carried on.

'I've put your suitcase next to the Aga. It's soaked through. You should get one of those hard-shell types that keep things dry – those canvas ones are about as much use as a chocolate fireguard. I didn't want to open it, but as soon as we've eaten, have a look, and see if there's anything that needs washing or drying. The clothes that you were wearing are in the washing machine, your coat I've hung in the outhouse. Did you know it's dry clean only pet? Nice coat mind, so that will have to wait until we get across to Alnwick or Berwick. I think your shoes have had it; beige suede is no match for the conditions around here. By the way, I've made vegetable broth for tea, wasn't sure if you were vegetarian?'

'No, I'm not. It smells delicious.' I smiled.

I heard the outer door creak open.

'Don't let that...' began Meg, as the cottage

door burst open and a black and white Collie shot in, followed by Bert. It made straight for the front of the Aga before giving itself a shake, spraying us in raindrops.

'I've told you a hundred times Bert, give her a rub down before she gets this far.'

I put my hand out, and the dog crept towards me sniffing gently, before laying its head on my knee and gazing up at me.

'Hello beautiful, what's your name?' I said, gently stroking her soft head, noticing her mismatched eyes, one blue and one brown.

'She's called Flower. Daft bloody name for a Collie,' said Bert. 'That's Grace for you, thinking it was funny naming her after a vegetable. We tend to call her Flo, much more suitable for her breed.'

'I think she suits Flower,' I said. 'Is she yours?'

'You'll soon come to realise that none of the animals here belong to any of us – we belong to them. We look after them, and love them all, but you can't help having your favourites,' said Meg, looking fondly at Flower. 'She stays in the cottage with us most of the time. She adopted us rather than the other way around. She was bred to be a working sheepdog and turns out she wouldn't even get down off the quad and is totally disinterested in sheep! Poor Harriet, who bred her, was devastated, as she had high hopes for her. Now we wouldn't be without her, mucky, messy blighter though she is!'

Ah, so Harriet was a shepherd. Great. I somehow could imagine Zen with a woman of the soil, or grass, or whatever!

Bert joined us at the table and Meg dished out bowls of thick vegetable broth.

'Would you like some bread? Made fresh this morning.'

'You made this?' I asked, taking a chunk and spreading it thickly with butter.

'No, not today pet. I sometimes make stottie cakes, but this is from the village. Zen's sister, Aurora, made it.'

'Mmm, it's delicious,' I said, dunking it in my soup. 'So, tell me, what's a stottie cake?'

'It's like a flatbread local to the northeast. I'm forgetting you won't know some of the things we say. Can you even understand what me and Bert are saying?' She laughed. Meg and Bert both had beautifully rich accents, singsong in tone and quite mesmerising. I could understand Meg more than Bert, who spoke quickly and had already used words I just didn't recognise.

'Kind of.' I smiled.

'Just you ask us if you don't understand or tell us to slow down if you lose track. Bert and I were born and bred here in north Northumberland, on this very island, and our accents are a little different to your Geordies from Newcastle.'

'Now then bonnie lass,' said Bert, 'if you're feeling up to it, why don't you tell us how you came to be crossing that causeway so near to high tide?'

And so, I started at the beginning and told them, warts and all, about Matt and Santa Paws and what led me to Lindisfarne.

'So, I didn't even know it was an island,' I admitted, when I'd finished telling them the entire story, 'otherwise I would never have tried to walk across the... the... whatever you call it. I was stupid for not finding out more before I left London.'

'You say the taxi-driver was Scottish?' asked Bert.

'Yes, from Glasgow I believe.'

'Aye that'll be Wullie Macpherson, and next time I'm up in Berwick, Wullie will be getting a piece of my mind, no fear about that!'

'Cake?' asked Meg, winking at me whilst shaking her head at Bert.

'Yes please,' I replied, already loving the pair of them. I'd been here no time at all, yet it felt like home already, and I had a feeling that I was going to enjoy my time on Lindisfarne.

CHAPTER 9

When we had finished eating, Meg and I went to the other end of the room and settled down on a comfortable sofa. Flower was stretched full length in front of the roaring fire and the theme music to *Strictly* drifted out from the television.

'Bert isn't interested in "that dancing bollocks" as he calls it,' said Meg. 'He goes to play darts in the *Crab and Oyster* on a Saturday night. It's the island pub. We only have the one, plus a hotel with a bar, and then there's the fishing club in one of the upturned boats. I've never been there and never want to if half the stories about what happens in there are true. They brew their own hooch. Don't tell anyone mind! I swear Bert went cross-eyed and his legs turned to rubber after a session there a while ago. He hasn't done it again since, thank God.'

By the time the programme started, Meg and I were engrossed in conversation, and I doubted we would be seeing much of the "dancing bollocks" that night!

'I can understand why you wanted a break away from London. Sounds like you have had a miserable time of it,' she said kindly, after I told her about Matt, and what brought me to the island. 'You've come to the right place. The island is so spiritual, very therapeutic and calming, and it will be such a change from your usual routine, Ellie. I only hope it's not too quiet for you. When you get settled, we'll show you around and tell you lots more about the history and why it's such a special place. Oh, and don't fret Ellie, neither Bert nor I will tell anyone about your reasons for coming to the island, so don't you worry about that.'

'Thanks Meg. You don't mind if I ask you things about my time here?'

'No pet, you go ahead, ask away, but before you do, hang on...'

She got up, went to a kitchen cupboard, and brought back a large box of chocolates.

'You help yourself. It's my Saturday night treat. I'll never be the shape of Claudia or Tess again – not that I ever was come to think about it!' She laughed, patting her middle.

'Nor me,' I sighed, 'too many takeaways on our doorstep.'

'Well pet, you are going to struggle to get takeaways from now on. Depending on the tides, you can travel to collect one, but, quite frankly, it's not worth the hassle. The pub and hotel do nice carry outs though, and sometimes the café opens on an evening, so you won't starve.'

'Tell me about the tides, Meg.'

'The island is cut off twice a day, every day. The sea covers the causeway and, that's it, you are a proper islander. Times vary as the tides change, but we have timetables – and you lot have those new-fangled phones that do everything except wipe your bum to tell you. Make sure you always take great care to carry the timetable with you every time you go to the mainland. I would not want you to go through that dreadful experience again.'

'Nor me, it was so scary. I thought I was going to drown.' I shivered.

'Well thanks to Zen and his blatant disregard for the tide times, all's well that ends well, but don't take a leaf out of his book and leave crossing until the last minute.'

In the couple of hours that Bert was at the pub, Meg filled me in on island life. It was very enlightening, and I was beginning to realise that I should have found out more information before I threw caution to the wind and basically bolted up north to escape.

'I don't really know many details about what's expected of me Meg, or even where I was actually coming to,' I admitted. 'It sounded like a fantastic opportunity, so I just went for it without stopping to think.'

'I'll give you a run-down of the basics, and the rest you will find out as you go along,' Meg said kindly. 'James and Grace are Lord and Lady Lindisfarne, and Grace is the sister of Lord Bamburgh, who you met at the charity. They live in the castle in an apartment. Me and Bert have worked for them for years. In fact, we have been at the castle since it was in the hands of James' father, God rest his soul. We help caretake the castle and lend a general hand around the place. In more recent times, Bert has been helping to look after the rescue animals that Grace has collected. They usually end up here as a result of a visit from her brother, with yet another waif or stray in need of a new home, or someone departing the island and leaving the animals here with us.'

'Tell me about the animals, Meg.'

'Oh, I'll leave that to Bert. They're his domain and I know that he has a list and instructions ready for you; but what I will say is that when James and Grace knew they were going to New York to meet their new granddaughter, Grace was adamant that Bert needed an extra pair of hands to help. He's had trouble with his hip recently – nothing too serious – but he can't do quite as much as he used to, and Grace, who has no airs or *graces* by the way–' she chuckled at her own joke, 'rolls up her sleeves and helps when she is here. So, when Lord B said he knew of someone who might help, we were grateful. I'll be honest though; we were a little worried about who we might get!'

'Wasn't there anyone on the Island who could lend a hand? Zen maybe?' I asked, purposely drawing him into the conversation. I didn't know what had come over me, maybe it was my near-death experience, but my protestations of never being interested in another man again, ever, were swiftly going down the pan. Those gorgeous coffee bean eyes had me fizzing like I had a quadruple espresso racing through my veins, and I was very curious to find out more about him.

'Yes, of course. There were lots of volunteers, but you will soon see how hard everyone works already. Island life isn't easy, and quite often people have more than one job or role. Zen hasn't been long back on the island, and he is working hard on building up his new coffee business.'

'Coffee business?' I echoed. 'That explains it. When he picked me up, all I could smell was coffee!'

'I don't just mean making drinks; he sources, roasts and is working on selling to other outlets on your internet thingy,' she said proudly. 'His sister Aurora runs the island café, *Northern Lights and Bites*. It can get busy, and Zen often helps. They both go over to Greater Reef when needed too, and it's a similar tale for a lot of island folk. The island has changed Ellie. When Bert and I were kids, it was mostly families who had lived and worked here for generations. Now about half the houses are holiday lets, and the number of us 'true' islanders is reducing all the time.' She sighed. 'Sad in some ways. It means house prices are increasing as people make money letting them out, so young islanders struggle to afford to find places to live on the island, and they inevitably have to move away to the mainland, further reducing the number of us islanders. Things change though, Ellie, and like it or not, we must change with it and move with the times.'

'You mentioned somewhere called Greater

Reef, where's that?'

'Bless you Ellie, here's me rambling away thinking you've been here ages because I feel like I know you already lass,' she said before popping another orange cream into her mouth. 'Greater Reef is a tiny island just across the bay from the front of the castle. You'll see it tomorrow. It belongs to James and Grace, and years ago they had it designated as a conservation area to ensure that it would always be a bird and sea life sanctuary. Zen and Aurora's parents, Mike and Simone, got the job as the first wardens and have been there ever since. Hippie types you know, but wonderful people. They were travelling the world in a camper van, but when the two bairns came along and Zen was school age, they took the job so the kiddies could get an education, and the remoteness and spirituality of this place suited their way of life, so they stayed. Me and Bert weren't blessed with bairns of our own sadly, so on the days when Zen and Aurora couldn't get to and from Greater Reef to the village primary school, we were delighted to help; they would stay with us, and very quickly all four of them became part of the family. Zen and Aurora are the grandkids we never had. When they got to high school and had to travel off Lindisfarne to go to Alnwick, they stayed with us all the time, or with my sister who lives over there when the tides were against us, going back to the smaller island with their parents on weekends.'

I reached for another chocolate and eagerly listened to her lilting voice as she went on.

'The island is made up of people from all walks of life, just like your street in London. Some you will get along with, others you won't, but I'll let you find all that out for yourself.'

At that, Flo sprang to life, cocking her head to one side. Bert stepped into the living room and Flo jumped up to welcome him home.

'Get down, daft bloody dog.' He laughed, gently shoving Flo away as he came through the door. 'I've told them our new mermaid helper has arrived, so it will be all over the island by now,' said Bert. 'I didn't tell them how you got here, Ellie lass, so don't you worry about that. If any of them bother you, just you tell them to, erm, well you know, to do one, if they ask personal questions or anything, because that's what it's like round here. A couple of the young bucks, and auld Maurice the oyster farmer already fancy their chances with you!'

'Older than grass he is!' Laughed Meg.

'Aye,' continued Bert, 'the lecherous git must have been scoffing too many of his oysters. There's not that many single people on this island, so you were always going to cause a stir. That said, they aren't aware of your situation lass. You might be married for all they know, and we won't be telling them. You just shout if any of them annoy you and I'll sort them out. Anyhow pet, changing the subject, you don't have to get up early tomorrow, it being a Sunday, but maybe after breakfast you and I can go through your duties and get sorted with the brood?'

'That's great Bert, thanks.'

'Breakfast at 8.30 a.m.' Meg smiled.

I looked at the clock. It was past 11 p.m. and I'd had a long and incredibly stressful day, so said goodnight to them both, gave Flower a big hug, and headed for my bunk bed in the tiny room.

As I lay in the narrow bed, I noticed how quiet it was compared to the busy street in Peckham, which generated noise day and night. I concentrated, but all I could hear was the wind blowing a spattering of raindrops against the tiny window. It was comforting, and even though I had arrived in a mess, the kindness of Bert and Meg had been overwhelming, and I hadn't felt this chilled in a long time. I thought about the causeway, not the danger I'd unknowingly put myself in – it scared me to think about it – but about the rescue by the intriguing Zen who had saved my bacon. Those gorgeous dark eyes which, even after the briefest of glances, were firmly imprinted into my memory. I'd felt more than a bit deflated when Meg mentioned someone called Harriet. I wondered if she and Zen were an item. I hadn't felt as drawn to anyone so quickly before. When I'd met Matt all those years ago, it had felt quite different. It was simply lust at the beginning with him. Lust was definitely at play with Zen, but there was something else going on too, something much, much deeper, which, quite frankly, was all new and alien to me. I had to remind myself that I hadn't even seen him properly yet, plus it sounded like he was in a relationship. Anyway, thinking like this was not conducive to becoming the new single and ready to mingle Ellie. Maybe I'd be better concentrating on a fling with old Maurice the oyster farmer!

At that, wondering which bunk Zen used, I fell fast asleep and dreamt of islands, castles and coffee bean eyes.

CHAPTER 10

I woke early the next morning to the sound of a cockerel crowing. Even the noise levels in Peckham, including hip-hop booming out of open car windows 24/7, were no match for the decibels this thing managed to produce. I was sure it must have been sitting right on my windowsill. Glancing at the time, I saw that it was only 5.30 a.m. and still pitch dark outside, so I pulled the pillow over my ears, buried myself under the duvet, and drifted back to sleep – at which point, the bird must have moved on to bother someone else.

Next time I awoke, light was streaming in through a gap in the curtains. It had just gone 8 a.m., so I got up, wrapped myself in the pink dressing gown and went in search of my clothes, which I found airing on the dryer in the kitchen. There was no sign of Meg or Bert, so I looked for the kettle to make myself a coffee. The only one I could see wasn't electric and I had no idea how to switch the Aga on. After a quick glance at it, I still wasn't sure, so I abandoned the idea. I was just about to go and retrieve my clothes when I noticed a large sheet of paper on the kitchen table and there was a list in spidery handwriting. I realised it was Bert's list that Meg had mentioned, so I sat down and began to read.

LIST OF ANIMALS

I'm not responsible for the stupid bloody names of this lot. They either came with them or blame Grace.

Alpacas: *Al Pacino and Al Murray – both canny things if not split up.*

Shetland Pony and Horse: *Hannibal Lecter, the Shetland – sodding villain, bites, kicks and won't come when called.* **CAUTION!** *Stout, the ex-working brewery Shire – huge bugger but placid, just don't let her stand on your feet or you won't have feet, pet.*

Donkeys: *Wonky and Jenny – Wonky is the darker of two. No love lost between them; they more or less ignore each other. Wonky tries to escape; seems he is smitten with another donkey called Wilma who lives on the far side of the island. Make sure he can't get out.* **CAUTION!** *(Wonky)*

Goat: *Nanny McPhee – Needs milking twice a day. Meg will show you. Noisy creature needs a friend, so bleats for attention. We are looking for another one, God help us.*

Chickens: *They don't know their names so don't worry about which one is which, but there's the lasses: Korma, Kiev, Curry and Tikka, who are ruled by Colonel Sanders, the Cockerel, until I wring his bloody neck for waking us up crowing like a good 'un far too early in the mornings.*

Turkeys: *Sage and Onion – not a brain cell between them and they'd be in the oven if it wasn't for*

Grace.

Cats: Cilla – ginger one, friendly (sometimes). Just watch your hands when you touch her. **HALF CAUTION!** *Lulu – tiny tabby one, butter wouldn't melt, but would scratch your eyes out given half a chance.* **EXTREME CAUTION!** *Elvis – big black and white bruiser, but best natured of all three and enjoys a cuddle.*

Dogs: Tripod (we call him Tri) – three-legged ex racing greyhound. Robson – Bedlington Terrier, looks like a sheep, and just as dozy. Flo – Grace calls her Flower. Collie lives with me and Meg.

All the dogs are proper softies, and a joy to look after.

I read it twice, not quite believing what I had seen the first time. Alpacas? Horses? Milking a goat? Oh my God! Surely this could not be for real. These were not just a few cute puppies. They were big for one thing, scary for another, and I had no clue about how to care for any of them whatsoever. I recalled the words of more than one person asking me what kind of animals I was going to look after, and me nonchalantly replying, 'Oh, just dogs.' Well, this was more like being a zookeeper than feeding and walking a few pooches. What on earth was I going to say to Meg and Bert? Should I just come clean and admit I had *no* experience whatsoever, except for incinerating a guinea pig?

I left the note on the table, collected my clothes, and slunk back to my room to ponder the situation. Meg and Bert were such kind people. I had come to help and, from what I understood, Bert needed support. I didn't want him to feel that he had even more work to do looking after me. No, this was time for the Bridget Jones extra-large knickers. I would listen carefully to what he told me; I would follow his instructions to the letter; I would watch as many videos as possible on caring for animals that I could find. And I would *panic in private*. It couldn't be too hard, could it? I mean, people looked after animals all the time, and I did have Bert to keep me right; and I was only the helper after all. Maybe it wouldn't be too different to a day in *Randy Parrot*. Quite frankly, that place was full of sharks and cows, and I'd survived them.

I looked through the scant selection of clothes I had brought with me, already realising after my experience of yesterday that they were probably inadequate to say the least. They all looked unsuitable for the freezing cold climate on an island, in the North Sea, in December. I threw on two vest tops, followed by a tee shirt, the thickest jumper I had with me, and a pair of jeans. The only footwear I'd brought, other than the ruined shoes, were my *Converse,* which, in fairness, was all I thought I would need to walk a few dogs. I had a lightweight cagoule that I had only ever worn once when we went to Dorset on a charity walk along the coastal path. The jacket had seemed perfectly functional at the time, but back then it had been July on the south coast.

I went back through to the kitchen, just as

Meg was coming in from outside clutching a bowl of eggs and a jug.

'Morning Ellie,' she said, putting her wares down on the table. 'It's Baltic out there today. At least the rain has stopped and it's bright, but that wind could cut you in two. Hope you've got your thermals on. How did you sleep, pet?'

'Great thanks, until 5.30 a.m....'

'Ah, bet that was Colonel Sanders, the cockerel. You get used to it eventually, but you won't have him to worry about when you go over the way. You're on the other side from the courtyard, but you'll get the sea birds squawking instead.'

'What do you mean by over the way, Meg?' I asked curiously.

'To your new temporary home. You couldn't be expected to live with two codgers like me and Bert. You need your own space. Plus, that spare room is far too small for adults for much more than a couple of nights. You're going to be staying in the guest apartment over in the castle. Grace insisted, and it's all ready for you. It's fabulous. You're going to love it, you lucky lass! Anyway, let's have a cuppa while I get breakfast ready, then I'll take you over later today, after you're done with Bert,' she said, picking up the kettle and shaking it to see if there was enough water. She lifted up a round, silver lid on the Aga and popped the kettle onto an iron plate. Agas don't require switching on, who would have thought it!

After breakfast, I put on the cagoule and

trainers and presented myself in front of Bert.

'I'm ready!' I said over brightly, a smile fixed on my face, frozen by fear, not the icy weather. 'I've read the list Bert, cool names.'

Bert looked me up and down, an astounded expression descending on his kindly face.

'Ellie lass, you can't go out there like that, you'll freeze to death. Where's your topcoat and a hat? Those things on your feet will be soaked through and filthy in seconds,' he said dismissively, looking down at my limited-edition footwear.

'Bert's right pet,' said Meg. 'You can't go out like that. Just a minute. I'll see what I can find.'

Meg came back clutching a huge yellow padded hi-vis jacket, the kind workmen wear while emptying the bins or mending the roads and suchlike.

'This will keep you toasty until we get you across to a shop.'

I took it from her. It was covered in splodges of goodness knows what, and had a pungent odour of, well of something I couldn't quite identify, but reminiscent of a petting zoo I had once visited. She handed me a brightly coloured knitted hat. It was in the style of a Viking helmet, with two woollen plaits hanging down the front and a couple of horns poking out of the top.

'Made with alpaca fleece,' she said proudly. 'Simone, that's Zen's mam, makes them to sell in the village gift shop. Mind, it's debatable whether Vikings had horns, but the tourists like them.'

To finish off my new look, she pointed to a pair of Bert's old wellies in the porch.

'Size 9 okay for you?'

'A bit big, but I'll manage.'

'Put these on. They're proper fisherman's socks and you'll be fine,' she said, handing me a pair of thick ribbed foot warmers.

'Right, you're good to go,' said Meg, as I pulled on the wellingtons and looked myself up and down in the porch mirror. Who was standing in front of me? The gang were going to love this, and no doubt ridicule me forever! I had a fleeting image of me walking into *Randy Parrot* dressed like this. It would be worth it to see the look on Anna's face.

Bert and I were just coming out of the cottage into the yard when I spotted him. Zen. He was still wearing the beanie, but the scarf was trailing around his neck and down the front of his coat, not muffled up over his face. And oh my God, that face! I couldn't help staring. There went that click again, my eyes locking into place as I walked towards him. He was the most beautiful man I had ever seen, and I was mesmerised. His eyes were still like the dark roast coffee beans of last night, but this morning, as they caught the light, I could see they had sparkling shards of golden demerara sugar in them too. They were set in a finely chiselled face, cheekbones like sharks' fins, and his skin was as pale as a mistletoe berry, with a wash of pink from the biting, cold wind. His hair was the colour of dark chocolate and was escaping from the sides of the beanie in long, loose tendrils. And his mouth – I could feel myself hyperventilating just looking at that mouth – it looked so, so kissable, his lips set in a semi-smile. He exuded an air of quiet confidence, casually dressed in faded denim and wool; yet to my eyes, more stylish than any model I had ever seen in all my years working amongst the movers and shakers of the London scene. I was gone. Like really, really gone and despite me thinking about playing the field, I got the feeling a quick fling with him would never be enough.

'Morning. Just popped over to see how you are after yesterday, Ellie?'
He may as well have been talking to me in Klingon. I heard the words but was just on to the bit where I was about to kiss those lips…

'Erm, yes, fine thanks,' I stuttered, having to drag myself back to real time. 'Slept well in your bed…' *Did I actually just say that out loud?* 'I mean your old bunk bed.'

He gave that half smile again.

'Top or bottom?' he asked mischievously.

'You choose!' The words were out of my mouth before I had time to stop them. Zen burst out laughing. So, despite his quiet demeanour, there was a sense of humour lurking in there.

'You should have been dressed like that yesterday. The hat suits you,' he said seriously, before turning to Bert. 'Is Meg in?'

'Aye lad, go on in and have a chinwag with her. She'd like to catch up with your news. Young Ellie and I are just starting our first lesson in animal care. Haway lass, best get on. Follow me.'

I said goodbye to Zen and shuffled off, trying to look as cool as one could in a coat that made you resemble a hot air balloon, a pair of giant wellies weighing my feet down like lead boots – not to mention the horned Viking hat. I'd only met Zen twice; yesterday I looked like something that had been dredged up from a swamp, and today, well, quite frankly, it didn't bear thinking about.

'Thought I heard your voice Zen,' said Meg from the doorway. 'Come in and have a cup of tea with me. I hear Harriet was over the other day. You can tell me all her news.'

And it was as if someone had pricked that hot air balloon, letting all the air out. I felt utterly, utterly deflated. There was that name again. *Harriet.*

CHAPTER 11

As the door shut on Meg and Zen, I tried to close my mind to the disappointment that Zen was unavailable. I didn't even know the guy after all, but it was as if an invisible force was drawing me to him and I was powerless to stop it. It was like I had been hypnotised. Maybe this place had ancient mystical powers which triggered the minute you crossed the causeway.

A weak sun was lighting up the unshaded areas of the yard, and for the first time, I took in my surroundings. The square courtyard was enclosed and overshadowed by the castle on two sides, with a range of outbuildings running around the perimeter. The big arched gate we had come through last night remained closed, and the only view of the outside world was from a five-bar gate at the top, with a view of green fields below and the sea in the far distance. The yard was cast in shadows, and with the predominance of old grey stone and cobbles, it looked medieval. There was a door set into the thick wall on ground level, and a flight of well-worn, stone steps led up to yet another door, leading directly into what I presumed was the back of the castle. The chickens were clucking about, pecking between the cobbles, and I noticed two turkeys huddled near the gate.

'I feel like I've arrived on a historical film set, Bert. It's ancient. My friend's boyfriend Toby would love it here. He's mad about history.'

'Aye pet, parts of it have been here since the 1500s when it was first constructed as a fortress. It has a chequered history like most of the castles around here. Its main job was to defend the lands around it and was largely unchanged until the early 1900s, when the outbuildings and our cottage were built. Tell you what, young Ellie, before we start on the introductions, let me take you to the front of the castle so you can get your bearings as to where you are. I'd forgotten you haven't seen anything yet.'

Bert headed towards the solid wooden door set in the wall and pushed it open. The wind rushed in and nearly blew us over, but I hardly noticed because I could not quite believe the view from the other side.

'Wow, just wow! Bert, the view... it's like something from a painting,' I said, gazing at what lay in front of me: miles and miles of Northumberland coastline, seemingly endless skies and the vast sea racing towards the rocks below. Perched high above the rocky beach, we were gifted a panoramic view.

'Aye pet, it is that. I've lived on this island getting on seventy years – at the castle for forty of those – and there's not a day goes by that I don't count my lucky stars. Every day is different. The view changes with the tides, with the weather, with the seasons. Winter is my favourite time. It may be cold enough to freeze your bits off, but there are fewer tourists, and the castle is closed to visitors, so we get this to ourselves. I'm a lucky old so and so, Ellie. I've got all of this.' He gesticulated; his arms wide open. 'And more importantly, I've got my Meg to enjoy it with.'

I could feel a tear in my eye as he spoke, his voice choked with sincerity. There was no doubt about it, Bert had what was truly important in life sussed.

'Look down that way, Ellie. That's Bamburgh Castle where Lord B lives.' He pointed into the far distance where a huge castle dominated the land, jutting out to sea.

'And that?' I pointed to a small island in front of us, where I could see a few small, whitewashed buildings and a red and white striped lighthouse.

'That's Greater Reef, the sanctuary Mike and Simone look after. The lighthouse was decommissioned years ago. The island isn't open to the public, although some of the tourist boats from Seahouses sail around it, weather permitting.'

I turned to look at Lindisfarne Castle, my new home. It wasn't huge, as castles go, almost square from the angle I was looking at, but it was captivating. As I followed Bert around the path, the view changed at every turn. For the first time, I got a sense of the island. I could see the village in the distance, what looked like upturned fishing boats along a stretch of beach, and the ruins of what resembled an old Abbey on the outskirts of the village. The place was magical.

'Bert, this is just stunning, I've got a million questions about everything,' I said, excitedly.

'Well lass, you've got a few weeks to ask them. Now is not the time. Those animals don't look after themselves, and we're already running late, so let's go and get on with it and you can come back here anytime. The castle's closed in winter, so you've got the place to yourself, Lady Ellie of Lindisfarne.' He laughed and made his way back to the door.

We went back through the gate towards the yard and Bert stumbled.

'You okay, Bert?'

'It's this blooming dicky hip of mine giving me jip today.'

'Why not go in and have a rest?'

'Can't do that, Ellie lass, the animals need sorting. I'll just pop in and take a couple of pain killers, won't be a tick.' Bert limped off towards the cottage.

A few minutes later, the door opened and out strolled Zen.

'Change of tutor.' He smiled. 'Bert took some persuading to have a rest – Meg all but had to pin him down – but you don't argue with Meg! So sorry, but you've got me instead.'

Sorry? I was absolutely delighted.

'I hope Bert will be okay.'

'He'll be fine, just in need of a rest. He does too much,' he said as he strode across the yard. I hurried behind, trying to keep up with his long legs, which was a struggle in giant wellies.

'Dogs first. Let them out for a pee as you start your rounds. If the weather is good, they'll potter happily around the yard, or take themselves back indoors. They stay in the kennel when James and Grace are away, otherwise Tri and Robson live in the apartment with them, then there's Flo of course. They've already been out this morning but let me introduce you.'

As we entered a warm, well-kept kennel, the three dogs all bounded towards us – even Tripod who, whilst on three legs, didn't seem affected in the slightest. Flo seemed especially pleased to see me.

'What happened to Tri's back leg?' I asked.

'Tri was a racing Greyhound. He fell and his leg snapped. It couldn't be mended, so when Grace heard about him, she offered to take him and paid for all his vet's bills. You wouldn't even know he was missing a leg now. I've got a proper soft spot for this boy and his tenacity. Dogs really show us humans a thing or two,' he said, stroking the sleek black animal who looked up at him in adoration. My heart was in danger of melting into a puddle on the cobbles at the sight of two pairs of dark brown eyes looking at each other with such love.

'And that's Robson,' said Zen, as a strange looking creature came trotting towards me.

The Bedlington Terrier was an odd-looking

animal. Part dog, part lamb! I didn't think I'd ever seen anything quite like him before. His coat was silver, the texture of lamb's wool, and he had a funny little face with a roman nose. That said, he was delightful, coming straight over and shoving his fluffy little body in front of me for a stroke.

'Meg is responsible for bringing Robson here. She was in Alnwick at the market and saw him tied up to a bollard looking lost and lonely. No one knew who he belonged to. They went down the proper channels but drew a blank. Poor dog was in a mess; his fur was matted; he was very underweight and scared. Grace immediately bonded with him and if she has a favourite, it's Robson. So, you obviously like dogs, Ellie. I suppose you have lots of experience with animals coming to help in a place like this?'

Did I tell him the truth or just fly by the seat of my pants? The latter seemed the easiest option!

'Err, well, I do love dogs, and err, all other animals,' I prevaricated.

'Has one ever stolen your heart?'

'You mean a dog?' I stuttered, thinking my heart was currently being stolen – by him!

'Dog, cat, giraffe. Any type of animal, Ellie.'

Maybe now was not the time to tell him about Buzz the guinea pig.

'Ah, well yes,' I answered without hesitation, back on safer ground. 'Nacho. He's arriving later today – you'll meet him. He's the most beautiful little dog in the world,' I said enthusiastically.

'I can tell you're smitten Ellie.' He laughed.

'Suppose anyone else in your life takes second place?'

Hmmm, was he fishing for information? I sincerely hoped so. I'd gladly be willing to do a joint first place – for him!

'Well, there's currently no competition with Nacho,' I replied, trying not to look too desperate.

'I hear he's part Yorkshire terrier?'

I looked blankly at Zen. I had no idea as to Nacho's breed and didn't really care. To me, he was just the cutest little dog in the world.

'You'll have to watch him for disappearing down rabbit holes, but he'll be a great help keeping the rats down.'

'What?' I gasped out loud.

'Ellie, the look on your face is priceless!'

'You'd better be joking. *My* Nacho is not going down a rabbit hole, and as for rats, that's just not happening – ever,' I said vehemently.

'It's what they were bred for Ellie, but we'll make an exception in Prince Nacho's case, eh? Right, on to the bird houses. The girls all came from a hen rescue trust,' explained Zen. 'The cockerel just arrived one day and hasn't left.'

'And the turkeys?'

'Christmas poultry sale. No one wanted these two scrawny weaklings, so Grace bought them, and here they are, weaklings no longer. Ready for the oven if you ask Bert.' He winked.

'Meg tends to look after the girls and the turkeys, collecting the eggs and keeping their houses clean. They're put inside at night although we don't have much of a fox problem here on the island. Colonel Sanders is left to his fate. He roams around wherever he wants and maybe he'll find his way back home with any luck. Right, come and meet the cats and Nanny McPhee.'

We strolled towards the next outbuilding followed by the dogs. I could hear her before I met her. She was one very vocal goat. As we entered her stable, she bleated even louder.

'I feel so sorry for her. She lost her mate and has made her presence known ever since. Her previous owners had neighbours and they objected to the noise. I can't say I blame them, but it's not her fault. Missing your partner is no fun, is it Nanny?'

He gazed at the goat, a faraway look in his eyes, and I guessed he wasn't just talking about Nanny. The pure white goat looked at me with unblinking pink eyes. She was pretty and looked like she was smiling, a cute little beard dangling from below her chin, but... she had fierce looking horns – put the Viking ones on the top of my hat to shame – and hers looked like they could do a lot of damage. I was beginning to feel quite anxious.

'Erm, does she headbutt you with those horns?' I squeaked.

'Hasn't done... yet... always a first time though, I suppose! It's important that she gets milked twice a day, every day, usually about eight in the morning and six in the evening. Meg takes care of that.'

I gave an inward sigh of relief. One less thing

to worry about, but it was short- lived as Zen continued.

'Have you milked goats before?'

There was no skirting around this one. I could not be let loose on a real goat without training, and even then, the whole idea terrified me.

'No, I've never encountered a goat before,' I answered truthfully.

'You need to learn; it will give Meg a break every now and again. I suppose I can show you now...'

He went to unclip Nanny but then stopped suddenly in his tracks, like he had one of those lightbulb moments.

'On second thoughts, maybe I should just leave this to Meg.' He started laughing, deep belly laughs. I looked at him quizzically, raising an eyebrow.

'You'll understand when you do the training Ellie. Let's just say there are only so many *double entendres* I can endure! Right, swiftly moving on. The cats. They all live outdoors, but they tend to sleep in this stall next to Nanny, and it's where we feed them. You read Bert's note – just make sure you give Lulu the tabby a wide berth, and don't be fooled because she is so cute – she's a proper little madam and would scratch your eyes out before you could blink. She's got a human equivalent on the island...' he stopped, mid flow. 'Sorry, that was uncalled for. I'm sure you don't want to hear me badmouthing someone.'

Oh, but I did! I was intrigued that this gentle man could have a bad word to say about anyone. It seemed so out of character, but then, I didn't really know him well – yet!

'Horses next.' He marched on, cutting the conversation dead in its tracks.

This was what I had been dreading the most. Horses were a mystery to me, and I was extremely nervous around them. They were big and strong, and I'd never had anything to do with them. As a kid, half of my friends were obsessed with ponies, but even though I liked animals, I hadn't ever wanted to learn to ride. We entered a stable with three stalls, one empty. In the first was an enormous creature. I swore it looked about the same size as a London double decker bus. It surveyed us, ears forward, hay hanging out the side of its whiskery mouth.

'Meet Stout. She's a beauty,' said Zen, mistaking my silence for awe. 'Eighteen hands of prime Shire.'

'Yes, indeed.' I gulped, pretending I knew what he was talking about. The big, brown horse continued to stare, motionless. It was quite unnerving.

'Came from the brewery in Newcastle when it shut down. She's about twenty-five years old – getting on a bit – but she's gorgeous, aren't you Stout?' he said gently, stroking her velvety nose. She whinnied and I swore I saw love in her big, brown soulful eyes.

We moved on to the next stall. There stood the

cutest little pony, all cream coat and dark mane and tail. It was tiny and very rotund, with huge, deep brown eyes framed by the longest lashes any self-respecting fashionista would be proud of, but its ears were flat to its head, and it watched our every move intently, as if weighing us up.

'Don't be fooled by him,' said Zen. 'Looks like butter wouldn't melt, eh? But I tell you what, he is a wolf in sheep's clothing. Trades on looking all demure, then wham! He'll nip you quicker than a crab in a rockpool. Never get too close behind him and keep your distance. They both go down to their paddock on good days. Han likes Stout – the only thing he does like.'

'Where did he come from?'

'They haven't had him too long. Grace was hoodwinked. A family in Bamburgh was moving and told her he was a sweetheart. When she saw him, she immediately fell in love, as she tends to do. Said he reminded her of some cartoon ponies she grew up looking at. I agree, he's cute, but then they learned the awful truth about the little blighter. Too late now. He's here, and they never move an animal on unless it's better for them. Anyway Ellie, we'll get these down to the paddock, which one do you want to take?'

I stared at the tiny devil pony in front of me. I swore it was baring its teeth like its namesake. It would be demanding Chianti next. And then I looked at the double decker bus in the next stall, feet like bin lids, and realised I was caught between a rock and a hard place with nowhere to hide. Zen burst out laughing.

'Ellie, your face is a picture. Don't fret. I'm not going to make you do that today – just my little joke! Bert tells me you've come to help with cleaning, walking and the jobs that his dodgy hip objects to. I'll take the horses down. You've earned a break, and it's coffee time, so go and see Meg and tell her to put the kettle on and I'll follow you over. Then after lunch, I'm sure Bert will be fit enough to take you down to the paddocks and introduce you to the last of the residents, the alpacas and the donkeys.'

There was no need for Zen to tell me twice. I was off, quicker than a thoroughbred out of the stalls, and back to the cosy cottage to see Bert and Meg. Hopefully, I'd have time to get out of these ridiculous clothes and run a brush through my hair before Zen came back.

CHAPTER 12

I went into the porch and was about to take off my coat and wellies when I heard Meg shout out.

'Is that you Ellie? There's someone waiting to see you.'

When I pushed open the inner door, Bert was sitting in his chair, clutching onto a tiny ball of fur. He gently placed it on the ground from where it launched itself at me. Nacho! He was wearing a big red bow around his neck and had clearly been groomed. I scooped him up and gave him a hug, kissing him on top of his scented spikey head.

'One of the lads from the castle dropped him off,' said Meg. 'What an adorable little dog. We've just got acquainted with him, Ellie, and I think he is going to fit in with us just fine.'

The door opened and in strolled Zen. He had taken off his coat and hat, and whilst most of my focus was on tiny Nacho, it was hard not to cast admiring glances towards the gorgeous man, whose personality seemed as beautiful as the rest of him. I maybe should have been grateful that Zen was taken, otherwise the new Ellie, the one that was supposedly going to play the field, might have been a very short-lived experience. If I was with Zen, I don't think I'd ever let him go.

'I can't tell you how much I've been looking forward to seeing Nacho again,' I gushed. 'From the minute I saw his photo advertising the charity on the internet, I was smitten.'

And now I was doubly smitten. I cast a furtive glance at Zen, who was watching me and Nacho intently, a wide smile on his face. It made him even more handsome – if that were possible. Looking at him literally made me feel weak at the knees, and there was me thinking that was some old wives' tale – it really wasn't, and I was sure mine were just about to buckle underneath me at any moment. He sat down on the settee and looked like he had been poured onto it; he was so languid, fluid almost. He looked so relaxed, his long limbs stretching out comfortably, totally at ease with himself. I noticed he had taken off his shoes and was wearing odd socks without any trace of embarrassment. This was a man who took casual to the extreme and despite me thinking I would never fall for someone so… so… well, casual, it would appear I'd done a total U-turn. Matt wouldn't go to the corner shop without fussing over his hair. I remembered Gran once saying, 'He's far too bothered what other people think about him, that one,' and it turned out Gran was right.

'I can see why you took a shine to him, pet. He's gorgeous,' said Meg breaking into my thoughts.

'He is that,' I agreed wholeheartedly, not sure

whether I was talking about Nacho or Zen.

'Meg, will you take a photo of me and Nacho please? I want to remember this moment.' I handed her my phone.

'Of course, pet. Go and sit on the settee next to Zen and I'll get you all in – I hope – because I'm not that used to these new-fangled phones.'

I smiled at Zen, wondering how close I could get to him without looking desperate. He was wearing a tight-fitting black V-necked jumper with a white tee shirt under it emphasising his broad chest. His sleeves were rolled up, exposing sinewy forearms, which were covered in fine dark hairs, and he was wearing a mish mash of wrist bands and ribbons around one wrist, and what looked like a silver coffee bean on a narrow leather cord hung around his neck. He was a total rock god and might well have just stepped off a band's tour bus.

'You in a trance, Ellie pet? Jump to it, haven't got all day!'

On hearing Meg's voice, I remembered to breathe and hoped I hadn't been gawping, or worse still, drooling, but I couldn't help it, he was mesmerising.

'Sorry miles away!' I laughed, placing Nacho next to Zen on the settee and sitting down at a respectable distance – I thought if I came into bodily contact with those taut thighs, I would literally melt on the spot. Once again, I could smell coffee, a strong expresso, but this time it was mixed with pine. I took a deep breath, filling my lungs with the heady aroma. It was like inhaling an essential oil, immediately hitting my senses, and putting me in the zone. Meg clicked the camera a few times and handed me the phone. When I looked at the photos, the realisation of what I looked like dawned on me. I had been so wrapped up in Nacho and Zen that I had totally forgotten I was wearing a stain splattered, yellow hi-vis coat and a hat with Viking horns. If I had any notion that Zen might find me even remotely attractive, then perhaps I needed to wake up and smell the actual coffee! Zen unfurled himself from the settee and reached out for his coat.

'Got to get off now and catch the tide in plenty of time. Don't want to risk being bollocked by Bert again.' Zen winked at the older man. 'Lovely to see you, Ellie. Glad you're settling in. There was no doubt of that really when you're being looked after by these two,' he said, looking at the pair of them fondly, before wrapping his long arms around Meg and giving her a hug and a kiss on the top of her head. 'Just give me a shout if there's anything you need, Ellie,' he said, pausing at the door.

'Oh thanks, I will,' I responded, keeping it brief before my foot had time to contemplate putting itself right into my mouth and telling him just what it was that I needed!

'This came with Nacho, Ellie. It's for you,' said Meg, handing me an envelope, oblivious to how flustered I was as I watched the door close on Zen.

I opened it up to find a card with Bamburgh Castle on the front. Inside, in beautiful handwriting, was a note from Lord B.

Dear Ellie,

I hope your journey north went well and that you are settling into your new temporary home. It probably all feels very strange to you after busy London. Bert and Meg are the most wonderful couple, and I knew after talking to you that a break in our beautiful county, with them looking out for you, could be just what you needed. Enjoy Northumberland, Ellie, and most importantly, your time with Nacho. In the few days he has been with us, he has been a joy, and my wife was very reluctant to part with him! Don't waste a precious moment of your time on Lindisfarne as it will be over too soon. If you make your way to Bamburgh, please do drop in – I think you will manage to find the castle.

Lance.

'Lord Bamburgh is such a nice chap, Meg,' I said, propping up the card on the table.

'He is that. Kind, like his sister. Grace is just the same,' she replied, handing me a cup of tea.

'Mmm, something smells good.'

'Sunday roast. We eat at 1.30 p.m. prompt every Sunday, tradition you know. You've got a while yet, so have your cuppa and then why not take Nacho for a little walk about, get him familiarised with his new surroundings? After lunch, Bert will take care of the introductions between the dogs, just in case there are any issues. Knowing the other three, and after meeting Nacho here, I don't think for a minute there will be.'

'Good idea Meg. I'm just going to my room to send a few messages while I have my tea, and then we'll go out.'

I lay on the narrow bed, Nacho curled up in a little ball next to me and looked at the photos Meg had taken. I sent a quick message to my parents promising to ring them later, and then, despite knowing what would happen as soon as they saw it, pinged a photo off to the group chat.

Happy Nacho Day to me! If this photo makes it anywhere near social media, I swear I will find every available Viking and come down there and sort you all out – I'm a hard girl from the north now, remember!
Love you all.
Ellie and Nacho xxxxxx

I made no reference to Zen and sat back and waited and, sure enough, three replies pinged back in quick succession.

Ellie, you don't look like our Ellie!
Stan and Alex xx

I'm getting bad twin vibes!
Sophie x

Good lord, they've drugged you!
Tara x

The little dots bouncing about on the screen informed me that they were all frantically typing away. Sophie got there first.

Why are you dressed like a garden gnome? Who is that absolute sex god next to you? Not seen him on Geordie Shore! What have they done to my bestie? Have they drugged you? Is the gorgeous guy the leader of a cult? I never trust men with long hair, although I'd make an exception in his case; it's super shiny and not too long. Do ask him what shampoo he uses. Do you want me to send Jake over to Bethnal Green and round up a few geezers from the manor? We can plan a Jason Statham style rescue. 7.00 p.m. vid chat Monday, non-negotiable, so I can scan the room and make sure you are not being held captive and you are telling me the truth, without mad people in cloaks forcing you to read from cards.

Love Sophie x

P.S. Nacho is just so cute!

Why are you dressed like a trawler fisherman? Whoever that is next to you, give him my number. I would relegate Toby to the past to massage his follicles. Thinking about it, Toby would probably be pleased with that deal – as long as it's back to Roman times! Is Mr Gorgeous there the gang master and has he disguised you as a fisherman so they can send you on a boat to a brothel in Amsterdam? Since Brexit, you hear of that happening all the time. Try and knock them out with a giant cod and make a run for it. I bet that Bert and Meg are in on it too and are currently counting their share of the spoils before running off to their villa in Marbella. 7.00 p.m. vid chat Tuesday, if you are not incommunicado that is. Toby said to tell you that

Viking helmets don't have horns.
Love Tara x
P.S. Nacho is just way too cute!

OMG! They are making you do the hard labour fixing the roads? That hat is so cool. Could you get me and Aleksy matching ones if they pay you wages for all that digging? Also, can you keep dirty coat when you finished? I think Aleksy dressed as motorway workman, all sweaty, shiny muscles, would be very, very sexy. Vid chat Wednesday 7.00 p.m. We all drink coffee and talk workman chic. Please tell us that gorgeous guy is gay. Our friend Curtis and him would be second power couple of Peckham – after me and Alex of course.
Kochamy Cie, Stan and Alex xx
P.S. Nacho is cutest dog in world x

My friends may have been hundreds of miles away, but I knew that wherever we all were in the world, we would always be there for each other. They creased me up and had supported me through thick and thin, as I had them, and thanks to the internet, I could get my fix on a regular basis, making the distance between us almost irrelevant.

'Right Nacho let's go and explore for half an hour,' I said as I went back through to the living room and looked for his lead.

'It's there,' said Meg, pointing to a funny, harness type thing. It was all loops and bits that clipped together and looked like a surgical aid. What was wrong with old style dog collars that just went around the neck?

I held up the contraption and studied it, Meg oblivious, beating Yorkshire pudding mixture like her life depended on it.

'Okay poppet. I think this bit goes here,' I said, and Nacho patiently let me lift his tiny front leg and pop it through a hole. I did the same with the next leg and stood back, full of self-admiration at my brilliance in tackling this new skill. Unfortunately, the metal ring to attach the lead was lost somewhere under Nacho's tummy, and I realised I had the thing on upside down. Attempt number two wasn't much better, with his legs both ending up in the same hole. I took it off again and, third time lucky, got it right. Nacho's bright hazelnut eyes were looking at me intently, and I swear he was thinking *idiot!*

'Sorry little one. It's a learning curve for me too.' I smiled, clipping on the lead and making for the door, Meg yelling, 'Don't forget the poo bags.' Yes, I had a lot to learn.'

CHAPTER 13

This time, I went through the door set into the big arched gates, following the steep road that curved around the castle. When we reached the bottom, I looked up at the ancient building perched on the top of a craggy mount, where it held a commanding position on the island, which looked almost flat by comparison. I went through the five-bar gate at the bottom, where a big notice informed people that the castle was closed for the winter. I walked along the road that Zen had brought me along the previous night, Nacho happily trotting next to me. Was it only yesterday that I had arrived? I felt like I'd been on the island for ages, yet it had been less than twenty-four hours. So much had happened in that time, and I had hardly had a minute to stop and take stock. What I did know was that, so far, apart from the causeway mishap, I'd enjoyed every single minute and couldn't wait to explore further and get to know the animals, minus the horses! With Meg's words about punctuality ringing in my ears, we walked only a little further along the road and onto a shingle beach, where we stood side by side, staring out to sea. Nacho's shiny, black button nose was in the air, breathing in the scents that were being carried along on the wind, and my mind was focused on what the next few weeks were going to bring, and when I might cross paths with Zen again.

A tall blonde woman of about my age, was walking towards me, and I was at once struck by how she stood out; on an island full of thermal bobble hats, she was a cashmere beret. She was a vision in near floor length powder pink faux fur, chunky studded biker boots, and what looked like a *Hermes* crossbody bag with a multi-coloured wide-webbed strap, casually draped over one shoulder. She would look quite at home strolling along the Kings Road. As she got closer, it was impossible not to notice how beautiful she was: fine features, pale grey eyes and a generous mouth, which sparkled with iridescent lip-gloss, her ice blonde hair in a fishtail plait, skirting towards her waist. This was a woman who cared deeply about her appearance, even for a walk along the beach on a tiny island in the middle of nowhere. I would have staked my professional reputation on it; this woman was a model. She drew level with me and was about to walk by without any acknowledgement when Nacho had other plans and jumped in front of her. She was forced to come to an abrupt halt, or trip right over his lead.

'So sorry,' I apologised. 'Nacho, come here,' I said, pulling his retractable lead towards me. 'I'm not used to this contraption,' I said, waving the offending item towards her.

'No harm done,' she said, in an accent that had only the faintest trace of northern in it. I could see her weighing me up, probably wondering where I had escaped from.

'Are you a winter security guard at the castle? Mind, that isn't much of a guard dog.' She nodded towards Nacho.

'Erm no, actually I'm staying up at the castle.'

'*You're* the woman from London?'

'Erm, yes, how do you know?'

'Everybody knows everything that's going on around here. You'll soon get used to that. Drives me bloody bonkers but that's island life for you. I'm Isla,' she said, holding out a hand clad in a baby blue glove made from the softest buttery leather.

'Ellie,' I replied, holding out my non-gloved hand, which I noticed was streaked with mud.

She withdrew her hand quickly before contact, the handshake equivalent of an air-kiss perhaps.

'So, Ellie, tell me, how are you related to the Lindisfarnes?'

I was about to answer when I glanced at my phone and noticed the time.

'Look at the time. Sorry to be rude but I've got to go, said I'd be back for 1.30 p.m.'

'That's a shame, but I expect Meg has been preparing your lunch. It must be lonely in the castle all on your own. I expect you are used to spooky old buildings though.'

'Err, not really,' I replied, wondering what she

was talking about. 'Nice to meet you, Isla.'

'Pleasure meeting you, Ellie. I've not been back on the island long myself. I was living in London, so it would be good if we could get together, exchange stories of life in the big city, talk about anything other than fish.' She grimaced.

'Great,' I replied. 'Where can I find you?' I asked, delighted that I might have made my first friend.

'Oh, I'll come up to the castle soon and we can arrange something.'
We said goodbye and went our separate ways. She hadn't patted Nacho – not once.

***

'Enjoy that pet?' enquired Meg when I got back. 'Nacho, okay?'

'He's a little star Meg, no problem at all.'

'Many people about?'

'A few walkers and a couple of families on the beach. Oh, and I met a stunningly pretty girl from the island called Isla. She seemed nice.'

'Isla? Oh, she's pretty, right enough,' said Meg scathingly. I could feel the drop in temperature as the atmosphere started to freeze over.

'Do I deduce you're not a fan Meg?'

'Listen pet, I think everyone has the right to make their own minds up about people, so I'm not going to gossip but… take it from me, keep your wits about you. She has a mean streak that one.'

Before I could ask any more, Bert came in,

minus his coat and wellies, but still wearing the tweed cap. I wondered if he ever took it off. I hoped I might get the chance to speak to Meg about Isla later, but I imagined it was subject closed for the moment.

Sunday lunch was fabulous. I struggled to remember the last time I'd had one that was homemade. Even Mum and Dad never bothered much these days, preferring to go to the golf club. And we would never consider making one at the flat, far too much like hard work and, quite frankly, would probably taste awful. I helped clear away and washed the dishes, whilst Bert had forty winks in front of the fire. When he woke up, the three of us put on our outdoor clothes. I clipped the lead on Nacho. I had decided the harness would stay on him throughout the day, thus reducing the number of times I could look like an idiot, and we set off towards our first stop, the kennel. Bert took Nacho from me and asked me to open the kennel door. The three dogs came bounding out, stopping almost in mid-air when they noticed the new arrival. After that, it was a melee of sniffing and waggy tails. This lot were going to get on well from the off, that much was clear.

'Wonder what he'll be like with my girls,' mused Meg, but as we walked towards the top gate, Nacho took no interest in the hens whatsoever, straining to keep up with the other three dogs.

'We won't let him off the lead for a few days yet,' said Bert. 'Once I'm sure he's going to be okay, and that he's got the scent of where he is, we'll test his recall in an enclosed paddock and go from there.'

We went through the five-bar gate which led outside the courtyard and followed a narrow cinder track down the steep hill to the flat land below the castle, where there were several fenced in paddocks, all with shelters.

'Meet Pacino and Murray,' said Meg. 'They are just the most adorable creatures; look into those huge eyes and tell me you don't get lost in dreams.'

'Do they spit?' I asked, looking at the pair of gorgeous, woolly animals, one black, one grey. They were actually a lot smaller than I had imagined.

'That's the first question anyone ever asks about alpacas. No lass, not usually. Llamas tend to do that more, but I'm not saying these two haven't ever. I have had the odd grassy clump fly at me. It's all to do with their digestive systems and where the spit comes from, and you don't want to be caught with any from down in their stomach.' She grimaced. 'Just keep on your toes, and if I can swerve them at my age, you shouldn't have any problems! Alpacas tend to be very friendly and easy to look after – well at least these two are. They enjoy carrot slices,' she said, giving me some out of her pocket to feed them. I nervously held my hand out, and they both gently took the carrot from me.

'They can live outdoors if they have a shelter, so we have made sure they have a nice weatherproof place to go if they need to, without bringing them up to the yard every night. They also like walks, especially to the village, so you can walk them around the island when you feel brave enough. Next time young William and Amelia come to take them out, you can go with them.'

'Walk? Alpacas? To the village?' I asked incredulously.

'Yes, you stressed city types pay a fortune to do alpaca walks. Meant to be very therapeutic and good for the soul – and you get to do it for free.'

This place was full of surprises.

Finally, I met Wonky and Jenny, the donkeys. Jenny was a sweetheart and came straight to the gate for some carrots and a nuzzle. Wonky, meanwhile, paced up and down along the far side of the paddock, braying loudly towards the fields beyond.

'Wilma, another donkey, is over there on the farm,' explained Bert, 'and Wonky spends his days shouting his love for her in donkey language.' He laughed.

'We are going to see about Wilma coming to live here with us, otherwise he is going to go mad,' said Meg. 'But the Willis family who own her, want to keep her alone until after the village nativity as she's playing a part – as are Pacino and Murray – they are going to be disguised as camels!'

It was dusk as we made our way slowly back up the hill towards the little cottage tucked away in the castle walls. Nacho was trotting along on his lead, tail wagging like a fan, the other three dogs all bounding about and chasing each other. Meg and Bert were ahead, arm in arm, laughing at something one of them had said. I looked across at the twinkling lights in the village, and the far-flung farms and houses which were dotted across the island. The gulls were circling above, noisily preparing for the night. Poor lovestruck Wonky was braying a bedtime lullaby to his beloved Wilma, and the rhythmic sound of the sea, ebbing and flowing, was a constant in the background. There really was something in appreciating the simpler things in life. After racing around London, hardly noticing anything, I had suddenly woken up and smelled the coffee. Which unsurprisingly brought my thoughts full circle back to Zen. How serious was it with this Harriet woman and what were the chances of her falling hopelessly in love with a travelling Aussie sheepshearer, and buying a one-way ticket to down under quicker than you could say 'G'day Sheila.' In the words of my favourite Australian ever, I should be so lucky!

CHAPTER 14

'Don't bother taking your coat off,' said Meg when we got back. 'May as well get you settled into your new abode,' she said, as she bustled about putting things into a basket.

I collected my belongings from the little room and felt a pang of sadness as I shut the door, casting a rueful glance at the bunk bed – I'd never found out if Zen preferred to be on top.

'Right, got a few basic provisions for both you and Nacho that will get you through the night. Then you can decide yourself about shopping, and whether you want to eat with me and Bert or sort yourself out.'

'Thanks Meg,' I replied. 'I'm sure it will all fall into a pattern – probably when I run out of food and am starving! Me and my flatmate are terrible at shopping, but then it doesn't really matter when you live on a street where every other shop is a takeaway.'

'Well, you'll need to get your act together here. It takes organisation.'

Nacho and I followed Meg across the courtyard and climbed the stone steps. She opened the door into the rear of the castle. A light came on automatically, and there was an area for boots and coats, a stone staircase leading upwards. I lugged my suitcase and a bag from Meg up the narrow, curving stairs, Nacho bounding ahead. At the top of the staircase was a landing with two doors next to each other. In the corner was another spiral stairwell.

'That one goes upwards to the roof terrace, and downwards into the castle,' said Meg. 'It's your other way out. Although you won't need to use it, except in the case of an emergency – just use the steps into the yard. I'm giving you my bunch of keys that will get you anywhere in the castle – so don't lose them!'

Meg put a key into the left-hand side door and clicked on the lights. The door opened straight into a large living room, with a small open plan kitchen at one end. The place was decorated impeccably; the fixtures and furnishings were high-end, five-star luxury, quite contemporary, but with some well-chosen period items and paintings.

'Meg, this is beautiful,' I said, gazing around the room. 'Surely, I shouldn't be staying here? It's like a suite in the Ritz.'

'Wouldn't know pet, never been to the Ritz, but yes, this is yours while you're here. Bedroom through there with an ensuite bathroom, and just wait till you see the bath, like a copper slipper it is, not that I could climb in and out of it these days.' She laughed.

I went across to the window; it was dark outside, but I could see the lights on Greater Reef and could imagine the view in daylight – the apartment was just above where Bert and I had stood that morning.

'I thought castles were old dusty places, not luxurious like this.'

'Just you wait until you see the rest of the place – suits of armour and everything. Even James and Grace's apartment is full of old junk, probably priceless objects, but dust gatherers just the same if you ask me! They went to town on this place, it being a guest suite.'

Meg showed me the basics of how things worked. It all seemed straightforward. Before she took her leave, she said, '8.00 a.m. sharp in the yard in the morning, Ellie, and don't forget to let Nacho out before you go to bed.'

'Understood Meg! I want to thank you and Bert for everything. You have gone way above and beyond in welcoming me, and I'm going to do my best to help you both as much as I can while I'm here.'

'You're more than welcome, Ellie pet. I'll be honest, we weren't sure when they said a girl from London was coming, but you've fitted in right away, just like one of the rescues.' She laughed, giving me a big hug before making her way down the spiral stairwell and back across to the cottage.

When she had gone, I looked around the apartment, opening drawers and cupboards, Nacho following me like a little shadow. The bedroom was as opulent as the rest of the apartment, with a huge bed. Shame it was probably going to go to waste.

'Come here little one, this must be as strange for you as it is for me. I'll let you into a secret Nacho,' I said, ruffling his spikey head. 'I've never lived on my own before, ever, so I'm pleased you're with me because I might get a bit scared.'

Because I didn't know what the rest of the castle interior looked like, my mind was running on overdrive. Could there be dungeons, instruments of torture, smugglers' tunnels that could be crept through in the dead of night? I was here in this ancient old building all on my own, and whilst Meg had told me that the island had a virtually non-existent crime rate, and that the castle was impenetrable to burglars, I was more worried about things that were already inside and had been for hundreds of years!

Glancing at the time, it had just gone 6.30 p.m., so I unpacked, put away the food Meg had given me, then had a long soak in the amazing copper bath. I put on my pyjamas and settled down to find something to watch on the television. One thing was for sure, it wouldn't be *Most Haunted* or a spooky film!

I nearly jumped out of my skin when, about an hour later, the intercom buzzed. Probably Bert bringing over something I'd forgotten.

'Hi, what have I left behind?'

'Hi,' said a woman's voice, laughing. 'Nothing as far as I know! This is Aurora. You met my brother Zen.'

'Oh hello! Yes, they've mentioned you. Come on up.'

I opened the door to a woman of about my own age, a similar height and build to me, with gorgeous dark chocolate hair poking out of her hat. Those tell-tale coffee bean eyes made sure there was no mistaking she was Zen's sister. She was clutching a couple of carrier bags.

'Let me take your coat,' I said, 'and please, sit down. It's lovely to meet you.'

Nacho was bouncing around her feet, desperate for attention. Aurora sat on the settee, scooped him up and gave him a hug.

'You must be the new boy I heard was coming. You're ridiculously cute and quite small. I hope the others don't trample on you.'

'Aurora, meet Nacho, and don't worry, the dogs all met earlier, and I think I know who's going to be in charge once he settles in!'

'I wanted to come across to welcome you earlier today,' she said, 'but we open on a Sunday. I run the local café,' she explained. 'It was busy because the tides were at times that suited the tourists. You'll soon work out all that kind of thing and how it alters the amount of people milling about the island,' she explained, whilst taking off her coat. She was dressed in the standard island apparel of padded coat, bobble hat and a thick scarf wrapped around her neck.

'Erm, yes, I'll be making sure I have my timetable tattooed on the inside of my eyeballs!' I laughed, hoping that she hadn't heard about my stupid mishap. 'Can I get you a tea or coffee? Sorry, I don't have any wine.'

'Coffee would be great, busman's holiday and all of that. I'm surrounded by the stuff all day, every day, not to mention my nerdy brother talking about little else.'

I put the kettle on whilst spooning some of Stan's favourite blend into a cafetiere, thinking her 'nerdy' brother could talk to me anytime he liked about anything.

'Try this,' I said, handing her a mug. 'One of my best friends in London has a mobile coffee business and dabbles in blending. He takes it very seriously.'

'Mmm, Ellie this is fantastic, so smooth. Did he blend this one?'

'Yes, he did, but I couldn't give you any details, except it's my favourite.'

'You must give Zen a taste, see what he thinks.'

'A taste? Yes, I most definitely will, at the earliest opportunity,' I responded innocently, trying to keep my face straight whilst my naughty streak sent me straight into the gutter. I blamed it on living with filter-free Sophie, who, according to my mum, was like a Navvy – whatever one of those was – but I could tell it wasn't complimentary. In my defence, unlike Sophie, I just thought things and I didn't say them out loud, well, most of the time that was...

'Anyway Ellie, if you feel that Bert needs extra support, please just give me a shout and I'll see if Zen can help more. He's not been back on the island long after being away for years, and he's just catching up on how we all muck in around here.'

'Where's he been?' I asked, intrigued.

'He left for university and then, afterwards, decided to travel, just like Ma and Pa at that age, keen to see the world, and then…' she trailed off. 'Anyway, he's back to stay, for now at least, so he needed a focus and started his coffee business. Like any new venture, it's almost a 24/7 commitment to get it off the ground. It's really keeping him busy, especially with the extra Christmas trade. Maybe he hasn't been over to help Bert as much as he should.'

'And I suppose it's quite time consuming for him and, erm, is it Harriet… his girlfriend… to see each other with her living on such a remote sheep farm on the mainland?'

'Harriet? Zen? An item? Whatever made you think that?' She laughed, clearly delighted by the idea.

'Oh, just something Meg said,' I mumbled, realising that, once again, my overactive imagination had clearly gone way off beam.

'Harriet's my best friend, and Zen is like her big brother. We've all known each other since we started high school. And seriously, whilst I know that my brother is total eye candy if you like the trippy hippie type,' she said, 'he's not Harriet's type at all – Harriet's gay.'

Any embarrassment I was feeling was quickly washed away by euphoria coursing through my veins. Harriet didn't need to relocate down under after all, and the mean girl I had imagined had now very quickly turned into the nice woman she probably was in reality. I couldn't imagine warm-hearted Aurora having a best friend who was anything less than lovely.

'I'll take you up to meet Harriet if you like,' said Aurora, breaking into my thoughts. 'Show you the Northumberland National Park where the farm is. It is absolutely beautiful and exceptionally remote.'

'Yes, I'd like that. I do want to see as much of the place as I can in the few weeks I'm going to be here, and sorry for the misunderstanding, I'm really good at that.' I laughed.

'My brother's single, Ellie, and whilst I wish he would meet someone, he doesn't think he's ready for another relationship yet, because for Zen that would mean serious. He's not the love 'em and leave 'em kind of guy. Let's just say, he came back to the island with a broken heart, and he isn't in a rush to go through that again. He's thrown himself into setting up the coffee business and it's his new love.' She laughed. 'Quite frankly, woe betide any woman who thinks they can take the place of a well roasted Arabica!'

We'll see about that!

I had a secret weapon – Stanislaw. I had much to learn about coffee, but he was an exceptionally good teacher and I'd learn quickly, and then Zen would fall for my expertise, and we would have happy times together, doing whatever you do with raw coffee beans. I could imagine Zen's arms around my waist as we crushed coffee in perfect tandem. The heady, intoxicating aroma of the beans fuelling our desire for each other... I had no idea how coffee was processed in the real world, of course, but in Ellie's world it was akin to *the* scene in *Ghost* as we ground together! My imagination was in danger of running totally out of kilter, but before I returned to planet earth, I indulged in a brief speculation about who had broken Zen's heart and decided she must be bonkers. Typical though, I'd managed to meet someone on my first day in Northumberland who had an immediate effect on me, but who didn't appear to do short term flings, and even though I was so interested in him, I was not ready for a long-term relationship myself... but sometimes you just had to go with the flow.

CHAPTER 15

'So apart from Bert, Meg, and Zen, have you met any other islanders yet?' asked Aurora, moving the subject away from her brother.

'I took Nacho onto the shore beside those funny wooden huts earlier, and I did meet someone called Isla. She said she lived on the island. What a stunning...' I trailed off, sensing an atmosphere creep in, just like it had when I had mentioned Isla to Meg.

'Aurora, is there something I should know about this Isla? When I told Meg I had bumped into her, I got the same response as I'm getting from you, positively frozen.'

'Erm, well, maybe you're asking the wrong person asking me, or Meg come to that. Let's just say, Isla is perhaps not as nice as she first appears, and you should be a little wary of her. She is very charismatic, I'll grant you that, but when the mask slips... anyway, you need to make your own mind up.'

'Funny, Meg said exactly the same! The thing is, Aurora, I've proved quite useless at reading people lately. I keep getting it wrong big style, so any forewarning you can give me might help.'

'If I start telling you, it will turn into a bitch-fest. I've only just met you and I don't want to come across as *that* person. Just take care and promise her nothing, otherwise she'll take everything.'

And on that cryptic note, Aurora moved the subject on.

'Zen mentioned that he had popped over this morning and that you were kitted out in Bert's smelly old hi-vis.'

My cheeks immediately began to burn, wondering if Zen had been poking fun at me. Aurora tuned in very quickly.

'Please don't think he was laughing at you Ellie – far from it – and whilst my brother can be a total bore at times, he is the last person that would make a joke at anyone's expense. He is as zen as his name suggests. He just mentioned the coat, and that you seemed to be struggling in wellies that were too big, so I hope you don't mind, but I've brought you one of my old jackets and a pair of wellies, size six, if they are any good to you?'

'That's really kind of you, and yes, I take a six too, so I'm sure they'll fit fine. As for the jacket, I'd be grateful to have something to wear when I leave the castle grounds. I think I'll continue to wear Bert's to help with the animals though, because it's as warm as toast and is already covered in... in... well you know what!'

'Yes, I do know what! Half of the village wear that coat from time to time when we come to help

Bert. It's communal, so be prepared to share!'

I liked Aurora already. She had an open, smiley face and was just so genuine.

'I'm pleased to hear that people come to help,' I said. 'Bert does an amazing job, but I did worry about his workload after watching him today.'

'We all worry about Bert, but don't fret, you'll soon meet lots of us, including my ma and pa, who lend a hand through the week when we can. I only wish I could do more as well, but I'm getting married in two weeks, on Christmas Eve, and that is just about taking every waking thought I have at the moment.'

'Wow, congratulations! Let me get you another coffee and you can tell me more.'

'My fiancé is called Jack. He's from a well-known local seafaring family in Seahouses. We've known each other since school, started dating when we were sixteen and have been together ever since – minus a couple of years when I went off to Newcastle to catering college. Although, we both knew that we would get back together, it was only a matter of time. I was two, and Zen five, when we arrived on the island. We grew up on Greater Reef over there.' She gesticulated out of the window. 'Ma and Pa had got jobs as wardens, and we stayed with Bert and Meg here on Lindisfarne a lot of the time too. I totally feel part of the fabric of this place and wanted to share the special day with my island family, so we're getting married in the village church and holding our reception in the village hall

– a small Northumbrian wedding which is exactly what we both wanted. Mind, Jack has been far more interested in the honeymoon!'

'And where is that going to be?' I ask curiously.

She burst out laughing. 'You are never going to believe it, but we are sailing up the east coast of Scotland – weather dependent of course – I may even borrow the communal coat! The honeymoon is my gift to Jack. He hates leaving his precious boats and I don't mind sailing, been around the sea all my life, but I wouldn't have minded a trip to the Maldives or somewhere else nice and hot. Sailing in December could be rough, even though one of his cousins is lending us a nice four berth yacht. And before you think it's something like you see on the French Riviera, it's not.'

'My bestie, Sophie, is off to the Maldives for Christmas,' I said, my voice breaking.

'No way! The lucky thing, although, tell me, are you not happy for her?'

'Oh yes, I'm absolutely delighted, just the circumstances are, well...'

And so, I filled Aurora in on Sophie, the gang, my life in London, about Matt, working for Randy Parrot, and the terrible time I'd had over the last few months, culminating in the engagement debacle. She was such a good listener and it all just came tumbling out. Once I'd started, I couldn't stop.

'Oh Ellie, I'm so sorry. You've really been through the wringer, eh? What a horrible thing to do to someone you've been with all that time. Sadly, you're not alone...' she trailed off. 'Don't you worry, I won't say a word to anyone about what you've told me. People eh, do we ever really know anyone?'

'It seems not,' I said, dabbing my eyes.

'London sounds like another world to me,' she continued, moving the subject on to more stable ground. 'Only been there a few times and, to be quite honest, I was like a fish out of water, pardon the pun. Far too many people and the noise got to me, but perhaps if I had someone like you who knew their way around showing me, I might actually like it.'

'I'd love that,' I said, and I genuinely meant it.

'I can't wait to show you around the Island Ellie and introduce you to people. I warn you in advance though, if you are looking for a new relationship, or even a holiday fling, we may have to cast our nets further than Lindisfarne. The standard of available men is not that great,' she said, her eyebrows knitted together as she pondered the island's single men.

'There's old Maurice, the—'

'—oyster farmer,' I finished for her, laughing.

'Or there's Dennis, who comes once a week to supply the butchers. At least you'd get an endless supply of sausage.' She winked lasciviously. 'Or maybe Ethan from the Willis farm. He's a bit young mind, like eighteen years young, and I don't think he's ever been off the island – not even to school – so you might have to mould him into shape, like a 'Christine' Grey type character!' she roared. 'Or if they don't float your boat, I suppose I could hook you up with one of Jack's cousins – these fishing puns just keep tripping off the tongue.' She laughed. 'No disrespect though, you don't seem a natural fit for a fisherman's wife.'

'Too right,' I said. 'I get seasick on the boating lake in Hyde Park!'

It was after eleven when she left, and we hadn't stopped talking. She was a breath of the freshest air, so open and likeable, but with a very naughty edge. Even though we had just met, I hoped that Aurora and I would become good friends over time. I'd arranged to go and see her in the café the next day, and as Nacho and I waved her off and climbed back up the staircase for the first night in our new home, I didn't feel half as lonely or scared. I was already looking forward to seeing her again tomorrow and totally intrigued about the glamourous but clearly dangerous Isla. No doubt it would all come out in the wash about her – Island life was proving to be far from boring!

Before I went to bed, I called Sophie. I needed to talk about Zen and who better to offload to than my bestie? We both screeched as soon as we saw each other. You would think we had been apart for months, not just days.

'Ellie! Oh babes, it's just so good to see you. The flat has been so quiet without you, and I miss you.'

'I miss you too, Soph. It's been hectic here, just getting to know people and learning about the animals and the island. I was just so unprepared for this, Sophie; I've got loads to tell you.'

'Well, before you do, let's have a look at your gaff. Is it awful? Have they put you in the broom cupboard?'

'Erm, not quite.'

I hadn't told any of the gang that I was living in a very Chi-Chi apartment in a castle. I scanned the screen around the rooms and Sophie's eyes widened.

'Oh My God Ellie, that looks like a suite in the __'

'Ritz, I know! Soph, you won't believe it but I'm living in this beautiful guest apartment which is inside Lindisfarne Castle.'

'A castle? Like the other one we found online?'

'Well, kind of, but smaller. Still a castle though. It's absolutely stunning, as is the whole island. I'll make a video and send it to group chat and show you around virtually.'

'So, what's the catch? Are you put to hard labour at stupid o'clock in the morning? How much dog shit do you have to pick up? Have you got to do kinky things with the old posh guy?'

'No, I don't do really early starts, it's too dark. There are all kinds of animals – not just dogs – like horses, alpacas and donkeys. Granted they all shit, but I don't have to collect it all myself, and no kinky anythings with anyone!'

I could see her eyes doubling in size before me at the mention of the eclectic range of animals.

'Please tell me you're joking. Babes, you hate horses and I'm not even sure what an alp... alpat... oh one of those things are, unless they're those spitty beasts! Shame about no kinky things yet, Ellie Nellie. I was rather hoping you'd already had an encounter with a sexy Geordie to report back on.'

'Err, give me a chance Soph, although as you well know, I'm not exactly into one-night stands – but I might make an exception if I get the chance. Remember the gorgeous guy in the photo, him with the shiny hair? I've fallen for him big style Sophie, even though I don't know him at all – the minute I looked into his eyes it was like I'd had a spell cast on me. Do you think I've lost my marbles so soon after Matt?'

'No Ellie, I don't and, quite frankly, it's probably a good thing, moving on. Remember, the new Ellie playing the field!'

'There appears to be one major problem though. Initially I thought he was in a relationship... with a sheep farmer...'

Sophie burst out laughing, which started me off, and we were soon both reaching for the hankies to wipe our eyes.

'A what? First the photo of you in that ridiculous hat and coat looking like... like... well actually there are no words to adequately describe it, and now you are telling me you have fallen for a man who's bonking a shepherd!'

'No, I got it wrong Soph. He isn't, although maybe it would have been easier if he had been. According to Aurora, his sister, he's back on the island with a broken heart and isn't interested in having a relationship with anyone, and definitely not a month long one. Apparently, he doesn't do quick flings, and I'm not supposed to be looking for serious!'

'Babes, you are gorgeous, funny and warm. It's impossible for him not to fall for you in my view, and only you can decide whether to stick to the plan of playing the field, or whether he might turn out to be the one – stranger things have happened, Ellie Nellie.'

I felt a little twinge of a tear plopping onto my iris. Sophie always knew how to boost my confidence.

'If he means that much to you, then you need to act on it. Or just enjoy his company during the time you are on the island and come back to London and find someone else. Oh, and by the way, the idea of you, the girl whose only experience with animals is incinerating the school guinea pig, helping to look after Noah's bleedin' Ark is priceless. Just wait until Jake hears about all of this!'

Two hours later, we eventually drew breath, and the call ended, after I'd filled Sophie in on everything.

'You two have a fantastic holiday. We can still do video calls, can't we?'

'Too right we can if you're okay with it? I don't want to upset you, considering it should have been you showing it off to me?'

'I'm fine Sophie. I'm actually very happy here so far, so I'll call you on day three as that's how long it will take for you and Jake to get the holiday sex marathon out of the way and make it out of your room.'

'Ha! Ha! You enjoy your freezing island babes. Joking aside, Ellie, it's great to see you smile, and I can see you're having fun. Find yourself a nice distraction from that Zen guy – by the way, what kind of trippy hippie name is that? Now listen up, you'd better not get too close to his sister, Zoflora, or whatever she's called. You can only have one best friend and that position is already filled. Love you, bestie.'

'Love you too, bestie. Safe trip.'

CHAPTER 16

I was woken up the next morning by birds squawking extremely loudly. It sounded like there were hundreds of them, all competing to be the loudest. Nacho was curled in a tight ball into the curve of my back – I don't think he had moved all night. I hadn't planned to let him sleep on the bed, and I wasn't sure it was the right thing to do, but feeling his warm, furry little body snuggled up to me was such a comfort. I had shown him his own bed on the floor next to me, but he must have had springs for legs, because for a tiny dog he could jump from a standing still position. We both slept like logs, despite my earlier worries about ghostly apparitions and drunken smugglers sneaking through tunnels in the dead of night. It was such a comfortable bed. I stretched my limbs and turned to look at Nacho, who was even cuter with ruffled bed-hair, reminding me of a spikey Rod Stewart.

'You wear it well, Nacho! Are we getting up then, boy?'

The room was bathed in orange light as I got out of bed and walked across to look out of the window. The sun was rising in the sky to the east, reflecting off the sea in hues of oranges, yellows, purples and pinks. I decided there and then that I was going to explore the roof terrace Meg had mentioned, and make sure that one morning, I was up there in time to watch the full colourful extravaganza happening right in front of me.

Throwing on the first clothes I came across, my mind flitted to London. I wasn't bothered about being coordinated or what I might look like – today was all about keeping warm. It was Monday morning and back home I'd be getting ready to battle my way through the rush hour, bracing myself for a full-on week of Christmas client events. I'd be dressed to keep old frozen-faced Anna off my back and exhausted from trying to dodge questions about Matt and Karen.

I looked at my adorable little Nacho, glanced around my fantastic temporary accommodation, and knew without any doubt I had done the right thing – for once. I had a quick cup of coffee, wrestled with Nacho's harness – it only took two tries this time – and we ran down the stairs, where I collected my hat, coat and wellies. We went out into the yard to meet Bert. There was no sign of him, so, checking my pocket for the to do list, I began my first morning of chores, going first to the dogs to let them out. They were all so pleased to see me and Nacho, tails wagging furiously. I made a fuss of them all and began sorting out their food when Bert appeared.

'Morning, Ellie lass. How was your first night?'

'Great Bert slept very well. I thought I would

be awake half of the night, terrified at every creak, but it was surprisingly quiet, just the noise of the sea. It was quite soothing. The birds woke me up this morning though. Not sure which is worse, Colonel Sanders crowing on the windowsill, or the bird noise which I think was coming mainly from Greater Reef? How do they ever get any sleep over there? It must be deafening the closer you get.'

'They're just used to it I suppose. They've been wardens over there for about twenty-five years and would have left long ago if they couldn't manage a few birds.' He laughed. 'By few, I mean that there could be upwards of 50,000 on Greater Reef, and the smaller islands further out to sea. We'll have to see about a trip across for you. Not many get to step foot on the sanctuary, and you can hear all about what they do over there.'

'*How* many birds? Good grief, no wonder they woke me up. I'd love to go across,' I said, already inwardly panicking about the boat trip. It didn't look far, but I was no sailor and distance could be deceptive, but what an opportunity, and if it arose, I wouldn't say no.

The morning passed in a happy haze of following Bert, learning where things were kept, watching him measure out food and him telling me the best way to muck out. Basically, hold your breath and shovel it up! As it was going to be one of my main tasks, I thought I'd better just learn to get on with it. I'd dealt with plenty of shit over Matt, so this would be a piece of cake in comparison.

'What time do you need me until today, Bert? Aurora asked me to go over to see her café this afternoon. She said it's shut on a Monday, but she does her baking when it's quiet. Hope that's okay?'

'No need to ask, pet. We'll be done by about half twelve. You go off and explore the Island. I expect Aurora will show you around. I'll take care of bedding the animals down later. You can do that chore tomorrow. Take Robson and Nacho with you, Ellie. They'll enjoy getting out, and those two will be easy enough to manage.'

'Yes, I will. Right Bert, I'm going back to finish cleaning out Nanny McPhee's stall, then I'll start on the horse's stables – once you've got them and their hind legs safely out of my way.' And off I went back to shovel more stinky poo.

Before I returned to the mucking out, I popped in to see the horses, having decided that I had to face my fear. Stout whinnied as I stopped at her stall.

'You certainly are a beautiful old girl,' I said quietly, bravely holding out my hand, flat like Bert had shown me. She gently took some carrots from me. Hand shaking, I tentatively stroked her long nose as she chewed contentedly. I gave her more and her velvety lips brushed against my palm; her mouth was so soft. I had always been scared of horses, but there was no doubt she was a magnificent animal, and those big brown eyes of hers looked like they might well hold the secret to the universe.

'See you later gorgeous,' I said, moving on to

the next stall where Hannibal – the devil pony – was eyeing me up. His ears were still flat to his head, but maybe marginally less so than yesterday, so I took that as a win.

'Morning Hannibal, you cute little beast,' I said in a calm voice. 'Now then, you and I are going to have a chat. Well, maybe I'll talk, and you listen.' The tiny pony stared up at me, his liquid brown eyes with those extra-long lashes fixed on my every word. 'You think you can intimidate me? Well, I've got news for you, you can't. I live in London and the place is awash with people who think it's okay to trample all over you. Believe you me, I've encountered more than a few good-looking charmers who make you look like a pussy cat – one like Elvis I mean, not like Lulu. She's the cat version of you, and I'll be giving her a talking to as well. I vowed that no-one else would get the upper hand – or maybe that's the upper-hoof in your case – over me again. Been there, done that and got the whole blooming kit and caboodle with my ex-boyfriend Matt, and I'm not taking any more nonsense. Right, lecture over. I have some carrots for you, but I'm not prepared to lose my fingers, so I'll just pop some down there for you to pick up. But before the four weeks is over, you will be taking it from my hand, without me losing my digits – have you got all that?'

'I think he might have got that loud and clear,' said a voice from the doorway, and I turned to see Zen leaning against the wall.

How much of that had he overheard? He must

be thinking I'm a mad woman talking to animals like that and combined with my bizarre appearance, we weren't getting off to a good start. I was way off my game if I had any chance of reversing his single status, but let's face it, I was well out of practice. My cheeks were on fire as I gawped at him, momentarily lost for words.

'Erm, just laying down a few ground rules,' I squeaked.

For the first time, I saw Zen smile – really smile – and it lit up his entire face, his wide grin showing even white teeth, his eyes twinkling, and oh my days, he was just so bloody handsome.

'He's a little devil right enough. I often wonder if it's a case of he just doesn't understand us. Apparently, he came straight from Shetland to Bamburgh, and I wonder if he only understands Shetlandic.' He laughed again.

'And there's me worrying that he might not understand my southern accent.'

'No problems there Ellie. You made yourself crystal clear!'

'Or maybe he doesn't understand Geordie; although your accent isn't as broad as Bert's.'

'That's because I left the island years ago, and the accent fades over time. It's a strange phenomenon though, the minute you meet a fellow Geordie, or you return to God's County, then you at once revert. You never lose it altogether and nor would I want to.'

'Hmm, well thanks for the tip. I'll maybe

learn some Shetlandic, if you're not winding me up. Seriously, is that really what the language is called?'

'Would I dare lie to you? Yes, that is what it's called. I would pay good money to witness the conversation between you and Han when you've learned some. Anyway, I'd better get on. I've come to lend Bert a hand doing a little of the heavy work getting the bales down to the paddocks. I need to make a delivery to Berwick, and I'd better not leave the crossing until the last minute, or I'll have Bert on my back again. I'm going over to Alnwick tomorrow afternoon if you fancy coming with me?' he said casually. 'I could show you where all the action happens on the mainland.' He laughed.

Oh my God. Had I just heard right? Was he asking me out… on a date? Whatever it was, I'd take it!

'That would be great,' I garbled. Perhaps a little too over-enthusiastically.

'I'll look forward to it Ellie.' He turned and strode off down the yard.

I stood rooted to the spot as I watched him go, his long denim clad legs striding out, dark curls flying out of the sides of the beanie – what I wouldn't have given to run my fingers through that gorgeous hair and who knew what tomorrow might bring!

CHAPTER 17

After a quick shower, I changed my clothes, slipping into jeans and a sweat top, which I knew was not really going to keep me warm. I decided I must ask Meg to take me to a shop where I could buy some more suitable things for my new life on Lindisfarne. I slipped on Aurora's jacket, which was pillar box red and matched one of the colours in my Viking hat – it was as near as I was going to get to being coordinated these days.

With Nacho and Robson by my side, we set off through the arched gates, down the steep bank that curved around the castle, and onto the road leading to the village. I was quite excited at the prospect of seeing it for the first time, and hopefully meeting some of the villagers and hearing a little about the island's history.

It was a bright afternoon, but very cold; the wind had a biting edge to it, coming straight in off the North Sea. There were people walking along the road towards the castle, and nearly everyone that passed said hello or wanted to pat the dogs. This was new to me; in London, strangers just didn't engage, and would go to great lengths to avoid eye contact with anyone. As we strolled along the road, Robson suddenly veered off to the left onto a path which looked like a shortcut to the village.

'Okay Robson, you know the way better than us, so you're in the lead.'

The path took us across a flat bit of scrubland following the curve of the bay. Randomly dotted about the grassy area were what can only be described as old wooden sheds, but not in the traditional sense. They were peculiar shapes for one thing and were various sizes. Staring at them, I realised they were all upturned boats of some kind. I guessed there must have been about fifteen of them, in various states of repair. I spotted one, set slightly back from the others. It was the biggest by far and looked in good condition, having been painted in the traditional seaside colours of blue and white. There were fold up tables and chairs stacked up next to it, alongside lobster pots and other fishing paraphernalia. I walked across to take a photo and saw a sign proudly proclaiming, 'Lindisfarne Fishing Club established 1974 – Members and Guests Only'. The famous den! I thought about the private members' clubs in central London where I had to go to for work purposes, how opulent and ostentatious they tended to be. I couldn't help but think that there was far more fun to be had in this old, upturned boat, with its supply of homemade hooch, than any grandiose building in Mayfair.

We continued until the path took us to a gate which led into a graveyard with ancient ruins beyond. The information board at the entrance told me that it was Lindisfarne Priory, built by monks nearly 1400 years ago. As with everywhere on the island, the view from the back of the graveyard was stunning, looking out across to the sea and the coastline beyond. I could see the tall poles embedded into the seabed that I had noticed when I first arrived. They looked to be in a long, straight line leading to the mainland and I wondered if they were markers to follow, but there was no road, so perhaps they were for people who walked across to the island when the tide was out.

We emerged from a gate at the other end of the path into a village square with a huge Christmas Tree in the middle, with Main Street leading off – it truly was picture postcard perfect – Insta ready without the need for any filters or edits.

There were cobbled lanes, houses and cottages in all sizes, shapes and shades, with an abundance of colourful winter plants and shrubs spilling out of baskets and pots and climbing up the cottage walls. Christmas wreaths adorned many of the doors, and there seemed to be a Christmas tree project going on, as there were small, rooted Christmas trees outside some of the premises, all in bright red pots with *Lindisfarne Tree Tuesday* written on them. There were a few small shops and a Heritage Centre, which I would definitely visit to find out more. I spotted the *Crab and Oyster* pub at the bottom of the street and a sign pointed in the direction of the *St Cuthbert's Way Hotel.*

The café was in the middle of the street. It was a large, whitewashed house, side on to the road, an advertising sign swinging in the wind from the gable end, showing the aurora in the skies above Lindisfarne and welcoming people to Aurora's *Northern Lights and Bites*. There was a doorway cut into a high, stone wall which led into an enclosed walled garden filled with tables and chairs. Running along the wall at the back of the garden was a stylish, wooden cabin with a long stainless-steel chimney poking from the roof, and I guessed that this was Zen's empire; the smell of coffee permeating the air was a bit of a giveaway. There was an empty gravelled area to the side where he probably kept his ancient campervan – he must have made the tide to cross over to the mainland.

'Aurora,' I shouted as I stood in the doorway. 'Are you there? Is it okay to bring the dogs in, or should I tie them up in the garden?'

I stepped inside the open double doors, which led into a large entrance hall with stone flagged floors, a wide staircase leading to the upper levels of the house, which had clearly been quite grand in its day. I noticed a cord across the stairwell with a sign saying *Private No Admittance*. Aurora appeared from a door at the end of a corridor, which must have led into the kitchen. She was wearing a navy-blue apron with the café logo on the front. Her dark hair was kept back off her face by a multi coloured headband and tied into a ponytail. Her cheeks were pink, presumably from the heat of the oven, and she was covered in a fine dusting of flour.

'Ellie! Just bring them in. We're dog friendly, plus we're closed today. Hope you're hungry. I've made us some lunch. You can test out a new tart I've been experimenting with.'

I let the dogs off the lead, and they made a beeline for the woodburning stove, which was throwing out much-needed heat.

'This is fabulous,' I said, as I gazed around the café. It was a big square room with tall windows overlooking the walled garden. It was far from being an olde world tea shoppe, or full-on seaside themed as you might expect. The floors were stripped wood; the furnishings were simple, painted in a matt grey. The log burner was a modern Scandinavian style. Each table had a tiny, real Christmas tree in the centre, with one solitary star on the top. There was a space cleared in the corner with boxes of Christmas decorations sitting on the floor, where the tree must have been going.

'I'm running behind this year because of the flipping wedding,' said Aurora. 'I've normally got the place ready for Christmas by now, so it's a very half-hearted attempt this year I'm afraid, but I quite like the minimal look.'

'It's fabulous Aurora, I love it.'

'I'm rather proud of it myself. We lease the building from James and Grace. You'll find that they own lots of property on the Island. I live in the flat on the first floor. Zen has the attic and runs his business from the Roastery, as he calls it; the posh shed, as I call it.'

My eyes were drawn to several huge canvas images displayed on the walls. Each one was an image of the Northern Lights, all different, unique to the night the magical event took place.

'Wow, Aurora, these take your breath away, they're fabulous,' I said, my eyes jumping from one to the next. 'Who took them and where were they taken?'

'Zen took them all. When he first came back to the island, he couldn't settle and hardly slept. He would disappear off in Ravi Shankar—'

'Ravi Shankar?' I raised an eyebrow.

'That's the name of the camper. Ma and Pa named it after an old muso they love. It's the original van they did their not so grand world tour in. God knows how it's still going. Me and Zen were both born in it, him in India and me in Greece. Anyway, Zen would go off for days at a time in Ravi and come back with yet another stunning capture, and it seemed to make him happier than anything we could do for him. Staring at the aurora and the stars is therapy. He still goes away every now and again, when he can fit it in around the business, but these days it's likely to be to Harriet's farm, so at least we kind of know where he is.'

I was beginning to appreciate that there was a whole lot more to Zen, but now wasn't the time to pry. Aurora continued.

'The images are taken from all over Northumberland. I don't suppose you have seen anything of our wonderful county yet. Well, that one,' she pointed, 'is obvious. It's *your* castle.' She laughed. 'And the other two castle images are from Alnwick and Bamburgh. Then there's a couple taken over Hadrian's Wall in the far southwest of Northumberland: one over the roman wall itself, and one over a famous tree in a place known as Sycamore Gap.' She pointed to a canvas showing a silhouette of a lone tree nestled between two hills, the aurora lighting up the image in hues of greens and pinks. It looked like a painting. 'Those two over there are taken from Kielder Reservoir and Forest. It's an amazing place – it has dark sky status and is really remote.'

'What, more remote than here?' I asked incredulously.

'This place is a metropolis compared to parts of Northumberland.' She laughed. 'I know the stars from here on a clear night are pretty spectacular, but the skies around Kielder are just mind blowing.'

The last two canvases were side by side. The first was the silhouette of a person standing on the brow of a hill, leaning on a shepherd's crook, sheepdog to their side, the Northern Lights in myriad colours dancing in the background. The second was of two people standing in between a circle of five huge stone obelisks, like a small Stonehenge. It was taken from behind. The couple were side by side, arms around each other's backs, looking into the distance at the surreal sky. I knew at once it was Zen. His hair was much longer than it was now, but it was blowing out from the beanie in his trademark style. Mesmerised, I stood looking at it; what I was seeing were two people who clearly cared for each other.

'The first one is way up in the Cheviots at Harriet's. She's from generations of sheep farmers; it's in her blood. The second is a photo Zen took of them both with a timer and tripod. They're at Duddo Stone Circle, just a bit further north from here. You can see for miles around from there, as far as southern Scotland. They were both having a bit of a tough time, and it was good for them to get off into the wild and just chill out and support each other.'

I was just about to ask what the bad time was all about when Aurora cut in.

'Right, let's have lunch. I've made a new type of tart – kipper pate and beetroot jam. The kippers are from a village called Craster, where there's been a smokehouse since the 1800s. The beets are from a farm on the island. I try to use local produce as much as possible.'

The tart was delicious, as was a huge slice of rhubarb crumble cake, and over many cups of tea we chatted non-stop about the forthcoming wedding.

'I'm going down to Newcastle tomorrow with Harriet if you'd like to come. See if we can find her some suitable shoes. You have no idea how long it took to find something she was prepared to wear. Harriet is not your usual bridesmaid.' She laughed. 'Still, because it's winter, it was much easier and we have gone for velvet, in a shade of green, like holly.

It may sound disgusting but it's really nice, and it matches the foliage in my winter posy, so we're both happy. Please don't get the idea that I'm some kind of Bridezilla, Ellie, far from it as it happens. A lot of the stress has been me battling with my eco-conscience about every aspect of the wedding. I'm a hippie child don't forget! Ma and Pa still hold all that they instilled into us as kids close to their hearts, probably even more so now the way the planet is going, so I've tried to get the balance between a wedding that I feel morally happy with, and one that Jack's family expect. Ssh, don't tell them, but both my dress and Harriet's outfit came from a charity shop specialising in second hand wedding dresses and outfits – or is that pre-loved? I can't keep up with Insta speak.'

'That's inspiring Aurora, and you will look just as beautiful! I wish I could come to Newcastle with you, but Zen has offered to take me over to Alnwick–' *and wild horses are not going to stop me from doing that.* 'Perhaps if you have time before I go back to London, will you take me to the city and show me around? I'd love that.'

'Of course, I will. But no wearing the communal coat. Lasses in the toon just don't wear coats – ever! Right, talking about looking around, come on, let's get those two lazy lumps away from that fire and I'll take you around the village, give you the low down. We'll just stick to the centre today; we're not going to be able to cover it all before dusk arrives.'

'How big is the island?'

'It's about two square miles and approximately 160 of us live here; although that swells by thousands if you include the visitors that come year-round.'

We walked down the main street and stopped to peer in the window of the gift shop at the range of exquisite crafts on offer.

'This is Imogen's shop. You'll meet her soon. She's originally from London too, and she's lovely! Lots of us on the island make things to sell in *Love Lindisfarne*. My family alone is like a cottage industry!'

'Really? What kind of things do you all make?' I asked intrigued.

'Well, I make jewellery from stones and sea glass that I find on the beach; my ma makes hats like yours from Alpaca fleece, which she sources from all over Northumberland, and my pa paints and draws original cards featuring the birds on Greater Reef. Zen has copies of his northern light images in there and has reproduced them onto mugs and cushions.'

'Wow, wish I could make something that someone would actually want. I've never done any kind of crafts, ever. I feel I've missed out.'

'Hey, well there's always time to learn. You should join the Crafty Lindisfarners, they'll keep you right!'

'Crafty Lindisfarners?'

'Local craft group, between them they could make anything.'

'I'll go inside for a proper browse next time, otherwise I'll be in there all afternoon.' I laughed as we strolled on, passing a butcher, an art gallery and the post office, which doubled up as a grocery store. We crossed to the other side of the street, where there was a large building which housed the Lindisfarne Heritage Centre.

'You must go inside when you have time. You will learn so much about the history of the island, far more than I can tell you. But basically, the island was one of the most important centres of English Christianity. Some old Irish monks came way back in 635 AD and a sort of saints' cult started. They celebrated a bishop called Cuthbert. Then the nasty, pillaging Vikings came and devastated the island – they were pagans, and a huge hoo-ha occurred because St Cuthbert hadn't stepped up to stop them.'

'I wouldn't have stepped up to the Vikings either!' I laughed.

'The monks packed up and eventually settled down in Durham. The Christian community did survive here though, and the place has kept its strong link to Christianity ever since. The other thing Lindisfarne is particularly associated with – and you may have heard of them – are the Lindisfarne Gospels which are now housed in the British Library in your London. Bloody cheek if you ask me. They should be here where they belong, but we do have examples of them in the centre. The gospels are amazing. The colours are so vivid considering they were created on an island in remote Northumberland in about 715 AD – no electric light to work under or popping down to the nearest art supply shop for ink. It blows my mind how they managed it.'

'Mine too. Life on the island must have been so different back then, and you can't imagine how they survived on a daily basis, never mind produce beautiful artwork.'

'And there endeth your first lesson. If you want chapter and verse on island history, just get Zen on the topic – yawn – he knows the whole shebang backwards!'

CHAPTER 18

By 4.00 p.m., we had completed a loop around the main village, Aurora introducing me to loads of people. I'd never remember all the names, but they knew mine already. As well as the shops, I'd seen the pub, churches, the tiny school, and the village hall. The one place we didn't go into was the St Cuthbert's Way Hotel. As we passed the impressive looking country house, set back from the road in its own grounds, Aurora casually mentioned it was owned by Isla's family. She said we didn't have time to visit today, but I knew instinctively that she didn't want to go in because of Isla. So, we strolled past, my curiosity growing. As we got back to the door of the café, I gave Aurora a hug.

'I've had a great afternoon. Thanks so much for the lovely lunch and the tour of the village. It was very interesting, and I know so much more about Lindisfarne now.'

'I've enjoyed it too, Ellie, and we'll be seeing lots more of each other,' she said, reaching into her pocket and handing me a piece of paper.

'What's this?'

'I've written you a list of the various

Christmas activities that are taking place over the next couple of weeks, and I expect you to come to all of them, except Santa Saturday!'

Christmas Quiz – Wednesday 8.00 p.m. – Crab and Oyster – Our team could do with someone who knows about current music and culture. We're stuck in the 1950s here.

Christmas Gansey Night – Friday 8.00 p.m. – Crab and Oyster - Get Meg to take you to the charity shops in Berwick and find the most ridiculously cheesy jumper you can.

Santa Saturday – Village Hall 3.00 p.m. – Avoid like the plague unless you have a small person tucked away.

Fishing Club Shindig – Monday – From 2.00 p.m. until the last person falls. A must in the Lindisfarne calendar – be prepared to see double, or triple, if you are lucky.

Nativity – All Saints Church – Tuesday 2.00 p.m. Plenty of tissues needed, just too cute!

Christmas Eve – <u>My Wedding.</u>

Christmas Day – And relax...

Here I was on a tiny island, in the far north of England, and I had a busier social diary than I'd had in London for months – I was liking Lindisfarne more as each day passed.

***

Surveying the contents of my wardrobe the next afternoon, I concluded that pickings were slim, so it was jeans, sweat top, Converse and Aurora's jacket. A dusting of makeup and that

was me done. If I'd read Zen right, he wasn't the type to particularly go for glamorous. I looked in the mirror and was quite pleased with the results. My cheeks were rosy, but I thought that might have been more to do with raised blood pressure at the anticipation of spending time alone with Zen.

'Okay Nacho, time to see your friends.' I grabbed my bag and was about to lock up when the intercom rang. I pressed to answer without looking at the screen.

'I'm about to put Nacho in with the other dogs and I'll be out in a moment. Really looking forward to our road trip to Alnwick!'

'Road trip? Alnwick? Great!' said a female voice, and I glanced at the screen to see Isla.

By the time I had sorted Nacho and opened the door in the gates, Zen and Isla were both waiting for me. Zen was leaning against the camper van, and Isla was so close that she was robbing him of oxygen. They looked like a pair of models on a photoshoot, and I felt the green-eyed monster tapping me frantically on the shoulder. I tried to shove it away and remind myself that, whilst she looked great, nobody seemed to like her, but it kept on coming at me because they looked *so* bloody good together. Her poker straight icy blonde hair was in total contrast to his dark chocolate curls. Isla was nearly as tall as Zen as she leaned in and giggled girlishly into his ear. He was wearing his black woollen coat but had accessorised it today with a colourful scarf, probably alpaca fleece, in similar colours to my Viking hat. Isla was wearing a black waxed jacket with gold trim and skin-tight leather leggings, which emphasised her long legs even more. They were paired with the latest cool trainers and yet another designer handbag with a chunky gold chain, which was draped over her shoulder. I may as well have been wearing the hi-vis, I felt so downtrodden by comparison. Zen heard the gate slam shut and looked up.

'Ellie, hi! You look lovely,' he said, and oddly enough, sounded like he really meant it.

'You never said that to me sweetie,' said Isla, stroking his arm like she was marking her prey.

Cow.

Were these two an item? I knew Aurora said he was single, but maybe they were a badly kept secret. I couldn't imagine a guy like Zen going for someone as obvious as Isla, but there was no doubting her beauty, and, quite frankly, most men (the ones I'd met so far anyway) were total suckers for a pretty face and a bendy yoga body. Zen didn't reply to Isla and moved himself away from the van – and her – towards me.

'Are you ready to go? We've only got a few hours before it gets dark.' He seemed keen to get away.

'I am.' I turned to Isla. 'Sorry, I didn't know you were coming across and Zen and I have arranged to go to the mainland. Perhaps you can come over another day?'

'No time like the present. I'm not doing anything this afternoon, so you don't mind if I tag along too, do you Zenny darling? It will give me and Ellie a chance to get to know each other.'

I could feel the tension seeping out of 'Zenny darling.' He was clearly not at all receptive to the idea, and I got the feeling that he shared the same views about Isla as Meg and Aurora.

'Well, the thing is Isla, it would be a very tight squeeze for three of us in there.' He pointed towards the van.

'Not a problem for me. I don't mind getting up close and personal,' she purred lasciviously. 'Maybe Ellie can sit in the back?'

'No, Ellie can't sit in the back,' he said sharply. 'No seatbelt.'

'Well then, she'll just have to squash in next to us in the front. I know the van takes three because you've given me and Harriet lots of lifts.'

'Oh yes, Harriet. I haven't forgotten her. It's a pity you seem to have conveniently put her to the back of your mind.'

Oooh tension. I was clearly not party to all the facts about Isla. I was beginning to get the measure of her though. She was like an angry wasp; no amount of swatting her away was going to do the trick – and that is how all three of us ended up on the bench seat of the old camper, with Isla thigh to thigh against Zen, and my face squashed up against the window.

We set off and were soon crossing the causeway. I felt my backbone shrivel as memories of my arrival came flooding back to me.

'You okay over there, Ellie?' Zen smiled, and I knew what he was really asking without giving anything away to Isla.

'Err yes, thanks. Tell me, what's that funny hut on stilts for?' It was the wooden structure I had noticed when I tried to cross the causeway on foot.

'That's where the idiot tourists end up,' said Isla, scathingly. 'They think they can beat the tide and *quelle surprise*, they can't, so they climb up there and wait to be rescued. Morons. We islanders never do that of course.'

'Of course, we don't,' said Zen, with what looked like a sly wink in my direction. 'Those that do are thicker than canteen cups according to Bert.' He laughed. 'It's officially called the refuge box, Ellie, and there may be some genuine reasons why people have had to use it in the past.'

'Well, I won't ever be needing it. That's a promise.' I smiled, and I genuinely meant it.

By the time we got to Alnwick, I had heard Isla's life story but suspected I only got the bits she wanted me to hear. She talked about her life in London as a 'supermodel,' emphasising that her agency hadn't worked hard enough to get her to where she deserved to be, so she had returned home to the island to plan the next stages of her career.

'I'm perfect for television presenting or acting,' she stated, without a shred of embarrassment. 'I lived in Chelsea, Ellie,' she crowed. 'I'm sure you know that area well. Hmm, let me guess about you...'

Her perfect brows knitted together in contemplation, and I was momentarily distracted by the thought that my brows hadn't seen the sight of a pair of tweezers since I got here. In fact, the animals had undergone more grooming than me.

'I've got it!' she squealed into my right ear, nearly perforating it. 'I bet you live in a serviced mansion block belonging to your family in Mayfair, penthouse of course. I'm right, aren't I?' Her decibel level was nearing eleven.

'Erm, flat in Peckham actually, but yes, a lovely Turkish family own it. They run the barber shop underneath us.'

Zen burst out laughing.

'So, I take it you're not related to the Lindisfarnes, Ellie? I did have my doubts when I saw you on the beach in those ridiculous clothes, but then the aristocracy doesn't really give a shit about what they wear.'

Patronising witch.

Before I had the chance to answer, Zen announced that we had arrived, and we pulled into a car park. It was obvious that because Isla thought I was related to the Lindisfarnes, I was worth her precious time. I had done as requested by Meg and Aurora and had made my own mind up about Isla. She was so far up her own backside she was in danger of turning inside out. And more than that,

165

it was clear to me she was after Zen. I'd left all that kind of toxic behaviour behind in London, and I wasn't going to have my precious time on the island disturbed by a self-absorbed cow like her. The gloves, soft kid ones at that, were well and truly off.

Alnwick was charming. Isla was not. She was like a petulant teenager.

'I don't know what you were expecting, Ellie, but this place is so boring. There are no designer shops, and the wine bar is a joke. I once asked for a bottle of Cristal and he didn't even know what I was talking about, oik, and everyone wears clothes from chain stores. It really is the pits.'

I could see Zen bristling but managing to keep shtum. He probably knew more about managing her behaviour than me.

'Well, I like what I've seen of it so far,' I said bluntly. 'Look at that Castle, how amazing is that?'

'It's the second largest inhabited castle after Windsor,' said Zen. 'It's amazing inside. The artwork is spectacular, but we haven't got time to do it justice today.'

'Thank God for that,' whined Isla. 'I can't bear the idea of trailing behind cagoule wearing neanderthal tourists, oohing and aahing at what basically amounts to old tat. I bet you want to go in though, Ellie. Now I realise you are not a Lindisfarne and come from East London, this must seem rather special to you.'

I could feel my hackles rise.

'I love living in Peckham. The people tend to

be upfront and honest,' I replied defensively. 'And yes, I would like to visit the castle with my fellow neanderthal tourists, but it's not that important when I'm already living in a castle. Not many people can say that, can they?'

Totally ignoring my sarcasm, she took Zen by the arm. 'So, are you taking me to the wine bar, Zenny?'

'My name is Zen,' he growled, shaking her off. 'And no, I'm not taking you. I thought Ellie might like to see around the castle gardens today. They're spectacular, even in winter, and the water features are stunning. Tell you what Isla, if that doesn't suit you, why don't you go and wait in the wine bar, and we'll give you a ring when we're done?'

She glared at me so fiercely, her pale grey eyes looked like they were about to glow red. She really was so devilish that I thought I might just wither on the spot.

'No, we can't split up. I suppose I'll come too.' She sighed. 'Can't leave you on your own with Ellie. I mean, what can you two possibly have in common?'

Zen turned and mouthed, 'I'M SO SORRY,' behind her back.

The atmosphere as we walked around the gardens was as frosty as the mid December air. It was incongruous that somewhere so beautiful was marred by someone so inwardly ugly. What Isla didn't realise was that her behaviour was drawing me and Zen together in conspiratorial support of each other against her! When she disappeared to the loo, Zen and I looked at each other and burst out laughing.

'Ellie, I'm so sorry. This hasn't turned out at all like I had planned.'

He had planned! Three little words that meant so much more. He had thought about our trip out and had wanted to make sure I enjoyed it.

'It's okay. Seriously, don't worry. She is truly awful, but I've met her type before. Lots of them!'

'I don't suppose you know just how awful she is…' He stopped as she came into view, once again leaving me wondering what else she had been up to.

She reappeared; her lips freshly glossed. 'Right, it must be time for afternoon tea now. I think if I see another plant, I might die of boredom.'

'Actually,' said Zen, 'we've still got the Poison Garden to go and there's not much time left. So, you choose Ellie, tea, or Hemlock?'

'Oh, Hemlock.' I winked. 'Any day of the week.' I laughed, wondering if it would be possible to acquire a few leaves for personal use.

CHAPTER 19

The next few days passed in a blur. I hadn't seen anything of Zen since our trip to Alnwick unfortunately, but on the upside, I hadn't seen Isla either. I had been dreading having to try my hand at milking a goat, but Bert was insistent I watch Meg and at least grasp the basics. It was the grasping bit that I was concerned about.

'Morning Meg. I've come to get to grips with the milking.' I laughed.

'Morning lass. I hear you went over to Alnwick, and a little birdie tells me a third wheel tagged along.'

I was beginning to understand that news spreads fast on the island.

'Err yes. She just invited herself. Meg, I did what both you and Aurora suggested and waited to make my own mind up about Isla. Because I spent time with her, it gave me the ideal opportunity and, quite frankly, she's a nightmare!'

'Aye, she is that. What Isla wants, Isla usually gets – not always, mind.'

'Tell me about her, Meg.'

'Well, Isla came to the island when she was

about ten. I don't think I'd ever met such a precocious child; I blame a lot of it on Gordon and Elspeth – her parents – they over-indulged her. She was a pretty slip of a thing, but so demanding. It's tough when you must be honest and say you don't really like a child; it's just not natural. Anyway, she left Lindisfarne when she was about seventeen, went to live with relatives in London, and she was spotted by a model agency – that was that. She was in her element. After a few years she was doing well, on the cover of magazines and flying all over the world, but as usual, it wasn't enough for Isla, and she messed up big time.'

'What did she do?' I asked, agog with interest.

'Isla decided her career wasn't at the level she "deserved" so she started sleeping around with anyone who could move her up the greasy pole, secretly making incriminating videos, often with drugs involved, and basically bribed them to get her bigger and better jobs. It worked, at first, until someone made a stand and outed her. Everything came crashing down, and she slunk back here with her tail between her legs, her career in tatters. Nobody will touch her with a barge pole now. The official line is she's taking time out to "refocus her career" but that's poppycock. She's finished.'

'How on earth did you find that out, Meg?'

'Elspeth, Isla's mam, drunk on gin one night. No wonder they call it Mother's Ruin! She blabbed to old Ethel, who took great delight in telling all the Crafty Lindisfarners.'

'Oh, the Crafty Lindisfarners. What happened next?'

'Well, Ellie, I think I will leave Aurora to fill you in on that. Let's just say, it didn't take long for the precocious miss to continue upsetting people once she got back to the island. Now then, Nanny needs milking,' she said, changing the subject. 'Best get on.'

It was difficult to concentrate with my mind full of Isla, but I was there to do a job, so I shoved the intrigue to the back of my mind – after working out how quickly I could catch up with Aurora.

'What you have to remember, Ellie,' said Meg, 'Nanny is quite happy to be milked. We are lucky to have such a compliant goat. Some of them can be difficult. Apart from the welfare of Nanny, one of the most important things is hygiene. We need to be scrupulous about sterilising the bucket and other equipment we use in the process, leaving no room for cross contamination.'

I gulped. This sounded serious already.

'Nanny is happy to go onto her milking bench. We put some food in the manger, make sure she is secure, and she'll hardly even notice what's going on at the business end. She will be too busy munching.'

Sure enough, when Meg opened her stall, Nanny went straight to the milking bench and jumped up, her head immediately into the manger filled with her food.

'Right. Next, we prepare her,' said Meg, settling down on a small stool. 'A quick brush to remove any excess hair – we don't want that in the milk. Then we clean her teats separately, never ever using the same cloth. I've a supply of them that I've washed at hot temperatures which are thrown away after use.' She pointed to a cupboard on the wall. 'All the paraphernalia is in there. I use warm water and a tiny splash of baby sterilising fluid and then rinse.'

I watched her gently wash Nanny's teats.

'Then, I get rid of the first bit of milk from her as this may contain bacteria.'

I watched as she deftly pulled, and the first expressed milk trickled to the floor.

'Then, my dear, it's all about the rhythm.'

I struggled to keep my face straight, eventually bursting out into peals of laughter, Zen's words about *double entendres* ringing in my ears. No wonder he didn't want to show me how to milk a goat!

'Sorry Meg, don't mind me, schoolgirl humour.'

'Lass, I was a schoolgirl long before you, but don't think I'm too old to understand what you mean. Now then, pick your mind back up out of the gutter and concentrate young Ellie.' Meg laughed raucously. 'Each milker has their own way of doing it,' she continued.

I bet they do!

She demonstrated a squeeze and pull technique using both hands, going from one teat to the other quite quickly. The milk squirted into the sterilised bucket.

'And that's it, pet, nothing to it really. Do you want to try?'

'Err, no, not today, Meg. I'll watch you over the next few days to make sure I feel like I half know what I'm doing.'

'Okay, Ellie, but don't be scared. It's perfectly natural and you're helping Nanny by doing it. She had a kid before we took her in, so her milk supply will last a while yet, and it needs to be dealt with.'

'I will try it, Meg. She's a lovely girl, and I want to help, but I need to know I'm not going to hurt her.' I was prevaricating, but with the aid of YouTube and more time watching Meg, I was confident I could master it.

'No problem, Ellie, just when you're ready. Finally – you can do this today – once the milking is finished you give her a wipe down with clean, damp cloths, then throw all the used ones away. Take the milk to the house, decant it into one of the sterilised jugs you have already seen, and get it in the fridge as soon as you can. Keeping it cold will help it from tasting too goaty. Then get the bucket sterilised.'

'Got it Meg,' I said, taking the bucket from her and sounding far more confident than I felt.

***

On Wednesday afternoon, Bert drove Meg and me to Berwick and I wandered aimlessly around the supermarket picking up items like tins of beans and soup and, most importantly, biscuits and chocolate. Meg followed me, looking into the trolley and shaking her head. She began pointing out things she considered 'proper' food. I had officially become a grown up. She then took me to a few charity shops where I bought an enormous Christmas jumper for the get together in the pub that was on Aurora's list of unmissable Christmas activities. On the front of the jumper was a drunk Santa attempting to climb down a chimney, his hat askew, bottle of Newcastle Brown Ale in one hand, saying, 'Whey Aye Man it's Crimbo.' I also treated myself to a couple of warm jumpers and thick leggings from an outdoor clothing shop, along with a pair of bargain brown horsey style boots, and my transformation to island girl was complete.

***

That evening, the Christmas Quiz took place in the pub, so I popped Nacho into the kennel with the other dogs. He had become the best of friends with Robson, and they curled up together, hardly noticing me leave. It was so heart-warming to see how happy he was in his new life, his eyes bright, and his feathery tail permanently wagging.

I opened the door of the *Crab and Oyster* to a full house, with lots of chatter and laughter circling around the place. It wasn't very big, and thankfully, the interior had retained its original charm to match the actual age of the building – without the aid of fakery as supplied by designers and stylists who did the rounds in London; they were changing the themes of pubs on a regular basis. It consisted of one main room with a couple of little snugs, dark wooden floors and a low beamed ceiling. The furnishings were simple, with round beaten-copper top tables, pew style benches and wooden chairs, and there was a huge inglenook fireplace at one end.

'Ellie!' shouted a voice from the corner. 'Over here!'

I spotted Aurora sitting on one of the pews, Zen next to her. She stood up as I walked across, gave me a hug, and gestured for me to sit down. I found myself sandwiched between her and Zen. The place was so full, we were crammed in like sardines, and I was squashed up to his side, thigh by thigh. I couldn't deny it was a very pleasurable experience, which made my insides feel all fuzzy, and I wondered if I should sit on my hands to stop them straying – the thought of stroking that soft, washed-out denim was overwhelming.

He was wearing a bright yellow tee shirt with a green trim and a small Brazil logo. It clung to his broad shoulders and taut chest. He smelled like his signature mix of espresso and pine. I don't know how I contained myself. The urge to bury my face into his hair and breathe in the delicious aroma was just too bloody tempting. I had to stop fantasising and keep my focus – thank God I wasn't drinking, or things could have gone pear shaped very quickly.

'What would you like to drink?' asked Aurora.

'Just a lemonade please. Promised myself no alcohol whilst in charge of animals.' I smiled.

'Oh, come on, Ellie, it's Christmas. Just the

one. What about a Prosecco? That doesn't count.'

'Hey, just get the lemonade, Aura. It's not cool to force alcohol on anyone, no matter if it is Christmas.' Zen smiled, noticing my embarrassment.

'I'm really sorry about the other day,' he said, as Aurora battled her way through the crowd to the bar.

'It's not your fault, Zen, and despite our uninvited guest, I had a really fun time, so thanks for taking me. At least she's not here tonight.'

'I'm not sure quizzes are Isla's thing. Not enough opportunity to grab the spotlight. Anyway, Ellie, perhaps we could go back to see inside the castle when we have time, without the passenger in tow?'

'I'd love that.' My heart began to calypso at the prospect.

'So, tell me, what brings a city girl like you to our tiny little bit of heaven in the North Sea?'

'Oh, that's a long boring story for another time,' I said, 'but I'm so pleased I came…'

He turned to me. We were nose to nose, his coffee bean eyes looking straight into mine. His proximity was giving me goosebumps on top of goosebumps. My heart was racing and my brain, well it had turned to mush. I could think of nothing but this gorgeous man whose face was about an inch from mine, his kissable lips within touching distance. I was convinced he was about to say something meaningful when someone tapped on the microphone. Ear-piercing feedback reverberated around the room, destroying the moment. I literally jumped when Aurora noisily plonked a glass of lemonade down on the copper table, and I had to drag my eyes away from Zen. I hadn't even noticed that a couple had come in and taken the two free chairs on our table.

'Ellie, remember Don and Moira from the Post Office? They're on our team. Don's our not-so-secret weapon. All the teams want him, but we got him! Right then, what's our festive team-name going to be?'

And that was that. 'It's Quizmas' as we called ourselves, came second to 'Island Past and Presents' because we didn't know the year *The Night Before Christmas* was first published. Like who would? There hadn't been another opportunity to engage Zen in anything other than quiz related conversation. It was a great night though, and as I said my goodbyes to my teammates, Aurora offered to walk me home.

We strolled along underneath the navy-blue night sky, a blanket of more stars than I had ever seen before. It was truly jaw dropping. Who knew, whilst I didn't usually consider such matters, maybe the universe might align mine and Zen's stars together?

'I had an interesting conversation about Isla with Meg,' I said as we walked towards the castle. 'I suppose you heard about her inviting herself along to Alnwick with me and Zen?'

'Hmm, yes, I did, the cheeky cow. She is truly awful, Ellie.'

'I know that now. I did make my own mind up by the way, saw her in action. Meg told me about what she had done in London before she came back here, but then alluded to her upsetting people on the island. She said you would tell me.'

'Well, if I'm going to do that tonight, I'd better come up for a hot chocolate if you've got any? We'll freeze out here.'

'I have as it happens, so come on, hurry up, I want to hear this.'

We were soon settled indoors, mugs in hand, and I listened as Aurora told me the tale.

'My bestie Harriet and I met at High School. Isla went elsewhere so they didn't know each other. A while ago, me and Harriet were in the *Crab* having a drink and Isla came in and joined us. At that time, Isla had toned the whole image thing down, probably as an attempt to slip back onto Lindisfarne unnoticed. I had warned Harriet that even though she might seem nice, Isla was probably still the same poisonous bitch she'd always been, but Harriet was totally drawn in from the get-go. Harriet knew she was gay from an early age, but as you can imagine, being stuck on a hill farm in rural Northumberland didn't give her many opportunities to meet women.'

'Biscuit?' I asked, absentmindedly shoving the plate in front of her, desperate to hear the rest of the story.

'Then suddenly, here was this extremely

beautiful woman showing an interest in her,' carried on Aurora through a mouthful of Jaffa Cakes. 'I can but imagine what Isla was thinking: daughter of a rich farmer – if only; tenant farmers, they haven't got two sticks to rub together. I told Harriet to be careful. I relayed the story about Isla's downfall in London, but all she could say was that she had nothing for Isla to use her for, and it was *different*. Harriet was hooked and quite powerless to step back. It was like she had been brainwashed. Harriet's quite shy, and Isla must have seemed so exciting. I just knew how it would all end, but we must let those we love make their own choices and be there for them when the shit hits the fan. It crippled me standing back and waiting for the first signs of carnage...'

'I bet it did. I get that. My bestie Sophie went through a wild phase before she met Jake, and I was forever sweeping up the fall out,' I added, picking up another Jaffa Cake.

'At first it was fine,' continued Aurora. 'They couldn't see that much of each other and when they did, they went to pubs and clubs in Newcastle, Isla never went up to the farm and they tried to keep their relationship off the island. If nothing else, it helped Harriet open up about her sexuality and see beyond life on the farm. She came out to her parents, who were initially shocked, but then dealt with it positively, as I always suspected they would. Then Zen suddenly came back, and true to form, Isla spotted an upgrade and dumped Harriet on the spot.

My brother is extremely good looking,' she said with pride, 'and I'm not just saying that because I'm his sister. He is gorgeous and has a beautiful soul too...'

I found myself nodding in agreement and was just about to say how I concurred, that he was indeed gorgeous, but I managed to stop myself just in time by shoving yet another biscuit in my big fat mouth to shut me up!

'Zen was in no place for a relationship with anyone when he got back. Quite frankly, he would rather live a monk's life like St Cuthbert than ever hook up with a woman like Isla.'

Aurora took a big gulp of hot chocolate to lubricate her vocal chords, then continued. 'Isla was oblivious to his disinterest however, and pursued him relentlessly, turning up at the door, sending him messages, gifts, you name it. Then her appearance changed from casual island girl back to full on vamp. It just shows how little she knew about Zen if she thought for a second that he would find that attractive, and the attitude returned alongside the spray on clothes. Zen would disappear off to Harriet's to comfort her. Naturally, she was heartbroken, as well as deeply embarrassed. Zen's like her adopted big brother; that's how she has always seen him, but he also went to escape Isla and to sort out his head. I'm not going to say anymore on that front. One day he may tell you his story himself, Ellie.'

'I don't quite know what to say, Aurora,' I mumbled, trying to take it all in. It seemed unthinkable to me that anyone could fall for Isla. Yes, she was staggeringly beautiful, but what an ugly personality. I kind of understood how difficult it must have been for Harriet in her particular situation living such an isolated life, and especially if the Isla back then was a toned-down version, but still...

'So, there you go. As you can understand, all of us who love Harriet found it exceedingly difficult to forgive Isla, but Harriet is over it all now and is fine. In fact, she's more than fine, but I won't say any more about that. Don't want to jinx it!'

'Anyway,' said Aurora, putting down her mug and shoving the last Jaffa Cake in whole. 'Time for me to go. I'm up early in the morning. Don't have nightmares about Isla.'

'I'll try not to.' I laughed.

I'd no doubt be lying awake, wondering if there was any chance of me and Zen getting together. I was sure I felt the vibes earlier at the quiz, but just didn't trust my instincts anymore. Besides which, it would appear we were at opposite ends of the spectrum of relationship requirements. Zen wasn't looking at all at the moment it would seem, especially not something casual, and I had come to the island wanting no more than uncomplicated fun. But that wasn't stopping me thinking about him – I could hardly think of anything else.

As I waved Aurora off from the back steps, I looked up at the sky, which was bursting with stars. There were two side by side, which seemed bigger

than the rest and were twinkling so much brighter –
if I was looking for a sign, then that could very well
be it. I turned to go back inside the Castle feeling
very confused.

'Hey Nacho, do you believe in the universe
being in control of our destinies? Hmm, too deep eh!'
I laughed, getting no response as he continued to
concentrate on his toy.

'Well, what about love at first sight? It
happened for me when I saw you.'

He dropped the toy and cocked his spikey head
to one side, his bright eyes looking directly into
mine, and I swear he gave me a little nod...

CHAPTER 20

The next morning, I was cleaning out the stables when I heard someone call my name. I went out into the yard to find two little kids waiting for me.

'Hi there, I'm Ellie.'

'I'm Amelia,' said the girl, looking up at me from beneath a hat like mine; it was a Christmas version, with reindeer antlers instead of Viking horns.

'Snap!' I said, pointing to my head and she giggled.

Amelia was a real cutie. Big green eyes, gorgeous freckles and two fat red plaits hanging from the sides of her hat. She was about seven, although you could write on the eye of a needle what I knew about kids.

'We've come to show you how to walk Pacino and Murray,' said the boy, who I assumed was William. He was a couple of years older than Amelia and sporting a Newcastle United beanie. 'Mam and Dad said it would be okay to come because you're dead canny.'

I was slowly learning the language up here and I knew canny to be a positive summation of a person's character.

'Ah yes, I met your mum and dad at the quiz last night. They're canny too! Let me go and get cleaned up, and you can show me the ropes.'

The alpacas knew both the children well and were delighted to see them, rushing across the paddock to greet us.

'I always take Murray, the grey one,' said Amelia. 'He never pulls and is so pretty.'

'Pacino is the best,' retorted William. 'He's very clever. I'm trying to make him do tricks, but it's not working so far.'

'Well, I think they are both beautiful. I love how soft their coats are and how wise they look.'

They showed me how to put the halters on and clipped them onto leading reins.

'They'll do most things for carrots,' said William. 'So always make sure you have them in your pockets.'

'Ok teacher, I will!' I laughed. 'Right, where are we going?'

'We always walk to the village and back when we are with a grown-up,' said Amelia beseechingly. 'Bert says we can only do the castle grounds if we are on our own. So, can we go to the village? Please? Pretty please?'

'Sounds good to me,' I said, quickly texting Bert to let him know.

We walked across a track, which led from the paddocks direct to the road, without the need to climb back up to the castle and down the other side.

Once on the grassy verge at the side of the road, we walked a few metres, and it soon became clear that it was going to take a long time. Every time we passed people, we had to stop, tell them about the alpacas and let them take photos.

'Good idea,' I said, handing my phone to William. 'Can you take one of me and Amelia please? Then she can take one of us two.'

We walked on and eventually made it to the village. I felt like the Pied Piper by the time we got there. We had a trail of people following us. Pacino and Murray seemed to know exactly where they wanted to go and headed down the cobbled lane and straight into the walled garden of the café. I disappointedly noticed that Ravi the camper was not in his space; Zen must be out.

'Are we okay to be in here with these two?'

'Yes, if we stay in the garden. They ran inside the café one time and Aurora was cross. We usually have hot chocolate while they have a rest. Their legs get very, very tired you know.' Amelia smiled coyly.

I think I had been had. By a seven-year-old!

'Hey Ellie,' said Aurora, coming out to the garden, now quite full of customers all wanting photos with the alpacas. 'These two are better than any sales campaign.' She laughed. 'Hot chocolates all round? On the house for creating the extra business. I'm going to have to send Pip out with her pad to take all these orders. Do you want a Christmas one with all the trimmings?'

'Ooh, can I have a white chocolate snow drift

please?' said Amelia.

'A ginger snap crunch for me please,' said William.

'They're Zen's creations, using natural products. He's very tetchy about messing with coffee but doesn't mind blinging up the chocolate.'

'Well, I'll take whatever Zen considers to be his finest chocolate creation.'

'That'll be extra dark chocolate with local honey and pine syrup for grown-ups. Won't be long guys.'

We were in the café garden for an hour whilst William and Amelia gave a masterclass in alpaca care to the captive audience. Bert had taught them well. Pacino and Murray enjoyed every minute. They were very placid animals, and I swore they were smiling, their beautiful eyes shining with happiness at every carrot slice.

'We'd better not give them too many,' I said.

'Bert showed us how many to put in our pockets and when they're gone then they can't have any more,' said Amelia indignantly. 'We know what to do. We love them very, very much and take care of them.'

That was me put in my place. I really liked the kids. They were clever, kind and naturals in front of an audience, who had rewarded them with all kinds of sweet treats to go with the hot chocolate. I knew exactly who was running the show!

As we walked back, Amelia came to an abrupt stop outside of *Love Lindisfarne*, the gift shop. She tugged on my sleeve, pulling me down to her level, then whispered in my ear.

And that is how I ended up concluding our trip in my new Christmas hat, reindeer antlers wobbling in the wind.

'You're my best friend now, Ellie. We look the same!' She grinned contentedly.

A bit further along and she stopped again, looked at me with her big green eyes, then held out Murray's rein to me. My eyes were in danger of springing a leak at her earnest little face and gesture of trust.

'Thank you so much,' I said as I took the rein. 'I will hold him properly and make sure he is okay.'

She put her sticky little hand in mine, and we continued towards the castle, me working out how to break the news to Sophie that she'd been overthrown!

***

Later that afternoon, I popped into the cottage for a coffee with Meg.

'Meg, it looks lovely in here, so festive.' I hadn't been in for a couple of days and the room had been transformed into a Santa's grotto. It was full of Christmas ornaments and decorations and looked so cosy. There was a small Christmas tree in the corner decorated in a traditional style. Most of its decorations looked like they had been handed down the generations. Sat on the top of the tree was a crinoline fairy. It reminded me of one of those toilet roll covers everyone's gran used to have, but I suppose, these days, it might be regarded as kitsch. There were snow globes and Santa Clauses dotted about the room, but what caught my attention was a huge bunch of mistletoe pinned above the door.

'You tried that out then yet, Meg?' I laughed.

'Hey, you cheeky young whippersnapper! Let me tell you, there's life in this pair of old dogs yet. We don't need mistletoe.' She cackled. 'Anyway, what do you make of these ganseys?' Meg showed me the Christmas jumpers that she and Bert were going to wear for the party. 'I bought a couple of plain ones and decorated them myself.'

'Meg, they're hilarious!' I giggled at the donkey themed jumpers.

'Ellie, because of it being Aurora's wedding on Christmas Eve, Bert and I are going to visit my sister in Alnwick earlier than we normally do, so we'll be going tomorrow afternoon and staying the night. Don't worry though, pet, we'll be back by 11 a.m. on Sunday morning, so you won't need to do anything out of the ordinary. You can help Bert sort the menagerie out early on Saturday before we leave, and just do your normal morning routine. Are you okay with that, leaving you flying solo for a little while?'

'I'm sure it will be fine, Meg. I'll do the dogs, cats, chickens, and turkeys as usual and make sure all the others are okay until you get back.'

'That's great, pet. Now then, are you looking forward to tonight?'

I was definitely looking forward to it because I was convinced that I would be seeing Zen again.

'I am, Meg. It sounds like great fun. I can't wait to see all the cheesy jumpers.'

We spent an enjoyable hour talking about everything and everybody on the island, but mainly Isla. And when the box of Belgian chocolate biscuits was empty, I made my way back across to the castle to get ready. I was brushing my hair when my tablet started ringing. It was Stanislaw, Aleksy and Tara, all waving at me from the boys' sofa.

'Hey, you lot. How fantastic to see you all!'

'You too, Ellie, but where is Nacho? We need our fix!' Stan grinned.

I called Nacho, who bounded over and jumped on my knee, shoving his whiskery little face into the screen. I knew my place in the pecking order these days.

'No Toby?' I asked, once they had stopped cooing over the dog.

'No, he's at a lecture at the V&A. He wanted me to go with him, but they could talk a glass eye to sleep at those things, so I thought I'd keep the boys company. Can I just say, you're looking fabulous, Ellie. Country life clearly suits you. You're glowing!'

'Are you being sarcastic, Tara?' I laughed. 'Is it windchill or whatever?'

'No, seriously, you're looking good.'

They could only see my face.

'Well, thanks, because I'm all dressed and ready to go out to the local in half an hour.'

'Give us a twirl, girl,' said Stan. 'Let's see the outfit. Is it your sexy black dress with the no back?'

I moved the camera so that they could see me in the Christmas jumper.

'Ta dah!' I threw my arms up theatrically.

Silence. The three of them gawped at me, open mouthed. After what seemed like an age, Stan eventually started to breathe again and came back to life, quickly followed by the others.

'What is that you are wearing?' said Stan. 'You can't be serious; you are not going to pub in that? You put it on for the call, eh, for bet?'

'I didn't know you were calling, did I?' I retorted. 'What's wrong with it anyway?' I asked, trying to keep my face straight.

I could see Aleksy peering closer at the screen to get a better look.

'What is that mean Ellie?' he said. 'I don't understand.'

'No, don't suppose many people down there would.' I grinned.

Tara, by this point, had put her glasses on.

'Okay, what have they done to our Ellie? Is there something in the water up there? You must be an imposter because there is no way on this earth that our Nellie would contemplate going out in that sack.'

'Hey, I'll have you know this is a genuine Geordie original. Cost me £2.99 it did. Fashion here is quite different, but I kind of like it – so there!'

'Bloody hell! She's really lost the plot.'

'Have you been drinking the bad northern cocktails?' asked Stan.

'Nope, not a drop has touched my lips since I got here.'

In the half hour I had with them before I went to meet Meg and Bert, I filled them in on Christmas jumper night, and more about life on the island and looking after the animals. They seemed satisfied that I wasn't quite certifiable yet.

'It's been so good to see you, Ellie. I miss your lovely face every morning asking for your cure in a cup. Tell me, have you had any decent coffee up in the north place yet?'

'Well, only yours,' I answered truthfully. I was yet to sample Zen's as I had only had tea and hot chocolate over at the café. 'Remember the guy with the hair on the photo? Well, he blends coffee right here on the island.'

'No, that can't be true. He can't be so good looking and blend great coffee.' Stan frowned. 'You send me some and I will tell you if it is good – right? We need to come to this island and taste it ourselves. Me and Aleksy need to see more of Britain than just Peckham.'

'Yes, I will send you a sample, I promise. And just for the record Stan, you are hotter than hot, yet you can still make the good coffee.'

'You've not asked about work once,' said Tara accusingly. 'Aren't you interested in what's going down in Randy flipping Parrot? Remember, the place you left me in all by myself at the busiest time of the year?'

'You know what, Tara? I seriously haven't given it much thought and no, I'm not interested in the slightest. Even if you were to tell me that Anna had smiled and her face didn't crack, it would be of no consequence to me.'

We did copious air kisses as we said our goodbyes, and for the first time, I actually felt that London life was about a million miles away, but that didn't matter at all.

CHAPTER 21

Once again, the pub was buzzing. The range of Christmas jumpers was fantastic, from downright rude and crude to hilarious home-made efforts, including many featuring the island. I met Maurice, the oyster farmer, for the first time. He was sporting a nifty little number with 'Oyster farmers do it better at Christmas.'

'You the lass from London then? You single?' he asked straight out. Before I could answer, he went on. 'Come down and see me oysters anytime. I'll give you a free sample. Great for bedroom action if you know what I mean,' he said, winking at me lasciviously.

'Alright Maurice, stop it, you dirty old devil,' interrupted Meg. 'I'm sure Ellie has heard all that palaver about oysters. Never helped my Bert; not that he needed help back in the day.' She cackled. 'Now leave the lass alone and find someone your own age to give your free samples to. I've just heard a whisper that Noreen Brannigan's old man has left her for Ted the kipper smoker's wife in Craster. They've run off to Sandy Bay in a caravan apparently. She got right sick of the smell of kippers I'm told.'

'Hmm, I bet he smells delicious under the

sheets.' I laughed.

'Stupid woman didn't quite think it all through, because Eric Brannigan works in the abattoir, and I know that Noreen often complained about *his* pungent aroma. From frying pan into the fire if you ask me. Anyway Maurice, I'm sure she'd welcome a bit of company for Christmas. She's always had the glad eye for you.'

'No smell from oysters.' He cackled and virtually ran out of the door to offer his services.

Aurora came in wearing a colourful jumper featuring Santa lost in the northern lights. Zen, behind her, was in a homemade coffee related effort with a printout stapled to the front with 'Santa's Bean' written on it.

Aurora gave me a hug and Zen leant in giving me the lightest of feathery kisses on my cheek. The espresso and pine nut aroma began to do its work and I was in danger of being transported to Nirvana. It took all my resolve to remain on terra firma. When he pulled back, our eyes locked into place and both of us seemed powerless to focus on anything other than each other. He was just so magnetic; I could feel a force-field of energy drawing us together. The intensity of the moment was overwhelming, and a warm glow washed over me – from my head, right down to my toes. I'd experienced nothing like it – ever. He was gazing at me with such depth, in a way that no one else had ever looked at me before. Not my Mum, my Dad and certainly not Matt, not even when he told me he loved me, although hindsight said that's probably because he was lying. It was like the world had stopped spinning on its axis, and both Zen and I were free-falling into each other's eyes, spiralling through a million stars, hurtling towards the unknown. I was sure we were both imprinting each other into our memory banks to tuck away for safekeeping. Whatever happened next, I knew that I would always be able to pull out that memory of Zen and recall everything about him, from the tiny chip on his bottom tooth to the faintest silvery scar just above his left eyebrow, and especially those soft kissable lips...

'So, what do you think, guys? asked Aurora.

I'm not sure how we managed it, but somehow Zen and I found the impetus to crawl back into reality. Drifting back together from our parallel universe, we both gawped at her, clueless as to what she was talking about.

'Err, sorry sis, miles away. I'll get us some drinks, eh? Gin and tonic for you and what's your poison tonight, Ellie? Will I see if they've got a nice Hemlock cocktail?' He laughed, nodding his head towards the door.

Isla had just made her grand entrance, no doubt timed to perfection so that everyone would see her. She had clearly not got the memo about the jumpers being ironic, or if she had, she had flouted the rules. Her grey eyes had a coldness about them as they darted round the room, until they aligned with Zen, who was leaning across the bar, and then they visibly softened. She looked like she should be selling houses in LA, not attending a cheesy jumper party on Holy Island. Her outfit consisted of a cropped red cashmere jumper with white angora trim – a fraction higher and she'd be in under-boob territory – a red PVC skirt so tight she could hardly walk, and the first pair of heels I had seen since I got here, and boy, they were high, taking her to over six foot tall. There was a hush in the room as the men stopped chatting, their drinks suspended mid mouth as they drooled. The women in their lives poked them in the ribs and threw knowing glances out to the sisterhood. Isla knew how to make an entrance, that was for sure. It took her exactly three minutes to drift over to our little group.

'Hi you three. Nice to see you all made an effort,' she slurred. She was drunk.

'The brief was funny, Isla,' said Aurora caustically. 'Although maybe you don't get that concept. What have you come as? A Christmas tart?'

I could see Zen's eyebrow twitching as he looked from his sister to Isla like he was trying to cross a busy road.

'Oh, save it for someone who gives a shit Aurora. It's about time you got over the Harriet thing. Easy come, easy go. And it's Christmas after all, season of goodwill, blah blah blah.'

'You're such a cow, Isla. Harriet's worth a million of you, you tragic trollop.'

Zen put his arm on Aurora's shoulder, telling her to let it go before it descended into all-out war. Isla turned her attention to me, and I braced myself.

'Actually, Ellie, congratulations. You look slightly more co-ordinated than you usually do, and when you are finished with that jumper, you can always use it as a tent, I suppose.'

Zen's other eyebrow shot up; he was just about to say something when Meg joined us.

'Good evening, Meg, the unofficial queen of Lindisfarne, or so you'd like to think. I see that you have a self-portrait on your jumper.'

'You fu...' I began, but Meg grabbed me by the arm before I could say any more. She turned to Isla and gave her a look that would sour Nanny's milk.

'I'd rather look like a donkey than act like one, you uppity little madam. I've roasted things in the oven with more brain cells than you. You're a disgrace to this island, Isla Thompson. Come with me, Ellie, Moira has something for you.'

'Thanks Meg, I think that might have ended up in a catfight,' I said as we walked away. 'And take no notice of her vitriol. She's pure poison.'

'I did warn you.' Meg winked. 'And don't worry, water off this old girl's back.'

Isla was the kind of woman who thought it was her right to have everything just fall into her lap at the click of her manicured fingers. Being exceptionally beautiful had not helped her cause and had fuelled her sense of entitlement. For the life of me, I couldn't quite understand why she was pursuing the quiet, eco-conscious Zen. Yes, he was the most gorgeous man on the island... and there it was, I had answered my own question. Isla was fickle enough to be drawn purely by physical appearances, but was that not a case of the pot calling the kettle black? Was my infatuation with him based purely on how gorgeous he was, and did that not just put me in the same shallow category as her? Or was I kidding myself? Was there more to whatever it was between me and him than just pure old lust? Had I felt something deep in my being? Might the universe be telling me that there was, just because *I might* have seen two stars twinkling brighter than all the others? Lots of questions, yet no real answers.

'Ellie, thanks so much for taking the kids out to the café with the alpacas the other day,' said Moira, when we eventually made it across to her. 'They had a wonderful time, and our Amelia hasn't stopped talking about you since. You are her new best friend! When she knew I was seeing you tonight, she insisted I gave you this,' she said, handing me an envelope.

I opened it to find a hand drawn card inside. On the front were me and Amelia in our matching Christmas hats with Murray between us. She'd decorated it in glitter and stickers – it was quite a work of art. I read the big, loopy writing inside.

To my best friend Ellie, I loved going to the café with you and I loved my hot chocolate and I love Murray and can we go again please please please? Lots of love, Amelia xxxxxxxxxxx

'This is just so lovely Moira. Please give her a hug from me and tell her we'll see each other soon.'

My phone vibrated in my pocket – a message from Sophie.

'Excuse me Moira, I'm just going to go outside and call my friend back,' I said, heading for the door.

I stepped out into the wintery night. It was bitter, and I could see the frozen breath from people talking, swirling into the still night air from behind the hedge of the pub garden. I was about to call Sophie when I heard Zen and Isla talking. I stood rooted to the spot, hardly daring to breathe.

'Oh, come on Zen. I was only joking. Won't do it again – pinkie promise,' she wheedled.

'Out of order, Isla. You crossed the line. Meg is one of the kindest people on the island.'

'Sorreee, naughty Isla – perhaps you should punish me. Let me make it up to you, Zen. You've been back on the island for ages and not a sign of a woman in your life. You must be sooo frustrated.'

'Take your hands off me Isla.'

What on earth?

'God, your legs are so taut, and long – I'd love to feel them wrapped around me. Darling, I'm brilliant in bed and I haven't had it in ages either, so let me show you what you're missing. I promise you won't regret it and you'll come back for more. Like friends with benefits, you might say. I'm not asking you to marry me, unless you want to, and why wouldn't you? We would make beautiful babies. We can do it here, right now. Come on, you know you want to. Outdoor sex is just sooo exciting.'

'Isla, we aren't friends, never will be, and there

will be no benefits, let me assure you. I'd rather go and live on St Cuthbert's island like a monk.'

'Aw, Zenny, don't say that. You're a red-blooded male, and I know you must find me attractive. There's no other woman...' she tailed off. 'Oh. My. God. Don't tell me you've fallen for that charity shop reject from London? That really would be scraping the barrel.'

Even though it was about minus two, my cheeks were burning, and it took all my willpower not to jump over the hedge and rip her hair extensions out. I tried to make myself move, to not listen to anymore. I knew I might not hear what I wanted to hear, but of course I didn't leave; I was far too curious.

'Her name is Ellie as you well know, and she seems a lovely woman, but—'

Oh God, there's a but coming.

'—there is no way that I'm going to start a relationship with her—'

I held my breath until I was in danger of bursting as I waited to hear what was coming next. The sensible thing would have been to leave at that point, eavesdroppers never hearing any good of themselves and all of that, but I was just so intrigued – plus the fact my legs appeared to have turned to concrete.

'—and not that it's any business of yours, but yes, actually I do like her – a lot. Thing is though Isla, I'm not like you; I don't just screw people for fun or what I can get out of them, and the timing just isn't right for either of us, so it's not going to happen.'

'Well, Saint Zen, all I can say is you've had a lucky escape with that rag bag. You don't know what you're missing with me though. There's nothing more fun than sex, and who needs all the complications of a relationship? The door is always open if you change your mind.' She laughed. 'I'd still love to get naked with you.'

I heard Isla's heels click-clack towards the door, which slammed as she went back into the pub, and Zen's soft footsteps as he left by the garden gate and headed towards home.

I took a few moments trying to absorb what I had overheard. He liked me. Zen liked me! The feeling was reciprocal, but he had sounded so matter of fact that it wasn't happening, and realistically, I had so much to think about too. It seemed so soon after Matt, who for whatever reason seemed to have disappeared from my head almost entirely, apart from the occasional thought about the thousands of pounds he owed me, which I quickly tried to shove to the back of my mind.

I just wanted to go back to the castle and speak to Sophie. My head was at sixes and sevens, and I needed to offload to my bestie, so I popped back in the pub to tell Meg and Aurora that I was going home. I was met with a death stare from Isla who had young Ethan pinned up in the corner. Poor kid would be scarred for life if she got her claws into him to provide her with a quick bunk up. That woman was positively vile.

***

'What's up babe? Slow down. You're garbling!'

'Sophie, I know you've just got to the hotel, and it's probably really late there and I hope it's lovely, it should be the amount it cost, but I just had to call you.'

'That's okay Ellie, we're both wide awake anyway, not adjusted to the time difference yet and yes, it is rather amazing, so thanks for having such great taste. So, what's up?'

'Oh Sophie, it's Zen.' I sniffed down the phone. 'I just overheard him saying that he likes me but won't have a relationship with me because the timing isn't right. I'm so confused Soph. It's hardly any time at all since Matt, and I think I must still be in shock because I'm not behaving rationally. What are the chances that the moment I set foot on the island, I meet someone who I feel so connected to? Surely that's impossible? You always said that we know 'the one' the minute we meet them. You said we would feel that the world was a new, brighter, and better place as a result of meeting that one person, that life was suddenly full of possibilities, and that we would know that no one else would compare. Not that I believed you at the time because I had never got those feelings over Matt.'

'Did I really say all that?' Laughed Sophie. 'Sounds far too deep for me! Joking babes, I did say it and I meant every word, but it was only something I believed in once I had met Jake, otherwise I would have laughed in your face if you had said the same to me.'

'Well, I've got all those feelings now, Sophie, and then some, but how can that have happened so quickly? Is it because I'm on the rebound? Am I just desperate? Oh Sophie, I'm just so confused! Not long before overhearing them talking, when I was in the pub with Zen, I experienced something I never have before. We literally locked eyes and the intensity was so powerful, I'm sure we created enough electricity to light up the national grid. It was just the most beautiful and romantic moment ever. Sophie, he was looking at me so intensely, like he could see right through me to my very soul. No one has ever looked at me like that before. I felt like we were free-falling into the universe amongst the stars. I know, I know, pure schmaltz, but of all the people in the world, I know you will understand. Then wham, I felt like I've been kicked in the guts after overhearing him because I know he's right; it is too soon. I don't know his story, but I know he's had his heart broken and is trying to invest all his time into his coffee business, and why would he want a short-term distraction at his busiest time of the year?'

'So many questions Ellie Nellie. Who was he talking to by the way?'

'He was talking to Isla. You know, the poisonous cow I've told you about? They didn't know I was there. She was coming on to him Sophie. The woman has no shame. She was offering herself up on a plate.'

'Tart. And?'

'He made it clear that he wasn't interested in her, thankfully, or else I would have truly doubted my ability to judge anyone ever again.'

'Oh Ellie, I wish I were there to give you a big hug. Now listen to me babes. Yes, finding 'the one' could happen the minute you set foot on the island, why couldn't it? These things aren't planned; we don't diary them in to happen at a convenient time. I mean, look at me meeting Jake out of the blue in that pharmacy when he was looking for corn pads and I gave him chapter and verse on foot care. Not the most romantic of encounters, but it was just meant to be. No, I don't think it's because you are on the rebound. Even though you and Matt had been together years, you'd not really been a proper couple for ages. As for desperate, never! You, my bestie, are gorgeous and have no need to ever be anything like desperate. I've not met this Zen guy, but I kind of liked him from your description, nothing that a haircut and some decent clothes wouldn't sort out.' She grinned. 'But honestly, If he's not interested in short term even though he obviously likes you, then maybe you just have to accept it and not let it spoil your time on the island. You could just talk to him, you know, stick your neck out and put it all out there.'

'Oh, I couldn't Sophie. Well, I suppose if the chance ever arose, but I don't want to admit listening in to his conversations.'

'Well then, what Auntie Sophie suggests is that you find a distraction. You've heard the saying you've got to get under someone to get over someone else? Well now is the time to put that into practice. Don't forget, you did say you wanted to play the field, and maybe that's the way you should go, you've got a lot of catching up to do in the dating stakes.'

'Soph, there's not exactly a surfeit of eligible men on the island to have a fling with.'

'Well, Ellie Nellie, maybe you should send a note up the chimney to Santa Claus. He always comes up trumps!'

CHAPTER 22

I woke up early the next morning, my head full of the night before. Maybe I should have taken on board what Aurora had told me when we first met – that her brother wasn't looking for a relationship. But something way beyond my comprehension had happened and I had literally fallen hook, line and sinker on the spot.

Because of Bert going away later that day, I had an early start, so maybe I would just get up and go and see if I could catch the sunrise – something I had been promising myself I would do. Perhaps it would help me put things into perspective.

'Come on Nacho, time to get up.' I gave him a little push and he opened his eyes, not looking at all thrilled at the prospect. I dressed quickly, putting on as many layers as I could. The weather had changed over the last couple of days; the wind had whipped up and the temperature had dropped considerably.

I made a mug of Stan's coffee, grabbed the massive bunch of keys Meg had given me, took Bert's torch, and went to see if I could get onto the roof terrace. I climbed up the spiral stairwell, Nacho at my heels, and got to a platform at the top with a locked door. About twelve keys later, I opened the door onto a flat roof that ran across the length of both apartments. A parapet about four-foot-high protected the perimeter. I was pleased, as it was so windy up there that I thought we were in danger of being blown over the top and into the sea below. I huddled in the doorway, sipping my coffee, and looked out across the sea. The darkness of night was turning to dawn as the first colours of the day began to appear. I could make out Greater Reef. The birds had begun their morning routine, exercising their vocal chords, and there was a faint orange glow beginning to rise on the horizon as I watched the day come alive. The sky was bathed in citrus light, which turned to a deep burnt orange, then literally glowed pillar box red. It reminded me of that saying: *Red sky at night, shepherd's delight. Red sky in the morning, shepherd's warning.* I hoped it wasn't an omen of things to come. It was well worth freezing my butt off for such a spectacular sight, although I wasn't sure Nacho would agree, his little body shivering in the cold. What he needed was one of those cute hand knitted Christmas dog jumpers that I spotted in *Love Lindisfarne*, which would keep him toasty. I locked the door and went back to the apartment for breakfast, before going out into the yard and starting my chores.

***

Bert and Meg set off for Alnwick that afternoon. We'd got all the animals settled down before they left, leaving only the alpacas and donkeys in the paddocks; and I would take the dogs out for a run later before the usual lock up routine. It was gone 2 p.m., so leaving Nacho with the other dogs in the kennel, I decided to go up to the apartment and make myself a sandwich.

As I approached the landing, I was horrified to see that the door to the Lindisfarnes' apartment was open. I stood stock still, not quite knowing what to do. I scrabbled for my phone, which was in a zipped pocket about two layers in – I was all fingers and thumbs trying to retrieve it. I didn't know whether I should get the hell back down the stairs and outside, or try to sneak into my apartment, lock the door and then call for help. Maybe James and Grace had come back early? Surely, they would have let Bert or Meg know if that was the case. I was still standing there looking down the long corridor of the apartment, when suddenly, a man wearing the top half of a Santa costume, the tiniest, tightest briefs and little else, stepped out of one of the doors and into view.

'Whoa, you gave me a fright!' he said, startled.

'I gave *you* a fright? My heart is going so fast I think it might burst. Are you a burglar looking to steal a pair of trousers?' I muttered indignantly.

He glanced down at his legs and burst out laughing.

'I'm Aidan, and you must be Ellie?'

Did everyone know my name around here?

'Don't just stand there woman, come in. I'm freezing my bollocks off here.'

I followed him down the corridor into a large

sitting room. He marched over to the huge roaring fireplace in the middle of the outer wall and stood in front of it, warming his very pert bottom. I stayed in the doorway, ready for a quick getaway, if necessary, and looked at him properly. He looked just like the Santa Paws I had imagined, the lead in a romcom. This guy would get the role hands down. There was more than a touch of Ryan Renolds about him!

'Have you finished gawping yet?' He laughed without a trace of embarrassment. His voice was deep and that was no local accent. He sounded quite aristocratic, or posh, as Bert might say.

'Err, sorry,' I replied, having to retrieve my eyeballs, which were out on springs, and pop them back into place. 'Aidan who? And how do you know my name?'

I concentrated on focusing on his face and the clothed top half of his body but was fighting a losing battle; his legs kept calling to me. He had dark blonde hair, piercing blue eyes and those long, lean legs which must have seen some sun of late; they were a lovely shade of golden brown and covered in sun kissed downy hairs. But it was those bright blue eyes that were the giveaway, as I suddenly realised that he was the much younger double of Lord Bamburgh.

'Aidan Bamburgh,' he introduced himself. 'James and Grace are my uncle and aunt. Papa told me all about you. Well in fairness to the old duffer, he didn't tell me much other than your name, and that you were here from London to help look after the animals. I didn't realise you were around my age. And I bet that there's a goddess lurking underneath that hat and coat, which I'm finding rather sexy. Nice antlers by the way!' He smiled, his bright blue eyes twinkling.

Aidan Bamburgh was a charming flirt, but ridiculously hot.

'What are you doing here in Grace and James' apartment?' I replied, my cheeks burning.

'Doing James a favour as it happens. It's Santa Saturday in the village hall today and James usually does the honours as Santa, just like Papa does for his worthy causes. Thankfully, I'm the spare and not the heir, so I won't have to dress like a prick every Christmas for the next half century.' He laughed. 'But I said I would step into the breach today and go in place of James. I started trying on the outfit but it's rather big and the trousers literally fell off me.'

It was all beginning to make sense.

'How did you get in here?'

'We keep a spare set of keys over at Bamburgh. I'm back for Christmas; I spend most of my time in London. It was like the proverbial fridge when I got here, and I know the heating system takes forever to throw out less heat than you'd get from a candle, so I put the fire on. People want to live in castles, until they have to live in them!' He laughed. 'They're bloody draughty old mausoleums. I mean, look at it in here. It's like a living museum; just like it is at home.'

I looked around the room. I would call it

country house shabby chic. Overstuffed sofas, side tables, and walls and surfaces adorned with the history of the castle and the family. I thought it was wonderful, but for Aidan it was clearly nothing new.

'How are you doing over there?' Aidan gestured towards my apartment. 'No wonder you're wearing a bloody hat and coat.'

'Actually, it's as warm as toast in there. I haven't even needed to put the fire on. The central heating works very well.'

'I'd heard they had splashed out to make the place nice for the prodigals and their families when they come home. I think it was all a ploy to keep the sprog out of James' way. He doesn't like distractions. He's like Uncle Quentin, the mad scientist in the Famous Five books, buried away in his study. Except he's a mad archaeologist. Anyway, how goes the time? I've got to be there by 2.45 p.m.'

'Better get a move on then. I'll leave you to it.'

'No! Don't go. Please, Ellie. Extend the Christmas spirit and help me get this costume sorted. I'm useless at things like this and if the trousers fall down while I'm on the job, so to speak, I'll ruin the family's reputation and it will be the end of us Bamburghs. Not to mention that dear old Papa will kill me.'

'I can imagine your trousers fall down quite often when you're on the job,' I quipped.

He burst out laughing.

'Oh, a quick wit. I like you, Miss Ellie; you and I are going to get along quite nicely. Now please help and I promise, I will make it worth your while.' He winked, a huge grin lighting up his handsome face.

'Okay, as it's Christmas and it's for the kids in the village. There will be an Amelia coming to see you, button cute, long red hair – you make sure she gets the best gift. That's my condition. Take it or leave it?'

'Done.'

I walked across to the fireplace and stood in front of him. He smelled like... well it wasn't espresso and pine, but whatever it was, it was rather delicious.

'Trousers? Put them on.'

I watched as he pulled the giant pair of red trousers over his gorgeous, tanned legs, all the way up towards the pair of very tight tiny briefs which showed every curve, and once again my eyes made their own decision and locked into position. It took all my strength and willpower to force them to look upwards. This time, there were no mystical powers involved. It was another part of my anatomy entirely controlling my senses!

'See what I mean?' he said, as he eventually covered his modesty. 'They're far too big around the waist.'

'Okay, have you got a belt?'

He went off to look and I was feeling so hot, I needed to take the hat and coat off. I wasn't sure if it was the heat from the fire, or my newly reactivated hormones flooding around my body like a tsunami in full flow. He returned with a belt and some other clothing in a bag, which he shoved at me.

'I was right about the goddess lurking underneath the hat!' he said, grinning at me. 'Now then, since you seem to care about the village kids, I just found this. It's Aunt Grace's elf costume. She always goes with James to help, so unless you have anything better to do, why not do your bit for the island and come with me?'

I couldn't really think of any pressing reason why I shouldn't. I didn't need to get back for the dogs until early evening, and everything else was taken care of.

'Tell you what,' he said, 'you come with me, and I'll take you out to dinner tonight – deal?'

Sophie's words ringing in my ears about needing a distraction, I didn't even hesitate.

'Okay, deal. Now then, I've had an idea re: the padding underneath your Santa jacket.' I handed him the big yellow coat. 'Pop this on underneath. You'll look like you ate all the Christmas mince pies. Right, let me go and change, and we'll be ready to head to the North Pole.'

I let myself back into the apartment, had a quick shower and got into the costume, which thankfully fit without the aid of belts and padding. It even came with outdoor shoes, which had little bells on the top. I popped on the hat and looked in the mirror, a vision in green and red with striped tights. Not bad at all except for one thing... I hastily put on a little makeup and drew two red circles on my cheeks with lipstick. Glancing at the clock, I had a couple of minutes to spare, so I picked up my tablet and called Sophie.

'Sophie, you will never believe this. Santa Paws is real.'

'Don't tell me, you sent a note up the chimney last night and this morning Zen was wrapped up with a bow and waiting next to the Christmas Tree.'

'I wish. No, I mean the one I thought Santa Paws was going to be. Y'know, the one like the lead in a romcom.'

Sophie was sitting in a beach bar, a scrummy looking cocktail in front of her. Taking off her sunglasses, she stared at me, a perplexed expression on her face.

'Slow down Ellie. What are you dressed as this time, by the way? Honest to God, I don't know what's happened to you since you got to that place. What time is it over there?' she said, checking her phone. 'Bit early for a fancy-dress party, isn't it?'

'It's Santa Saturday.'

'Santa what? How many Santas are there on that tiny island?'

'Oh, never mind, but I'm telling you, this Santa Paws, I mean Claus, is real. You should see his legs…'

'I won't even ask how you have seen under his robes. Honestly, Ellie, you're not making much sense – do you think you've had too much sun?' She hiccupped, gulping down the bright pink drink.

'Err, no, because I'm not in the bloody Maldives, am I? It's freezing here.'

'Well, I did tell you to ask Santa and it seems like he has come in person to be your distraction therapist.'

There was a knock on the door.

'That's him! Got to go. Love you Soph.'

'Ellie, I need to hear more; don't you dare cut me....'

Click.

CHAPTER 23

It was blowing a gale as we went down into the courtyard.

'We can't walk in this,' said Aidan. 'Better go in the Landy.'

We went through the door in the big arched gate and into the car park, where an old green land rover was parked. I climbed in gratefully, and we set off on the short journey to the village hall.

'So, how do you know my old man?'

'Well, actually,' I said, 'coincidentally, he was dressed just like you when I met him.'

I explained about the *Dogs Are For Life* Christmas bash, missing out the bit about all my embarrassing email messages.

'You have a lot to live up to because your dad is an amazing Santa. He makes sure that everyone gets the gift they ask for. I asked him for a new life – an impossible request you might think – but he arranged this trip to Lindisfarne. It's a temporary new life, granted, but nevertheless, he's amazing, and I can't thank him enough.'

'No pressure then. Let's hope I'm a chip off the old block. I'll let you into a secret, I'm not that great around kids. The poker-faced little darlings freak me out when they do the death stare thing. I'm rather hoping that with you by my side it will be okay – just drag them off me if the going gets tough. Should we have a safe word? How about "Santa's not real!"'

'Relax.' I laughed. 'It'll be fine.'

We pulled up to the side of the hall, and Aidan put on the beard and arranged his Santa suit.

'You make an exceptionally fine Santa Claus,' I said, smiling at him.

'And you are quite the hottest elf I've ever seen. Would you like to sit on my knee and tell me what you want for Christmas? I know exactly what I want.' He smirked, looking directly into my eyes, his face breaking into a wide grin underneath the fluff.

Oh, my days, he was easy on the eye, even in the costume. And he was interesting. And he was interested...

'Hey, enough of the flirting. We're going into a kids' party, remember. Now concentrate on the task at hand.'

'Okay Ellie Elf, I will – but only if we can concentrate on a joint task later?' He winked.

I swiped him with my handbells. If I was looking for a distraction from Zen, then I had found one for sure. The universe, or whatever, wasn't at play here. It was a pure case of good old-fashioned lust. There were none of the magnetic feelings that I got when I saw Zen, but if I was looking for a fling, he was right here next to me.

We snuck in through the back door and took

our places on the stage behind the curtain. The noise coming from the front of the hall was deafening. There weren't that many children on the island, but they were managing to create more decibels than you'd get at a thrash metal gig – no doubt an overload of candy cane sugar and the excitement of Christmas fuelling them to run amok.

'Have you heard the little darlings? I feel like the condemned man going to the gallows.' Aidan gulped, mopping his brow. 'I'm about to melt inside this stinking old coat and costume. I need a drink. Pop to the pub and bring me a pint back pleeease, Ellie Elf.'

'You can't drink on duty. Now stop whining and I'll give the signal to Mrs Brown. She'll get things underway.'

Aidan turned out to be a natural. The safe word wasn't instigated once. He listened carefully to the children and was particularly good at not promising the earth when they were asking for the impossible. When Amelia saw it was me, she rushed over and gave me a big hug, her huge green eyes taking in my costume, clearly impressed that I knew Santa personàlly. Even though it didn't seem possible, I had gone up yet another notch in her estimation.

'Santa,' I said, 'remember I mentioned Amelia? Well, here she is, and Santa always keeps his promises – right?'

'Of course, Ellie Elf. Now then Miss Amelia, come and sit on the stool and tell Santa if you have been nice, hopefully not naughty, then we can discuss what Santa might bring you on Christmas day.'

She sat on the stool, looking up at him. She was wearing her party dress. It was Christmas themed, with little trees and sequinned lights that twinkled, and she was wearing a pair of fairy wings, her red hair hanging loose in waves. She looked adorable.

Aidan established she had been nice; Amelia explained all about how she helped Bert look after the animals and wasn't scared of shovelling up poo. She finished by saying, 'Please don't tell the others, but I love Murray the best.'

Aidan asked what she would like for Christmas. She looked at me coyly, and then did her little thing of whispering in his ear so I couldn't hear.

'Okay, Miss Amelia, got it. Now Santa can't promise that, but what I can promise is that I will try my absolute best.' He gave her the biggest box in the sack, and she skipped off back to her friends, no doubt full of pride that she was best friends with an elf!

Sitting in the *Crab* after we had finished, Aidan gulped down a pint and removed the coat, which was practically welded to his skin. We looked at each other and burst out laughing. His face was the same colour as his suit.

'Your cheeks look like roadkill splatters.' He grinned.

'Hey, you don't look so great yourself. You're the colour of a boiled lobster! And as for that delightful child throwing that glitter all over us, we'll be finding the stuff in every orifice for weeks to come.'

'Don't tell a living soul,' said Aidan. 'It will ruin my reputation as a man about town, but I enjoyed that. If Papa got to find out, I'd be put out to tender. He's always saying I need a proper job. Although,' he scratched his red face, 'Santa only works one day a year, so result!'

'What do you do?' I asked, sipping my mineral water.

'Truth Ellie? Well, I ponce about in the family firm. We have various business interests and I'm supposed to look after our London portfolio, but more often than not, I just schmooze. Before you get all, "that's not a proper job" on me, it is you know. Bloody arduous work having to spend time with some of the odious nobs that I have to. What about you?'

'I'm in public relations. I have to schmooze too, and yes; it is bloody hard work having to spend time with you nobs. Anyway, enough talk about work.' I didn't really want to tell him about the London me. It felt right to keep it to the here and now, to make this about the me he had met on Lindisfarne, so I changed the subject.

'Santa, are you allowed to tell me what Christmas present Amelia asked for? I can pass it on to her mum if it's something she hasn't already got for her.'

'You can't buy what she asked for Ellie. That kid has impeccable taste by the way. Hmm, now then, can I divulge? I need to refer to my Santa handbook,' Aidan said, laughing, holding up an invisible book and thumbing the pages.

'Okay, here it is, according to page 4, paragraph 9, subsection 2a, it seems I'm allowed to tell you, as long as it stays just between Santa and his chief elf.'

'Absolutely, I promise,' I said seriously.

'Amelia said that if I could arrange that you stay on the Island forever, she wouldn't need any other gifts this year. You heard me tell her I couldn't promise that, but perhaps you need to work out if you can help make her wish come true.'

My eyes filled up. I'd never really had a closeness with a child before, and it was magical, but quite a responsibility too. How could I promise her that? The longer I was here on the island, however, the more attractive a proposition it was to stay. The idea of going back to London was filling me with dread. I had nothing to go back to. No job, nowhere to live, no boyfriend... Aidan put his arms around me and gave me a hug.

'You've made a big impression there, Ellie Elf, and you're making one on me too.'

As we hugged, the door opened and in walked Zen. Even though I was in the arms of a nine, my stomach did the usual flips on seeing his curls and the coffee bean eyes, and all thoughts of what I had heard last night were shoved right to the back of my head. He may not have thought the timing was right, but I still wanted him; there was no doubting that.

'Well, look what the bloody cat's dragged in!' shouted Aidan amiably. 'Zen Chambers! Good God, it's years since our paths last crossed. Come and join us. Let me get you a drink.'

Zen's eyes twinkled as they went from me to Aidan, taking in the costumes and the bedraggled appearance of us both.

'Aidan Bamburgh, you posh prick, how the hell are you?' He laughed.

Aidan let go of me and they fist bumped each other before merging into a man hug.

'So, you bloody hippie, you need a haircut by the way, how's...' he stopped abruptly and turned to me.

'Sorry, Ellie, how rude of me. Do you two know each other? Let me introduce you.'

'Oh, we've already met,' I said wistfully, not taking my eyes off Zen.

'Pint of Lindisfarne Lil?'

'You remembered Aidan, thanks.'

Aidan went to the bar and Zen turned to me.

'I didn't know you and Aidan knew each other.'

'We don't. I only met him this afternoon. He seems nice.'

But then so are you and look how that's turning out.

'He's charming, Ellie. I wouldn't have thought he was your type though.'

'Oh, and what type would that be?' I raised my eyebrow.

He had the grace to look embarrassed.

'Sorry, none of my business. I shouldn't presume to know you well enough to make that kind of judgement.'

No, you made it abundantly clear that you didn't want me to be your business.

'But as your erm... friend,' he seemed to struggle to find the word, 'I'm just looking out for you, so be careful, Ellie. He's great fun but a bit...' He tailed off.

'Well, thanks for the advice, I'll be sure to take it on board.' Sarcasm dripped from my every word.

'Ellie, what's wrong, you sound angry with me?'

I looked into the normally bright coffee bean eyes, which were now as cloudy with confusion as a flat white. I had to remind myself that this was not his fault. He seemed a lovely, genuine guy, who had his reasons for not wanting a short-term fling, and realistically, I wasn't ready for another long-term disaster. But then again, who's to say it would turn out a disaster? My insecurity was driving me, and no matter how I tried to push it back, it just kept on pulling me, like a dog with a very large bone. How on earth did I trust my instincts again when they hadn't served me well thus far? Maybe the best course of action would be to accept that friend-zoning him would be the best way forward, and perhaps if I had some fun with Aidan, it would help me break whatever weird mystical bonds were tying me to Zen.

'Sorry Zen, I didn't mean to snap. I'm not angry, but maybe don't presume to know who I should spend time with. I'm a big girl. I'm sure I can work that out for myself.'

I really couldn't, but he wasn't to know that.

He nodded, an air of dejection almost sinking him under the ancient floorboards, but before I could say anymore, Aidan bounced back from the bar. I spent the next twenty minutes having to listen to them catch up and reminisce, without being able to contribute anything at all. Then Zen finished his pint and left with another man hug for Aidan, and nothing more than a half-hearted nod in my direction.

'Shall we just stay out and go straight from here for dinner?' continued Aidan, oblivious to me staring at the closing door as Zen marched through it, my fixed smile turning upside down.

'Erm, I've actually got to go back and do the lock down for the night, give the dogs a quick walk.' I needed some air, some time to think.

'Can you drive?'

'Yes, I've passed my test, but living in London there's no need, so I don't really get behind the wheel very often. Why?'

'Well, you take the Landy. Go back and do what you need to do. Leave me here and pick me up on the way past and we'll go to the hotel. Oh, and Ellie, don't get changed. That elf costume is rather sexy, and it wouldn't be fair if I have to stay dressed up like this!'

'Won't we need a reservation for dinner?' I asked.

'That is one benefit of being a Bamburgh – round here anyway – guaranteed to find us a table.'

'What? Dressed like this?'

'Oh yes, believe you me, it wouldn't matter if we went in there naked – now then, there's a nice thought...'

I had never driven a Land Rover before. It took me ages to get going and once I did, it was like it was filled with kangaroo fuel. It lurched along the road, but at least there were no other vehicles to contend with. The wind had gone up yet another notch; it was howling, so I quickly went into the yard, sorted out the chickens, and Sage and Onion. Colonel Sanders was back, so I left open the hatch to where he sometimes went to sleep. I saw to the cats, giving Lulu her daily chat as she spat the others out of the way of the food. Then I fed the dogs, gave Nacho an extra big hug, and let them into the yard.

'Sorry guys, there's no way I can take you out. We'll get blown away. So, you'll have to make do with a run around here.'

The yard was quite sheltered thanks to the high walls surrounding it. I checked on the horses, topping up their hay nets, and gave the devil pony extra carrots, as for once, he hadn't tried to kick me.

I popped in to see Nanny, who was all snug in her stall. Meg had arranged for Don to come across and milk her that evening and she would be back to do it herself in the morning, thank God. I still wasn't sure I was up to that challenge yet. I did wonder about the alpacas and the donkeys down in the paddocks in the wind, but Bert and I had fed them earlier and they had their shelters.

I hastily washed my hands under the stable tap, scrubbed my face with a wet wipe to get the lipstick off, and went back to the Land Rover. I sat quietly for a few minutes, taking stock, the wind howling around me. I looked up at the night sky for guidance, but it was devoid of stars thanks to heavy cloud cover – it was as if it was trying to tell me something. My two bright shining stars were nowhere to be seen. Aidan was great. He was gorgeous, funny, and utterly fanciable, but seeing Zen had thrown me. It was something I couldn't really explain, even to myself. What would Sophie say if I was to ask her advice? I could almost hear her voice – just like she was sitting right next to me.

You need a good old no strings romp babe. It's Christmas and you're on holiday, so forget the trippy hippie and have some bloody fun.

Imaginary Sophie may well be right. I started up the engine and lurched my way back to collect Aidan.

CHAPTER 24

'Here she is,' shouted Aidan as I walked back into the pub. 'My favourite elf.' He was holding court in the middle of the room, a crowd of locals around him, and by the way he was swaying about, I guessed he must have had more than a few drinks.

'Santa Claus is ready for you Ellie Elf.' He grinned. 'Let's go to the North Pole, or maybe the *St Cuthbert's Way Hotel*. The sleigh hasn't got much fuel in it!'

'Everything okay over the way, Ellie?' cut in Don. 'I had a quick scout around when I went across to milk Nanny and all seemed fine, but I'm a bit concerned about this forthcoming storm. It's due to hit at about 2 a.m. and it's going to be bad according to the forecasts.'

'Everything seems fine, thanks Don. Hopefully, all will be well. Bert and Meg are due back in the morning. I'll shout if I need you if that's okay?'

'No problem, Ellie, anything for my Amelia's best friend!' He laughed.

'Right Santa, let's be having you.'

'Ooh Ellie Elf, not in front of the locals please. Night chaps. See you all again soon.'

By the time we crossed the hotel car park, we

looked even more dishevelled than ever, if that was possible. My hair, underneath the elf hat, had done its usual of springing into frizzy waves. Aidan had to hang onto the Santa hat to stop it blowing away, and at one point I thought his trousers were going to be back around his ankles.

We literally fell through the door into reception. The hotel was as smart on the inside as it was on the out. A little too manicured for its location perhaps, with a colour coordinated Christmas tree in baby pink and blue, so full of baubles there was hardly a branch showing. I immediately thought that Isla had probably had a hand in the design. The woman behind the reception desk looked down her haughty nose at us – the windswept Santa and Elf, looking like they had crashed the sleigh and got pissed on the bottles of sherry that were waiting to be distributed. I could see a distinct likeness between her and Isla. She was an older version, dressed a little more sedately, thank God – it had to be her mum.

'Yes, can I help you?' she muttered, sounding like anything but a welcoming host. She obviously hadn't recognised Aidan underneath the face fluff and suit, and I hadn't met her, so there was at least one person on the island who didn't know who I was in advance of my arrival.

'Yesh, you can, and may I say you are looking particularly ravishing tonight, Elspeth,' slurred Aidan.

The woman's eyebrows shot up.

'Do I know you?'

'I know everyone in the world; it is my duty. Now then, we would like your finest table for me and my chief elf here. We are doing a trial run and decided to land on your rather splendid island for some supper.'

'Do you have a reservation?' she asked tersely.

I poked him in the ribs and whispered, '*I told you so.*'

'No madam, I don't; however, do you not know who I am?'

I literally cringed – not that old chestnut. Only pricks of the highest order spouted that line. Aidan had just plummeted down in my estimation.

'No sir, I don't.'

'I'm Shanta Claush. Are you a non-believer? Look, it is me. I exist and I am shtanding right in front of you.'

I burst out laughing, thank God, he hadn't used *the line*! The woman glowered at me disdainfully.

'Well, deeply sorry to disappoint you *Santa Claus*, but no reservation, no table. May I suggest the *Crab and Oyster*? I would imagine it to be more your kind of place; although I'm guessing you've been in there already,' she said sourly. She reminded me more of Isla as every minute passed.

'We have indeed, and an exceptionally fine hostelry it is, but I promised my chief elf a nice meal and Santa always keeps his promises.'

At that, a chap came through from the dining

room and again, it was easy to see from the family resemblance that he was Isla's dad.

'Can I help you?' he asked brusquely.

'I hope so, Gordon,' said Aidan, whipping off the hat and fluff and shaking the man's hand. 'Have you got a table please?'

'Aidan, how wonderful to see you, and your, err, elf. Follow me, I'll give you your father's preferred table,' said Gordon, leading the way across the dining room.

'Happy Christmas.' I smiled sweetly at the woman whose eyebrows had knitted into one long frowny line. 'May it bring everything you deserve.' And I trotted off behind the men, shoe-bells tinkling, trying not to combust with laughter.

'It's quiet in here tonight, Gordon. You're usually full at the weekend.'

'It's this storm Aidan – put lots of people off coming to the island. Businesses have had cancellations, but that doesn't stop us having fantastic choices on the menu. Chef has an amazing oyster and chorizo dish, thanks to Maurice over there, supplying wonderful local oysters.'

I looked across the dining room to see Maurice in a suit and tie, hair flattened to his head with gel. He was dining with a grey-haired woman of about his own age, who was wearing a sparkly turquoise dress and an overload of costume jewellery. Maurice raised his glass at me, and I waved at him and the woman, who I assumed to be Nora Brannigan.

'We also have seabass on tonight, and a top-draw selection in the cellar, which I'm sure you will appreciate,' said Gordon, who was so far up Aidan's arse he was in danger of disappearing.

Aidan winked at me and whispered, '*I told you so.*'

'Do you know the daughter?' I asked once we were settled at our table.

'Ackshually, I feel like I do. Those two utter snobs tell me about her any opportunity they get, but she's never been around when I've been here, which isn't that often. I think they have me lined up as a potenshal hushband though,' he replied, two glasses into an expensive bottle of chilled Sancerre. 'I've never met her in the flesh.' He burst out laughing. 'But I would like to meet you in the flesh one day very soon, Ellie Elf...'

Ignoring him, I continued. 'She's worse than the pair of them put together. I hope she's not around tonight.'

'Well, if she is, then I will tell her that she is wasting her time against an elf with the most magnificent pair of... ears.' He pointed, laughing.

'By the way, how are you getting home tonight?' I asked. 'You won't be able to drive now you're over the limit.'

'Swim? I think I've mished the tide anyway. I'll crash at Aunt Grace's – or Aunt Grace's guest apartment, if I'm really lucky, and Ellie's a naughty little Elf,' he said suggestively.

My phone pinged. It was a text from Meg.

I hear that you are out with Aidan Bamburgh. You be careful, pet, that one could charm the habit off Mother Superior. Love Meg x

News travelled fast on the island. About five minutes later, it pinged again. Aurora.

I hear that you're in the witch's den with Aidan. He's a charmer, Ellie, a philanderer, but an incredibly good looking, eligible one! Hope poison Isla isn't around. Have fun x.

We were mid-way through our main course, the seabass as delicious as promised, when my phone rang. *Who was it this time?* Had news travelled to London, or even the Maldives? It was Bert.

'Ellie pet, I'm worried about this storm. It's supposed to get bad in the night and I'm scared the shelters in the paddock aren't up to the job. They've been fine in the past but, if the weatherman's got it right, this could be the worst for twenty years.'

'Oh, that sounds bad Bert.'

'I hear Aidan is around. Can you get him to give you a hand and get the alpacas and donkeys up to their stables in the yard? It's about time that young rake did something useful.'

I looked across at the 'young rake' who was quaffing back the wine like his life depended on it. Bert might have had a point.

'Yes, Aidan's here Bert, so don't you worry. Between us, we'll get them sorted. I'll ring you when we're done, but it might take a while, so don't panic.'

'Ellie lass, you're worth your weight in gold. Now you take care and I'll speak to you later.'

'Aidan, that was Bert. You've met him, I take it?'

'Yesh, lovely fellow, salt of the bloody earth.'

'Well, he's worried about the storm during the night, and I've got to go and get the animals up to the yard. Will you be able to help, or do you want me to call into the *Crab* and see if I can round anyone else up?'

'What sort of animals?'

'Alpacas and donkeys.'

'Well in that case, I'm your man. If there's one thing us posh lot know all about, it's horshes, and they're more or less the same. All got four legs and bloody big teeth.'

'Are you capable though? You've had a lot to drink.'

'We Bamburghs are always capable, Ellie Elf. Our motto is—'

'—strength and valour,' I replied.

'Good God, you know our motto? Ish it ackshually possible for a chap to fall in love in one day? Because I think I just have. Anyway, I digresh. I'll have you know; I can hold my drink like a camel. Now, if you had asked me to help with *them*, I might have had to be ungallant and refuse, as they stink. Have you ever ridden one of the humpy-backed, bad-tempered bastards?'

'Err, no, can't say I have. Come on Aidan, eat up. We are really going to have to go and do this now, before the weather gets any worse.'

***

We were soaked by the time we got from the Land Rover to the stables; the rain was almost sideways; such was the strength of the wind. Aidan's legs seemed to have taken on the consistency of jelly, and he was wobbling all over the place. It didn't bode well. I opened the stable, switching on the light. There were three stalls: one for Pacino and Murray, and one each for the two donkeys – Wonky didn't like to share. Probably wouldn't object if it was with Wilma though.

'Right Aidan, you stay there a minute until I go and grab the reins, some carrots and find us something more suitable to wear, or we will seriously be in danger of hypothermia.'

'Ok chief. I will jusht lean here against this wall and wait for further instructshions. Perhaps I could have a little lie down on that straw?'

'Don't you dare. I need you to stay awake.'

I ran across to the store, where we kept the gear, grabbed what I needed and took a couple of old fisherman's oilskins that Bert sometimes wore in the rain. When I got back, Aidan was propped up against the wall, eyes closed, Santa hat askew. The facial fluff had blown away and was now probably halfway to the North Pole.

'Aidan, wake up, put this on,' I said, shoving the oilskin at him. It was clear to see that he wasn't even going to accomplish that simple task without help. It was like trying to dress an octopus. I tried to bundle him into the oilskin, his arms like tentacles wrapping around me, and as I peeled one off, another seemed to come out of nowhere.

'I just want a hug, Ellie Elf; Santa needs a hug to keep him warm.'

'I'm cold too, and wet, but we need to get this done,' I said, eventually getting the oilskin on him. 'Right, we're sorted. Now all I want you to do is support me in the wind as we go down the bank. Understand?'

'I do, boss. Lead the way.'

We literally crawled our way down the steep bank towards the paddocks, the full force of the wind in our faces taking our breath away, our eyes streaming from the constant force battering us. We had to stop every now and again to catch our breaths by turning our backs, and then we were nearly getting blown back up the bank. My elf hat blew off, my hair wrapping itself around my face, and I had flashbacks to the causeway, the night I had arrived on the island.

'Let's get the donkeys first. They are going to be the most difficult. The alpacas are sweeties,' I shouted in his ear over the noise of the wind, sounding far more confident than I was feeling. The brute force of the gale seemed to have sobered Aidan up slightly, and he nodded in understanding. I opened the gate to the donkey paddock, but there was no sign of them. The sensible creatures had taken themselves inside the shelter. We went into the wooden structure, and for the first time ever, they were huddled together, scared by the noise, their shelter rattling in the wind. I was terrified it was going to blow away. I quickly attached the lead reins and we headed to the gate. I passed them to Aidan, telling him to stay put and hold on tight until I'd collected the alpacas and we could make our way back up the hill. Pacino and Murray were also frightened, cowering in the corner, necks wrapped around each other.

'Oh, poor loves. Please don't be scared. I'm going to get you up to the stables where you'll be safe.' I stroked them both, offering carrots, which they refused point blank. Things really were bad; they never refused carrots. I led them out of the shelter and across to where Aidan was waiting, clutching tightly onto Wonky and Jenny's reins with one hand. He held his other hand out towards me, and I grabbed it, Pacino and Murray's reins in the other. We began our way across the field towards the cinder track leading back up to the yard. Aidan was wearing wellingtons as part of his Santa costume, but I was wearing the elf shoes with the tinkling bells and Wonky took exception, rearing and trying to pull away. Aidan hung on to the donkeys, but slipped and fell, and I swiftly followed, and we sat, soaking wet, in about six inches of thick brown mud, clutching on to our charges for dear life. Trying to get up was ridiculous; Aidan with his jelly legs, and me with the stupid shoes. I ripped the bells off so they wouldn't spook Wonky again. By the time we were both on our feet, I swore we could have been mistaken for mud wrestlers; we were unrecognisable.

'Shit! Just shit!' exclaimed Aidan. 'Aunt Grace is going to kill me for ruining the costumes.'

'That's the least of our problems,' I yelled back. 'We'll both be killed if we don't get a move on.' And as quickly as we could, we got on the cinder path, wind behind us this time, and literally blew up the hill.

We made it to the stable and I got the animals settled. Aidan had slid down the wall in a crumpled heap, and was sitting on the floor, back against the stable wall, looking like he'd been dug up. I sank down beside him, waiting for my breathing to return to something near normal, while watching my charges as they began to calm down and start pulling on the nets. While we were waiting, I got my phone out and took a selfie of me and Aidan – the gang were not going to believe this.

Once I was sure that all four animals were settled, I offered them carrots and I knew we were good when they happily took them, even Wonky nuzzled my hand. Thank God.

'Come on Santa, time to go. We'll do a quick check on the others on the way, and I'll collect Nacho.'

I was confident that all the animals would be okay during the night. The solid stone stables had been built to last and were protected in the yard by the high castle wall. Once I was happy that all was well, I collected Nacho, made a fuss of the other three dogs who were all happily curled up next to each other, seemingly oblivious to the weather, and we made our way back up to the apartments. We got to the landing and the two apartment doors. Aidan and I looked at each other and began to laugh until tears were running down our faces, causing wide tracks on our muddy cheeks.

'Ellie Elf, may I just say that you are the first woman to ever wear me out without so much as a snog. I'd ask you for one now, but I'm absolutely broken. Even if you were the naughtiest elf in the world and demanded my body and offered me all manner of sexy things, I'm afraid I would have to turn you down, but please never tell anyone that.'

'Don't worry, I won't. I'm feeling a little broken myself.' I smiled.

'Rain check? If you pardon the dreadful pun.'

'Rain check,' I agreed.

'I shall look forward to that. Me and this mud are going to crash out. When I wake up it will probably have hardened and you will need to chip me out in the morning, but I can't be arsed to care about it right now. I just need to sleep. Night, night, Ellie Elf.'

'Night, Aidan. You really did help, so thanks.'

We hugged and he kissed me briefly on the lips. He tasted of salty soil. Then he staggered next door, waving as he went.

I went straight to my bathroom and peeled off the soaking, ruined clothes. It was like déjà vu to the night I had arrived on the island. I left them in a heap in the bath and had a quick shower before ringing Bert.

'They're all inside and safe, Bert, so don't worry. But I'm so, so sorry, I feel like I should have got them up much earlier.'

'Ellie pet, it's not even ten yet, and the storm isn't supposed to hit hard until the middle of the night. If anyone's to blame, it's me. I should have got you to move them up at teatime. Don't you worry, they're safe now, and those outbuildings have been there as long as the castle. It will take more than this to shift them. As long as you're okay?'

'Yes, I'm fine.'

'And did Aidan help, or was he as much use as a chocolate teapot?'

'He's the colour of chocolate come to think about it,' I replied, 'but yes, he helped, and I would have struggled without him. Night Bert. See you and Meg tomorrow.'

As I lay in bed, I couldn't sleep. The noise was deafening. The old windows of the castle were rattling in their ancient frames and the sounds coming from the sea were like nothing I'd heard so far, the waves crashing and thrashing onto the rocks below. I wondered what it was like on Greater Reef and hoped Mike and Simone were okay over there, comforting myself with the thought that the lighthouse must have seen worse storms than this and was still standing. Nacho was distressed by the noises, and I cuddled him as my mind whirled like

239

the wind. I thought about Aidan. We'd had a brilliant day. He was fantastic company, made me laugh and no one could deny that he was bloody gorgeous, but my mind kept creeping back to Zen and the sadness in his beautiful eyes. I liked him, I really did, and if it was friendship or nothing, then I'd take it even though I knew it might never feel enough. But in the meantime, I needed time to find me, the fun Ellie that had been long lost to Matt's manipulation and control.

I eventually drifted off into fitful sleep, Nacho curled in a tight little ball underneath the duvet, my arms wrapped around him.

CHAPTER 25

I awoke with a start the next morning; I'd hardly slept because of the noise from the storm. My phone was ringing, and the intercom was buzzing at the same time. It had just gone 7 a.m. I leapt up, threw Meg's pink dressing gown around me and went to the intercom at the same time as answering the phone.

'Bert! What's the matter?' I yelled down the phone. 'Is everything okay with Meg?'

'Meg's fine, but haven't you heard lass…'

The intercom continued buzzing.

'Bert, two seconds, there's someone at the outside gate. Let me look and see who it is.' I peered at the camera screen. 'It's Aurora. What's she doing here so early?' I exclaimed, as I pressed to let her in. She must have run up the stairs two at a time as she got up so quickly.

'I'm so sorry for turning up at this time in the morning Ellie,' she panted. 'I was coming across to see Meg when I remembered she wasn't on the island. Everything's ruined!' She burst into tears.

'Aurora, don't you worry about coming here. I'll be with you in two ticks, I'm just on the phone to

Bert.'

'Bert, what on earth's going on?'

'That's what I'm trying to tell you, lass. In the middle of the night, the storm was so strong that it caused a sea surge, and a huge pile of silt and debris has blocked the causeway. It's impassable. The island is cut off!'

'Oh my God. Bert, Aurora is terribly upset, so I need to talk to her. I'll call you back soon and don't worry, everything will be fine here.' I replied with my fingers crossed.

'No problem, pet.'

'Ellie, the causeway is blocked, and the storm has nearly taken the village hall roof off. It's got huge holes in it, and it's flooded. All of the things I'd collected to dress it for my wedding are ruined.' She burst into yet more tears; distress etched on her face.

My head was spinning. The implications of this were not at all good, but until we knew the facts, it was probably best not to panic, at least not in front of Aurora. First things first though – I went across to Aurora and wrapped my arms around her.

'Listen, don't get upset. It may turn out better than we think, and the wedding is three days away yet. I promise you; we will come up with a Plan B. I'm a hotshot PR executive don't forget, and party planning is second nature, so this will be a walk in the park,' I fibbed – well at least about the party planning bit which wasn't my department. 'You go and make us some nice strong coffee and put the toaster on, and I'll get ready.'

'Is Aidan here?' She sniffed. 'I saw his Landy in the car park.'

'He's in the other apartment. We had a bit of a crisis here last night, but I'll tell you all about that later. Have you spoken to your mum and dad? Are they okay? I was worried about them in the night. The wind coming in off the sea was like nothing I've ever experienced before.'

'They're fine. They embrace storms. To them, it's nature's way of cleansing the atmosphere. They were up at the top of the lighthouse in their hideout, watching it roll in, clutching crystals no doubt.' She smiled, wiping tears from her cheeks.

'Ah that's good. And what did they say about the potential wedding issues?'

'When you meet my ma and pa, you will see that they don't do stress. They live in the firm belief that what will be will be, and that everything will always work out in the end at the behest of the universe, so no point worrying. Whilst that's wonderful for them – and in the main is probably true – it would be nice if occasionally they had the odd rant like me. Ma just said to take deep breaths and do some meditation, focussing on the thought that everything will work out. Great, eh? At this point, I'm just after practical solutions.'

'Well, I think we should try both approaches. If one doesn't work, we try the other. I'll just go and give Aidan a knock and tell him what's happened.'

But no sooner had I spoken, in he strode, his bed-hair sticking up in muddy clumps, his face still streaked with dirt. But even so, he looked devastatingly handsome, his bright blue eyes shining. He was casually dressed and dangling his car keys.

'Papa just phoned me and told me the news. What a dreadful thing to happen just before Christmas. He's coming down with my brother, Lance, and a few of the guys from the castle to see if there's anything they can do from their side, so I'll get over to the causeway and help the locals on this side of the divide.'

'There's lots of villagers over there. Zen has been rallying the troops, but I'm not sure how much they can do,' said Aurora, bursting into tears again.

Aidan looked at me aghast.

'Shit, was someone hurt... or worse?'

'No, nothing like that,' and I briefly explained about the wedding. 'Here take this,' I said, handing him a travel mug of coffee. 'You look like you could do with it. You're looking a bit pale underneath the mud stripes.'

'I haven't even had time to shower yet.' He laughed. 'I literally just fell out of bed when Papa rang. I look like one of the specimens James digs up. I'm still covered in mud, and I've ruined Aunt Grace's sheets, as well as her Christmas costumes.' He shrugged, took the mug and went out of the door.

Aurora sipped her coffee and eventually calmed down after I convinced her that even if the worst came to the worst, we could salvage things.

'Right, as for now, I'm sure that you need to go

and open the café and take some refreshments over to the causeway. They must be freezing, and I need to get on and sort out the animals. Come back over later today when you close. Bring us the leftovers and we can eat your delicious food and make plans. We should know what's happening by then. How does that sound?'

'It sounds great. Thanks so much, Ellie. I was in such a tizz. I got halfway here to cry on Meg's shoulder before I remembered they weren't even at home. I haven't known you long, but I have a feeling that we are going to be good friends,' she said, giving me a big hug.

I waved her off and it was only then that the penny dropped. If the road was closed, then how would Bert and Meg get back? It could prove to be even more problematic than I first thought.

I rang Bert back. He had more news than me, even though he was in Alnwick on the mainland. His friends on the island were keeping him updated.

'It's going to take a lot of hard graft to clear the road Ellie, and then no-one is sure what the surface is like underneath. The refuse box will also need checking by structural engineers. Diversions are in place on the mainland and the causeway has been blocked off. Christmas is not the best time to have this kind of catastrophe, and it's not totally classed as an emergency in the sense that we could still get medical help on the island via the Air Ambulance if needed. And we can get food deliveries and access to the mainland by boat; although that is very much down to how the weather goes.'

'I don't know what to say Bert. What does that mean for you and Meg?'

'It's a case of seeing what happens, lass, and we will be back as soon as we can, even if we have to get Jack to bring us by boat. Now then, how are you going to manage the animals? If you can get sorted this morning, I'm sure you will be inundated with offers of help, but people are tied up with the crisis at the moment.'

'Don't you worry about that Bert. I'll manage, and if I can't, there are plenty of people I can call on. Oh, and Aidan, he won't be able to go home either, will he?' I said, as yet another dimension came in to play. I had thought that after this morning I wouldn't be seeing Aidan again. It was quite reassuring that I wouldn't be alone at the castle. Aidan was great company, if a little full on, and we were due to have that rain check after all!

Bert gave me a run-down of what to do – basically feeding and cleaning out the animals and instigating a rota of who could wander around the yard with who. I had no idea what state the shelters were in, so the paddocks were out of bounds until he got back.

'Here's Meg. She wants a word. Speak to you later.'

'Ellie lass, are you okay? Will you manage to milk Nanny this morning? I know you can do it. Time to try. But if you can't, please find someone to help within the next couple of hours as she'll be uncomfortable otherwise.'

'Don't you worry, Meg. One way or the other, I will make sure she's milked,' I promised, hanging up to go and get on with my tasks.

I worked my way around the animals and somehow against all the odds, had managed to start to milk Nanny, when my phone pinged to let me know there was someone at the gate. I opened the app and there was poison bloody Isla – the last person I expected to see.

'Yes,' I shouted tersely. 'Can I help you?'

'Ellie, it's Isla. I thought I would come and help you, all hands to the pump at times like this.'

There was nothing else for it but to press to let her in. I walked across to the door in the gates to meet her. At least she wasn't wearing six-inch heels today. She was appropriately dressed for the weather in a belted silver padded parka coat. I knew from the Italian designer monogram that it wasn't from the charity shop in Berwick. She sported a gorgeous pale grey cashmere hat and scarf covered in delicate sequinned snowflakes, and I got footwear envy when I saw her boots – mega expensive designer riding lace ups, in black suede and leather. Who would have thought I would be envious of what was basically practical footwear? How things had changed. I was in my usual uniform of yellow coat, antler hat and my second-hand wellies with the frogs on them from Aurora. The contrast between us, as usual, was stark.

'Is Aidan Bamburgh here?' She waded right in,

as was her customary style of cutting to the chase to get what she wanted. 'I heard you were both in the hotel last night. Well, I'm assuming it was you as the description fit. You have your own *unique* style, Ellie.'

Bitch.

So, she was on the prowl looking for Aidan and, presumably, Zen had been side-lined after he'd declared his lack of interest in her. Aidan, I supposed, was a much bigger catch. I didn't know whether to be pleased about it or not.

'He's over helping on the causeway, but it's so kind of you to come and help me,' I said sweetly, knowing that she hadn't for one second thought she would have to do anything. 'I'm just finishing milking the goat, but if you could perhaps clean out one of the horses, it would be a real help to me,' I said, trying not to smirk.

'Oh, err, well I'm not sure. I'm not that experienced with horses.'

'Ah, it's just I see you're wearing riding boots, very nice by the way,' I replied caustically.

'These? More of a fashion statement, actually.'

No, you don't say.

'I was scared of horses too when I first arrived. Tell you what, leave the big brute to me. She's massive and quite ill-tempered,' I lied, acting like I was doing her a favour, 'but the Shetland pony is tiny, hardly any bigger than a dog, and quite a sweetheart. I'm sure even you can manage him, and you did say you'd come to help; you'd be doing me such a favour,' I gushed. 'You'll find the brush and shovel in the empty stall. Just give it a quick once over and pick up the shit.'

You should know all about that as you appear to have been stirring it for years.

'You are kidding me, right? I can't pick up horse shit, not in this coat.'

'Oh, you won't even need to touch it, just sweep it up and pop it in the wheelbarrow,' I said, like I cared. 'Careful of your *expensive* boots, though. Don't step in any. But that's what they're actually meant for, I suppose.' I shrugged.

'People who can afford boots like these, can afford people like you to pick up their shit for them,' she muttered, marching towards the devil pony's lair.

Cow.

'What's it called?' she asked as she slunk off.

'Hannibal Lecter,' I replied, so quietly that she had zero chance of hearing me.

I collected the half bucket of milk from Nanny's stall. It turned out milking was nowhere as difficult as I had thought.

'I'll not be long, gorgeous,' I said, tickling her cute beard. 'You just look out there and enjoy the show!'

I crossed to the stable, leaned against the wall and waited. It didn't take long. There was a scream and Isla came belting out like she was being pursued by a pack of hungry wolves.

'It's a monster! It's got my scarf. It's pure

cashmere, and that hairy dwarf is eating it. When I tried to get it back, it kicked me. Thankfully, I've got my padded coat on which softened the blow. It better not have damaged it because this cost *serious* money. Has it?' she demanded, turning round to show me. There was the evidence – a shitty little Hannibal sized hoof print on the back of her coat.

'Oh, that's nothing. It'll wash off,' I said dismissively.

'Wash off? Don't tell me that evil little bastard has got shit on my coat?' she screamed angrily. 'It's vicious! It should be sent to the knacker's yard.'

'Let me help,' I said sweetly. I hurried towards her and, oh dear, my clumsy feet somehow *accidentally* managed to trip over a cobble, and whoosh, the bucket of warm, pungent goat milk went all over her.

'You did that on purpose!' she screamed. 'I know you're jealous of me. First you try to take Zen away, and now you've got your claws into Aidan. All I can say is that you must be good in the sack, because for the life of me, I can't fathom out why either of them would be interested in a... in a... fluorescent bloody Teletubby like you,' she raged, stinky milk dripping down the designer coat.

'I take it you mean the yellow one, so Laa-Laa here is going to go and get your scarf before Han chokes to death on it,' I said, ignoring her outburst.

'I hope it bloody well does.'

The scarf was lying on the floor of the stall when I went to make sure that Hannibal was okay. He was munching his hay like nothing had happened.

'Hey little man, I owe you big time.' I whispered. 'I think you and I are beginning to understand each other. I'm like your Clarice.'

I gave him extra carrots, noticing that his ears were nearly as far forward as they could be – progress indeed. I went back into the yard and handed Isla the scarf. It had teeth mark holes in it and the tiny sequins were dropping off.

'You've got to be kidding,' she said, pushing it back at me. 'It's ruined, no good to me now. You mend it and wear it. It'll be the most tasteful thing you own. I'm going home. I need to get this coat sorted.' She marched off towards the gate.

Poisonous bitch.

'Oh, by the way,' she said, turning, 'tell Aidan I'll be back. I know he can't wait to meet me, and I imagine he might need somebody who is on his level to keep him company during his enforced stay on the island.'

Once she was safely through the gate, I dissolved into laughter, but it was short lived as my phone rang and it was Bert. He sounded distressed.

'Ellie, are Wonky and Jenny safe?'

'Yes, they're both fine. Why? What's happened?'

'I've just had a call to say that a donkey is stuck in a sand bank near the accident on the causeway. It must be Wilma, but her owners are off the island as well. Poor little mite. It doesn't look at all good. She's exhausted and isn't responding to encouragement to move. I feel bloody useless being stuck over here. I should be there helping.'

'Don't you worry, Bert. I've had an idea. Keep your fingers crossed and I'll be back in touch as soon as I can.'

CHAPTER 26

I ran across to the tack room, fished out Wonky's bridle, and headed for his stable.

'You and I are going on an adventure to see your Wilma.' I stroked his woolly neck as I slipped on the bridle. He looked at me with huge, brown unblinking eyes and I swore he knew what I was saying – he seemed eager to go. 'See you later Jenny!' I shouted, closing the stable door.

We ran across the island to the causeway, made easier by Wonky pulling me and running with the wind at our backs. I could hardly breathe by the time we got there. The sight that met my eyes would stay with me forever. Apart from what looked like tons of debris blocking the road, there was Wilma, buried up to her chest in deep wet sand piled up to the side of the causeway by the storm. Her head was drooping, and she looked so forlorn, like she had given up. It was pitiful.

As soon as Wonky saw Wilma, he started to bray loudly, and it was then that I noticed Zen standing next to her, up to his waist in the wet sand, a rope tied around his middle. Don and some of the other guys from the island were holding on to him.

He looked like he had used every ounce of energy, his usual translucent face flushed with exhaustion, his lips almost blue with the biting cold. He was clutching a rope which had been tied around Wilma, whilst stroking her gently and talking to her. My eyes immediately filled with tears at the sight. Aidan came dashing towards me.

'Poor animal. She was struggling like mad to try and get up, but couldn't, and I think she's so exhausted that she's given up and it's making it more difficult to try and get her out. Zen's been in there ages with her. He must be freezing,' shouted Aidan above the noise of the wind, still howling, sharp sand swirling and peppering everything in its path. 'I've tried to encourage him to come out and let me take over before he gets hypothermia, but he's not having it. We can't get the tractor near enough for all the debris in the way, so we've been doing a human chain pulling on the rope. Poor old girl was too distressed, so we decided to let her have a rest before continuing.'

'I thought if she saw Wonky, it might encourage her a little,' I said. 'Let's take him a bit nearer.'

Aidan grabbed my arm. 'Don't go beyond the tarmac Ellie; it's just not safe,' he said, taking my hand and leading us as near to Wilma as possible. Wonky started braying louder and Aidan and Ethan from the farm took him from me, one on each side of his halter to make sure he didn't make a dash into the sand towards Wilma.

As I got nearer to Zen, I could see the stress etched on his face as he continued to try and pacify the small donkey. The bouncy curls were gone, replaced by strands of soaking wet hair which hung down the sides of his exhausted face. Our eyes locked and he gave a shy smile, probably wondering what response he was going to get. I'd been a right moody cow the last time I'd seen him. My entire being just wanted to get to him, hold him tight and give him all my body heat and energy. I yearned to gather him up in my arms and never let him go ever again.

'Okay, this is far enough,' shouted Aidan, breaking my train of thought. Wonky continued to bray and Wilma ever so slowly began to lift her head. She looked at Wonky in much the same way as I looked at Zen, and then whinnied softly towards us. Wonky brayed back and Wilma found her inner strength and began to bray back louder, whilst starting to move her legs. It was all systems go from that point. The guys slowly began to pull, holding tightly on to the rope, and Wilma began to rise to the surface as Zen got behind her and gave a final push. Suddenly, she was free, and a big cheer went up across the rescuers.

'Oh, thank God!' I shouted at Aidan, giving him a hug before taking carrots from my pocket to give to Wonky as a treat. 'I'm going to spoil you rotten today, you little star,' I said to the donkey, rubbing his woolly neck. He hadn't taken his eyes from Wilma once. 'You really love her, don't you?' I whispered in his ear. 'Well, I know what that feels like, and I promise that you will be together soon. I'll make sure that happens before I leave this island.'

The guys were all patting Zen on the back, and someone had wrapped a survival blanket around his shoulders. He was shaking with the cold and totally depleted of energy, and just about to climb into the coastguard truck to go home.

'Zen.' I smiled, moving towards him, wanting to hug him but holding back. 'You were amazing. You saved Wilma's life, just like you saved me, nearly on the very same spot. Any more heroics and you'll be awarded a medal.'

'Ellie don't underestimate your idea to bring Wonky across. Without that, I think Wilma would have had to be pulled out against her will and may not have recovered from the experience. We make a good team you and me, you know.' He smiled shyly at me. Our gaze held for what felt like eternity, yet was a few seconds at most, and once again, I almost forgot to breathe. I was so fixated on Zen that life going on around me had temporarily ceased. That was until Aidan came across and threw his arm around my shoulder, smashing the moment into a million pieces – a bit like my heart – and I was brought back down to earth with an almighty bump.

'Let's get you and this little chap back to the castle, Ellie.' Aidan nodded towards Wonky. 'I'll help you sort out the other animals. Chambers, you're a stubborn sod, but I doff my cap at you. Well done, sir, you've got stamina. I'll give you that, you old hippie!

Let me buy you a few drinks later.'

Zen nodded, then without another word, turned and climbed into the truck.

We got back to the castle where I put a very belligerent Wonky in his stall, probably wondering why Wilma wasn't there. Aidan helped with the morning chores until he got a call to go back to the causeway, and I continued to do my rounds in a daze, my head all over the place. I couldn't get the image of Zen from my mind, and I wondered how he was doing. I couldn't shake the overriding sadness at the awkwardness between us and wished I had been brave enough to have thrown my arms around him and given him a well-deserved hug.

Aidan reappeared at lunchtime.

'We're not going to manage to clear the causeway ourselves Ellie, we need machinery, then Health and Safety will have to come in and do some checks before the road can re-open. An emergency committee has been set up; we're meeting in the *Crab* at two and linking up by video to the various authorities to see if we can get a clearer picture.'

I handed him a sandwich.

'Cheers Ellie Elf, you're a lifesaver. My hangover is just starting to lift, and I'm starving. I'm going to have this and then go and get that much needed shower. Any chance you can scrub my back?' He laughed suggestively. 'These are the only clothes I have with me.' He indicated his rugby shirt and chinos. 'And I've got them covered in mud now. I'll have to rifle through James' wardrobe and borrow some. No doubt I will end up looking like the bloody aristo I studiously try not to – James is partial to pink moleskin trousers, checked shirts and tweed! By the way,' he said, his eyes scanning the room, 'this place is rather smart. They must have pawned some of the family silver to pay for it. I was in too much of a hurry to notice before, but I could happily stay in here instead of the mausoleum next door... it's cold and draughty in there, Ellie. Okay for one night, but who knows how long I might be holed up here? And we've had a shock; we need to comfort each other,' he wheedled.

'I know what you are trying to do, you chancer!' I laughed. 'Tell you what though, I will help, if you dump the dirty clothes and bedding at the door. I'll wash it all for you. Can't have you going around looking like a posh prick for too long! Oh, and by the way, you had a visitor earlier this morning when you were across at the causeway. Didn't get time to tell you before.'

'A visitor? Me? Who?'

'Poi... I mean Isla, your future intended. Come to offer you moral support, her being on your wavelength and sharing your social standing and all that crap.'

She wished.

'Isla? Oh God, you mean her from the hotel?'

'I do.'

'Jeez, they mean business. What's she like, by the way? Should I be interested in her as my future bride?' He grinned, strumming his chin with his fingertips.

'Depends on whether you like vacuous,' I replied. 'No one can deny she's easy on the eye, but she is self-absorbed and devoid of any kind of warmth or humility.'

'I can tell you aren't a fan, Ellie, but you had me at the easy on the eye bit. So, she's fit, eh? Clearly, I'm shallow too but, in my defence, I have no control over what happens in the business department when I see a good-looking woman. Sounds like Mr and Mrs Shallow might make a good pairing, so just as well I'm not interested at the moment, isn't it? I've got my eye on a rather nice elf who does a mean line in cheese sandwiches. Right, I'm off to the mausoleum for a cold shower, feel free to join me...'

'Not a chance, Mr Shallow. Just dump your washing. I know my place!' I curtsied, laughing.

I sat and chilled out for a while, looking through the photos from last night. I sent the gang a couple of me and Aidan in our costumes pre and post mud.

Is that the famous Santa Paws? Okay, I believe you, he is real! I hope the second photo was after you had been rolling around in the mud having an orgasmic time with him! He's a good eight and a half if I ever saw one babe. You should def have a ride on his sleigh. Those blue eyes are killer – I bet he scrubs up well. Love you, you make a lush elf, Sophie x P.S. Forget the hippie!

Ellie, your photos never fail to disappoint! Are you staging them for our benefit? Toby says he hopes you have been helping in an excavation to get so dirty. I'm going to kill you because, since you went to your Holy Island, he has been giving me chapter and verse on the history, about some old monks carrying a coffin all over the place with a dead Bishop called Cuthbert inside. Macabre if you ask me. Btw, despite all the detritus, your Santa looks very fanciable. Those blue eyes are amazing. Tara x

We love his blue eyes. We think you both need a bath – hopefully together. Where is coffee? Missing you lots like the jelly tots. Kochamy Cie, Stan and Aleksy xx

After his shower, Aidan came back to my apartment carrying a load of washing. He was wearing nothing but a tiny towel. His hair was still damp and swept back off his face, and those long golden legs were just as mesmerising the second time around. He may have been a massive flirt, and I had no doubt he could charm the habit off a nun, as pointed out by Meg, but it was quite clear how he had the power to do so. He dumped the washing and came over towards me.

'What do you think of this?' he said, leaning in towards me.

I took a step back. Talk about forward.

'Err, eye watering just about covers it,' I said gulping, trying, and failing to make my eyes look away.

'Eye watering? Is that bad for an aftershave? It's James's, not my usual brand. Do you like it?' he said, stepping forward again. This time I stood stock still.

'Oh, you mean your aftershave! It's rather nice, very citrusy,' I said, feeling stupid as I smelled his neck, my face an inch from his.

'That's good, because it matters to me what you think, Ellie Elf.' He put his arms on my shoulders and looked directly at me, his blue eyes full of intense desire, flashing like they were on a 999 call.

'I probably smell of warm donkey.' I laughed, embarrassed. It possibly wasn't far from the truth.

'I like warm donkey,' he said, pulling me into his chest, and snaking his arms around my back. I found my hands encountering his smooth, golden, and deliciously naked skin. He kissed my neck and whoosh, we had lift off. It was like a blowtorch had been directed at my libido, which suddenly ignited, bursting into life. Was this really happening? I knew that before too long, I would be past the point of being able to stop it and I tried to reason with myself whether I wanted this with Aidan, because it called into question my feelings for Zen. But as he continued kissing my neck with such delicate featherlight kisses, his forefinger lightly trailing down my cheek, I was putty in his hands, my hormones firmly in control, shutting down my abilities to make reasoned choices.

'I want to kiss you like this all over, Ellie. I want to kiss you here,' he said, his fingertip tracing around my lips. He then trailed the finger down to my neck. 'And here. Then here,' as he stroked my shoulder and down my arm. 'Then I especially want to kiss you here,' he said, his hand caressing me with the lightest of touches, and I heard myself moan in pleasure. 'Oh God, I want you so much,' he groaned, continuing to kiss my neck in between telling me where he wanted to go next. 'Then I want to kiss you here,' he continued the finger journey, stroking down my stomach, stopping just short of his intended target, teasing me without contact. 'And most of all,' he murmured, 'I want to kiss you *there*, for a *very, very long time*,' he said. I let out another groan, shuddering with an urgency I hadn't felt in ages. He took my hand and began trailing my fingers down his body, and I mimicked him by kissing his neck lightly. His lips found mine and we shared our first kiss, which began gently, finding our way around each other's mouths. He tasted of the citrus aftershave that had drawn us together in the first place. Tentativeness became urgency as we progressed quickly into full force snog mode, hungrily kissing, our tongues meeting, our hands moving across our bodies in tandem. He was covered only by the flimsiest of towels and my fingers lightly brushed against him as he shuddered. 'And I want you to kiss me *there* for a *very, very long time*,' he whispered. We stood still for a moment, nose to nose, but not touching, our arousal increasing even more with the brief halt in proceedings.

'Ellie, I want to see your body, to feel it skin to skin against mine,' said Aidan as he took me into his arms again, breaking the interlude, the tempo increasing ten- fold, as he frantically tried to remove my clothes. It was not perhaps the most romantic situation to be in – I had several layers of thermals between me and what was promising to be a glorious experience. I was desperate to feel his hands – and lips – on my bare skin as I began to help him by hurriedly struggling out of the first layer.

'Hurry up, Ellie,' he groaned. 'I'm going to lick every inch of you until you are begging me for more.'

I was just about to remove the second layer, when I heard the outer door creak open and two little voices shouting up from the ground floor.

'Ellie. Ellie. It's us! We've come to see you and Pacino and Murray,' yelled Amelia, as she and William began to race up the spiral stairwell.

'Oh my God, it's the kids,' I said horrified, trying to pull myself together, blood coursing through my veins. My hotspot was on fire, literally burning its way through my thermals, I was so turned on, my brain as scrambled as a breakfast egg. 'Quick, you go in the bedroom and shut the door,' I stuttered. 'We can't let them see you in that tiny towel.' At least I was clothed. We'd only managed to remove the top layer.

'No! No! No!' grumbled Aidan, running into the bedroom. 'I'm so ready for you, Ellie. I'd say get rid of them, but I've got to go to the meeting soon, so this is to be continued later this evening. Maybe you can lose some of the layers first in preparation? I like a striptease, but not one that will last until I'm a bloody pensioner,' he said wryly, closing the bedroom door behind him.

I stood, trying to control my breathing, waiting for the kids to burst in. Suddenly, a niggle, that I had tried my best to suppress, popped up uninvited into my psyche. Was Aidan really what I wanted? My still pulsating body would argue yes, and it had been a deliciously erotic experience, but perhaps the me and Aidan thing was wrong. I knew it would be a temporary fling, that the sex would likely be frantic and orgasmic, and I could hear Sophie shouting at me to go for it, but hand on heart, was that what I wanted? No, I wanted Zen, which was the truth of it, but that wasn't going to happen. I'd come to Lindisfarne determined to be a more spontaneous me, to stop clinging on to familiarity and enjoy experiences I'd missed out on because of being with Matt for so long. Maybe I'd hung on to him because I liked the idea of being in love. However, looking back, I wasn't sure that it was love at all. The all-encompassing feeling when Zen was anywhere near me was like nothing I had experienced before. It couldn't be love already, surely, but I knew that whatever it was, it wasn't going to go away any time soon.

I needed some time to think. Since I'd arrived on the island, I'd hardly had time to breathe. The irony was that I was living somewhere synonymous with peace, calm and tranquillity, a place where people came to reflect and heal, and that was exactly what I needed. Later today, if I got the chance, I would find somewhere sheltered, look out to those big skies spread out in front of me like a huge comfort blanket, and just lose myself to whatever thoughts came to me – hopefully, it might help me work out what to do about Zen. All I knew then, was that I was so pleased that the kids decided to call when they did, because Aidan, despite how ridiculously sexy he was, was not for me.

CHAPTER 27

Once the kids had gone, thankfully unaware of what they had missed, I rang my mum to tell her and Dad about the storm.

'You'll never guess what? I'm trapped on the island. A storm surge has left the road impassable.'

'Oh, my goodness! How do you feel about that, darling? Sounds a bit of a nightmare being there on your own with the old couple away. You should come back for Christmas if you are going to be alone.'

'Erm, Mother, I've just said I'm stuck and can't get off, not that I want to. I'm not really on my own. I've made some great friends since I got here, and you are never alone on Lindisfarne.' I decided not to mention Aidan staying in the castle too. 'I don't know how long it's going to take them to mend the road yet. It may look worse than it is. I'll find out later. The only thing is, I'm disappointed I might not get to see much of the rest of Northumberland while I'm here if it remains closed. I had imagined I would be able to get out and about and see how beautiful it is for myself. I've seen photographs and begun to learn about places, but so far, I just haven't had the time.'

'Oh, that's such a shame, Ellie. Like I told you, I feel I know Northumberland through the *Vera* programme. Talking of, did you know she lives there?'

'Where? Here on Lindisfarne? You mean the actress who plays her?'

'No, the real Vera.'

'Vera isn't a real person, Mum!'

'Well, maybe not, but her house in the programme is real and I just found out it's on your island. You must find it and take photographs to send to me. Take the dogs you constantly talk about for a walk there. I'm sure they'll like it. Has little Nacho settled in? I don't know anything about dogs, but he looks extremely cute.'

'Yes, he fit in from day one. He is gorgeous Mum; a proper little sweetheart.'

'So I can see from the million photos you have sent me.' She laughed. 'It's going to be a wrench for you saying goodbye to him, Ellie. You can't possibly bring him back to London. You know that don't you?'

I felt like my heart had been pierced with a very sharp skewer. I knew she was right in what she was saying, but, quite frankly, the idea of leaving him had never entered my head. Since he arrived, he had been my shadow. I shared him with Robson, Flo, and Tri of course, but he was my doggie soulmate, and I couldn't even begin to contemplate leaving him behind.

'I hear you, Mum,' I said, without any conviction. 'Right, I promise I will find Vera's house once the wind has settled down, and if she's in, I will ask her who the next victim is going to be. I can think of one suggestion if she's looking for candidates from the island!'

'Ooh that sounds intriguing darling, but Vera will find out you did it; she always does.'

'I might take my chances! Anyway, I've got to get on, Mum, speak soon.'

'Okay darling. Going to miss you at Christmas. Dad sends his love.'

The intercom went off at about 6 p.m. It was Aurora and Zen. Suffice to say, the day had been a blur of animals and crisis management, peppered with total embarrassment over the Aidan encounter. It washed over me periodically like hot oil, making my face burn. My longed for me time losing myself to the skies just hadn't happened.

'Hey, how's the hero?' I smiled at Zen. 'You looked absolutely done in earlier.'

'I'm fine.' He smiled shyly. 'It was no big deal. How's Wonky? I bet he wasn't too pleased at getting so close to Wilma and then being dragged away.'

I know exactly how that feels.

'He's fine. Because they're not in the paddock, he can't see across to the farm which has helped, along with lots of treats of course. I'm going to talk to Bert as soon as he gets back and see if we can make arrangements for Wilma to come and live here after the Nativity.'

'Good idea. It's not fair to stand in the path of true love. Even if they are donkeys,' said Zen, with more than a touch of melancholy in his voice.

'No, it really isn't,' I replied dreamily.

'Listen to you two.' Aurora laughed. 'You'll be setting up *Donkey Date Mates* next. Swipe left if you think they're an ass! But meanwhile, back in the real world, where's Aidan?'

'Not come back from the *Crab* as far as I'm aware, unless he's next door in *his apartment*,' I said pointedly.

'He was still in the pub when I left,' said Zen. 'The meeting had long since finished, but some of the guys stayed on for a pint or three.'

'Leftovers,' said Aurora dumping two big bags on the table. 'Hope you're both hungry.'

She began unpacking as I got Zen a beer and opened a bottle of wine for Aurora. Nacho had jumped on Zen's knee and was sitting quite contentedly as he stroked his head and whispered to him, his feathery ears flapping up and down like a burlesque dancer's fan mid routine. They just looked so right together, my beautiful boy and the gorgeous Zen, and I felt quite emotional watching how gentle he was with the tiny dog, and how Nacho clearly adored him. Zen's trademark curls were back to their usual bounce. He was wearing a black tee shirt; the usual faded denims and the silver coffee bean was twinkling around his neck – I took a breath. Just looking at him my oxygen levels were suddenly saturated. My mind cruelly wandered back to earlier in the day, when I was standing with Aidan's arms wrapped around me on the brink of having sex with him – just next to where Zen was sitting now. If for one minute I thought the relief at being interrupted was nothing to do with my infatuation for Zen, then I was only trying to kid myself.

'Okay guys, come and have some tea,' said Aurora, breaking me out of my reverie.

I had yet to get used to the northern names for meals, where tea was supper and dinner was lunch. It was all highly confusing. Aurora had brought a selection of delicious home cooked treats and despite the fact she was devastated about her wedding, she was quite buoyant, and we were like three old friends who had known each other for years, not weeks.

'Do you ever drink alcohol, Ellie?' asked Aurora. Once again, I was drinking water, having refused a glass of wine.

I felt comfortable enough in their presence to tell them the story about my drunken outburst at the Christmas Party and the subsequent emails, and making the decision to have a dry spell when I got to Lindisfarne whilst I was looking after the animals. Aurora burst out laughing in sisterly solidarity, saying she would have thrown more than a drink over Matt and Karen. Zen sat quietly, taking it all in. He put his hand gently on my shoulder, and I swear it was like being struck by a force field of energy from a million of those stars I kept staring at in the sky. My entire being was tingling as power surged around my system.

'Ellie, if you don't mind me saying so, he sounds like a prick, and whilst it was awful for you at the time, it brought you here into our lives. Otherwise, we may never have met.'

Never have met. The very idea of not having met either of these warm, kind-hearted people was inconceivable. I had more recently questioned whether these traits still existed outside of my small circle of close friends and family. Yet here on Lindisfarne, I was overwhelmed by the warmth of most people that I met. However, there was one notable exception.

'I was talking to my mum today. It struck me that I may not get to see the rest of your wonderful county in the time I have left now the causeway is closed. I had been so looking forward to going to Newcastle with you, Aurora, and up to meet Harriet at her farm. And I wanted to visit some of those places in your stunning photographs, Zen.'

'And I would love to show you them, Ellie,' he said, a huge smile lighting up his face. My heart began to rattle out a calypso that seemed so loud, I half expected the pair of them to get up and dance.

'If we can't make it work this time, then you will just have to come back,' said Aurora. 'Although, I wish you could just stay.'

We chatted about their favourite places in Northumberland, Zen telling us such a tale about how he went walking along Hadrian's Wall and was chased by an army of fully kitted Roman soldiers.

Turned out he had stumbled across a history re-enactment, and they thought he was one of the actors playing a Pict!

'Think it was the hair.' He laughed.

We were all giggling at the thought of Zen running for his life when Aidan stumbled through the door. He'd had his pint or three, that much was clear. I at once began to feel uncomfortable, hoping he was more discrete than I expected him to be considering he was quite merry.

'Evening all. The high-level talks are finished, and the conclusion is… we are stuffed, for now at least, until the wind drops. But the good news is that the experts feel that it looks far worse than it is. Once they can get the machinery in, then we might only be talking a matter of days. Until then, we can sail our way off this desert island like Robinson Crusoe, but maybe that depends on whether we have unfinished business to conclude.' He winked at me suggestively, and I swore I saw Zen bristle.

'Help yourself Aidan,' said Aurora, gesticulating towards the food. He sat down with us at the table, poured himself a glass of wine and loaded up his plate.

'Do you three know each other well?' I asked, trying to steer the conversation onto safe ground.

'Yes, of course,' said Aidan. 'Well, in fairness, more when we were young kids, when me and my siblings used to come and play with our cousins here on Lindisfarne, and Zen and Aurora were staying with Bert and the lovely Meg. We drifted apart when the parents shipped me off to bloody boarding school, but since then, we've caught up at various island events when our paths crossed – before he went on his extended world tour to find himself, or whatever it is hippie types do!'

'Did you like boarding school?' I asked.

'Not initially, but once I'd established my place as someone who took no prisoners, I began to enjoy the experience and what the school offered. It was moderately warmer in the dorms than at home, and the food was much better. Mrs Spencer, our cook at the castle, can't boil an egg, but Mama keeps her on out of loyalty. No wonder they're all like sodding stick insects over there,' he said, shoving another sausage roll in his mouth. 'Aurora, these are delicious. If you are ever looking for a job, my brother Lance says he is sacking Mrs Spencer the minute he takes over from Papa. I'll put a good word in for you.'

'Erm, thanks but no thanks. Right, are we going to salvage my wedding?' She asked, changing the subject.

'Yes, we are. I've got my pen and notepad at the ready. Let's get this sorted,' I said, desperate to keep Aidan away from conversations revolving around him and me, and what he was hoping for later. If I had thought about one thing in between shovelling shit this afternoon, it was Aidan. It had been a far less complicated issue to resolve than Zen. I had concluded that I needed to friend-zone him. There would be nothing happening later, or ever. I just needed to work out how to tell him.

CHAPTER 28

'So, what do we know to be the facts?' I asked, pen poised.

'Well, we know that the causeway is closed and won't be re-opening in time for the wedding as it was originally planned. That's a cert,' said Zen.

'And what about the weather?'

'The winds are due to drop tomorrow, and that's straight from our reliable shipping forecasts. If that's the case, then we know that Jack and his immediate family can get here onto the island and the church service can go ahead at least. We know the village hall is out of bounds due to the holes in the roof, thanks to the storm.'

'The whole thing might be off if the weather doesn't play nice. Jack might not even get here. I'm missing him so much,' wailed Aurora.

I hadn't met Jack. I'd seen lots of photos and almost felt I knew him after listening to Aurora. I just knew I was going to like him. He sounded like a genuine, down-to-earth guy.

'Would it not be sensible to just cancel the whole shebang and reschedule?' Aidan asked.

Zen threw him a look which said *you really*

aren't helping, and Aurora burst into tears.

'No, that's not what I want. I want to marry my Jack as we planned. I love him, and I want us to get married at All Saints on Christmas Eve.'

'Aurora,' I said gently, taking her hand. 'You more than most understand that there's a teensy chance that it may not be possible, because no matter what we do, we can't alter the weather. But remember, what will be will be, and we're going to believe it will happen and make plans – right?' I gave her hand a squeeze.

'Right,' she responded, returning the squeeze before wiping away her tears.

'Here's what I think I'm picking up. You don't want to cancel. You want to get married in All Saints with close family, friends and islanders around you?'

'Yes.'

'So, we find another venue for your reception, dependent on Jack and his
family being able to get here of course.'

'And Ma, Pa, Bert, Meg and Harriet.' She sniffed.

'Listen, Aurora, everyone will understand that these plans hang by a thread. You islanders know that the weather is in charge, and if we must cancel, then everyone will be fine with that. Those of us on the island can still have the party anyway, like a pre-wedding celebration.'

'So, if the weather is kind to us,' she said, 'Ma and Pa will be able to sail across from Greater Reef, and we can arrange for Jack and his family to bring the others from Seahouses.'

'Great planning,' said Aidan, filling up his wine glass. 'Anyone for another? Now then, where are you going to hold the most important bit, the wedding breakfast, more commonly known as the piss up? I hope I'm invited, since I'm a captive here.'

'Yes, of course you're invited.' Aurora smiled. 'I want as many islanders as possible to come. It will be a chance to all get together after the shock of the road, which has derailed a lot of Christmas plans. We're all in this together.'

'The pub?' I threw in the first venue suggestion.

'Too small.'

'St Cuthbert's Way Hotel!' shouted Aidan gleefully, thinking he had solved the problem.

Three sets of burning eyes bored into him until he was in danger of melting, and a unanimous, 'No way,' bounced off the walls.

'Ah, the daughter. I need to meet this woman. I'm intrigued. Hey, don't shout me down on my next suggestion – I do seriously want to help you know – so how about here?'

'Here? As in this apartment?' I asked. 'It's way too small.'

'No, here, as in downstairs, in the castle, specifically in the dining hall. It's an amazing room and, with a little decoration, I'm sure it would look splendid and would be an incredibly special place to hold a wedding celebration.'

Aurora's eyes suddenly brightened, and I saw a ray of hope descend as she took in the possibility.

'Aidan, I could kiss you. Do you think James and Grace would let me do that?'

'I'm absolutely certain they would and do feel free to kiss me anytime.' He grinned. 'The castle is closed; the island is cut off – what better way to get all the villagers together on your special day?'

'I haven't even seen the main part of the castle yet,' I mused. 'Just not got around to it.'

'You what?' said Zen incredulously. 'You mean you've been living above it yet don't even know what it's like down there?' He gesticulated to the floor.

'Nope, and in some ways that suited me, because if it's seriously creepy like the haunted castles you see in horror movies, then I'd rather not know!'

'Have you got the keys?' asked Aidan.

'Yes, I've got Meg's main set.'

'Come on then. No time like the present. Follow me,' said Aidan, leading the way, picking up Bert's big torch from the table.

We descended the narrow, curved stone stairwell, losing the light from the landing on each bend. Soon it was pitch black, except for a faint beam coming from the front, which was useless to me at the back.

'Any chance of putting the lights on?' I shouted.

'Sorry, Ellie, the electricity will be switched off, so until we get down there to the main fuse board, it's just the torch, I'm afraid, unless any of you have got your phones?'

None of us had, so Aidan led, followed by Aurora, Zen and then me. They had all been inside before and knew the layout well, but for me, it was like entering the house of horrors at the fair. I was just waiting for a hand to grab me around the throat!

'There's a rope running down the wall to hold on to on your right, Ellie. Some of the steps are really worn and sloped, so hang on tight,' said Zen.

'Okay, thanks. I can't see a thing and it's so cold,' I replied, seeking out the rope, my teeth chattering.

'Not many more steps to go, then a long corridor before we get to the entrance hallway at the front of the castle,' he said encouragingly.

We made it down to the bottom of the stairs. It was freezing and had that musty smell that old buildings always seem to have. There was no rope support there now, so gingerly, I began to feel my way along the wall.

'Whoooohooooooo!' came a sudden loud ghostly screech from ahead, and I just about jumped out of my skin, my heart residing somewhere in my throat.

'Man up, Ellie!' howled Aidan. 'You wouldn't get Daphne out of Scooby Doo all scared when they go prowling around castles. Zen, that's just reminded me. Can you remember us pretending we were the members of the Mystery Machine seeking out the spooks?'

'Blimey Aidan, yes, now you have said that I can remember. You were always Fred I seem to recall.'

'Well, what do you expect? Even then I was tall, blonde and a natural born leader,' he said modestly.

'Can you remember us trying to recruit girls who were here on holiday to play Daphne and Velma, but they were all too scared to go around the castle in the dark?' Zen laughed.

'I can indeed. Not even my youthful charm offensive could persuade them,' responded Aidan. 'But we have our girls with us this time. You be Daphne, Ellie. She was the stuff of young boys' fantasies, one of my first ever crushes, all curves in that tiny mini dress, the saucy minx. You remind me of her, Ellie. I spent many happy times under my bedclothes...'

'Eww, far too much information Aidan!' I butted in, before he got the chance to say anymore.

'So, I suppose by process of elimination, that means I'm bloody Velma Dinkley. Why have I got to be the plain one in the big shapeless jumper?' Aurora sniggered.

Just at that moment, something ran past my leg, and I let out a blood curdling scream that would have woken up the dead – and I was sure there were plenty of those in here.

'Whoever did that, just stop, it's not funny.'

'Did what, Ellie? I'm in front of you, and I promise no one did anything,' said Zen.

'Well, something just brushed past my leg. Oh my God! Maybe it was a giant rat. Or is this place really haunted?'

'Ellie, it was only our very own mini Scooby Doo, in the shape of Nacho. He's followed us down.' Zen laughed.

'You'd get the chicks these days, Shaggy,' said Aidan. 'My sister, Violet, tells me you are the embodiment of some character that used to be on the television called Poldark – all dark curls and smouldering eyes apparently. Just as well for you that she's betrothed to a dullard earl called Humphrey, otherwise you would be a potential brother-in-law. God forbid.' He laughed raucously as my mind strayed to a very pleasant image of Zen, shirtless, cutting hay with a scythe in the sunshine!

We continued until we came to the end of the passageway. Aidan shone the torch around the walls until he found the fuse box and suddenly, the place was illuminated. We were in a cavernous entrance hall, with a huge open fireplace on one wall, the room full of ephemera of the castle's history, the walls displaying old maps and portraits.

'Wow, I feel like I've landed in Hogwarts. It's amazing – so old.'

'That's the front entrance door that leads in from the terrace,' said Aurora, pointing to massive, studded oak double doors. Guests will come through there and into this reception hall. The dining room is just over to the right.' She pointed at Aidan, who was opening the door.

The door swung open, and he flicked on the lights. I had been expecting a huge, grand hall, high ceilings, tapestries, formal dining furniture, a sense of grandeur, but the reality was far different. The room was much longer than it was broad, rectangular in shape. The ceiling was not at all high but was bowed, the old stonework forming into an arc, meeting in the middle of the room, and it at once reminded me of the upturned fishing boats on the shoreline, but on a much bigger scale.

'It's like being in an upside-down boat in here,' I gasped. 'It's charming, and so unique.'

'It's called the Ship Room,' said Aidan, pointing to a wooden model of a boat suspended from the ceiling. 'That's the Henrietta of Amsterdam and is how the room got its name. It was originally used for musical recitals, but James and Grace turned it into more of a dining hall or entertaining space. It's mainly used for a variety of charitable events these days.'

'It's perfect, Aurora,' I said. 'Imagine when we get it all dressed up with lights and tasteful Christmas decorations. The good thing is it's quite empty in here so we can perhaps bring in some small tables and chairs...'

'There's loads in the village hall,' she said.

'And keep the food simple.'

'I'd already planned the menu, and it will be as easy to serve from here as from the village hall,' she said, smiling. 'It's simple Northumbrian fare like broth, stottie sandwiches and Christmas traybakes, and I already have my wedding cake. We can really do this, can't we?' she squealed excitedly. 'Quick, back upstairs to the planning!' and she hustled us all out of the door.

We got back to the apartment, and Aidan disappeared next door to phone James and Grace. He returned clinking several bottles of wine, as he handed the phone to Aurora. It was set to video call, and we could all hear the conversation.

'James and I would be absolutely delighted for you to use the dining hall. We've known you since you were little more than a baby and you are like one of the family. There are cases of champagne in the castle cellar. Please don't give Aidan the key – I can hear he is already raiding our wine rack. As our gift to you, take what you need, and make sure all the villagers have a glass on us. I can't think of a better way to bring everyone together after this terrible business with the causeway.'

Aurora gave her thanks and Grace asked to speak to me, so she handed me the phone.

'Hello Ellie, it's nice to put a face to the name eventually. Thank you so much for taking such good care of our animals. I'm sorry that you have been left in the lurch, however I'm sure you'll be getting lots of help. Bert tells me you are a natural around the animals and that even Hannibal has warmed to you more than he's ever taken to any of us.'

'That's kind of you to say so, Grace. I'm enjoying every minute and I want to thank you and James for giving me – a stranger – the opportunity.'

'I trust my brother implicitly, Ellie, and if he says you are a good egg, then you will be a good egg! I do hope our paths cross when we get back. I'm not sure of dates, but let's hope so.'

'She is just lovely,' I said as I hung up. 'And how beautiful is she? She reminds me of Grace Kelly. They even share the name.'

'She is,' agreed Aurora, filling up their glasses.

'Okay, we've done food, furniture, we have champagne, what else?' I asked, before they were all too drunk to take part in the planning.

'Music,' said Aidan. 'Got to have music. Shall we make a playlist and try and rig something up to play it through?'

'Actually,' said Aurora, looking at Zen, 'I want you to play for me.'

'Me?' asked Zen. 'I'm not sure I would be right for your wedding.'

'You perform, Zen?' I asked, intrigued.

'You always were a dark horse,' said Aidan. 'I haven't heard about this.'

'Err, I used to play, but these days I just play for me,' he muttered shyly.

'He was in a band,' cut in Aurora, clearly proud of her brother. 'They were just about to get signed but then...' She stopped mid-sentence like she had said too much. 'Anyway, yes, he can play the guitar, and sing. Tell you what, big bro, as a compromise, will you join up with Dean and Eric? They were the guys at the gansey party who do the Northumbrian stuff,' she explained, 'and they were already lined up for the village hall. Please...'

'Okay, how can I refuse my little sis? I'll join them on a few songs, I promise.'

'Great, that's the music sorted, and tomorrow we will put a shout out about the plans onto the village group chat and stand back and watch the rush of help that will come forward. Just you wait Ellie, it's going to be full on.'

Half a bottle of something dark red and unpronounceable later, and Aurora went from the highest of highs to the lowest of lows and was sobbing drunkenly on my shoulder.

'Ooh, Ellie, we must ashk the weather to be kind. Shall we go up to the roof terrash now and ashk the stars?'

'Erm, I don't think that's a good idea at the moment, Aurora. It's still blowing a gale out there. Maybe leave it until the morning.'

'I think I should get you home,' said Zen, who had also hit the wine when the beer had run out.

Aurora got up and then immediately sank back down onto the chair.

'My legsh don't sheem to be working.' She giggled.

'Listen, why don't you both just stay here? It's wild out there and a long walk when you have wobbly legs.'

I could see Aidan glowering at me, shaking his head behind their backs.

'Maybe a brisk walk in the fresh air will do her good,' he suggested, full of self-interest rather than concern for Aurora's welfare.

I knew that he was trying to get rid of them to reconvene our earlier encounter, but the moment had passed, and it was never going to happen again.

'Good idea, Ellie, if you're sure that's okay with you?' asked Zen.

'Fine by me,' I said. 'Aurora can sleep with me, and you can have the settee.'

'So, I'm back into the frozen wasteland all on my own,' whined Aidan.

'Well, it's either that or the floor. Take your pick.'

'You're a cruel woman, Ellie.'

I went to show him out and he pulled me into the hallway with him, closing the door behind us.

'Ellie! What are you doing to me?' he whispered in my ear. 'I've been turned on all day.' He clasped my shoulders, pushing me against the wall, his body against mine, and I could feel that he wasn't lying. He began to kiss me on the lips, his hands travelling down the length of my body as he groaned gently. 'I seriously can't wait much longer...'

I stepped to the side. 'Not tonight when the others are around Aidan. Go and get a good night's sleep,' I replied, removing his hands, which were clasping my hips as he pushed himself against me. 'Let's just wait and see what tomorrow brings, shall we?'

I knew I was prevaricating, but there was no point in trying to tell him he was friend-zoned when he had so much alcohol on board.

'Tomorrow it is then, Ellie, and believe me, I'm going to make up for lost time,' he said determinedly, as he slunk through his apartment door, banging it shut behind him.

By the time I went back into my apartment, Zen had crashed out on the settee. He'd had an exhausting day and was fast asleep. I took a throw and gently placed it over him, looking at his beautiful face, his pale skin, with the hint of a five o'clock shadow making him even more attractive. I wished I'd dared kiss him goodnight, but I didn't, so I switched off the light and left before temptation got the better of me. Aurora was already in my bed. At least she had managed to remove her boots, but otherwise she was still fully clothed.

'You still awake?'

'Nearly,' she chuckled.

'Let's get that heavy jumper and your jeans off you at least,' I said, helping her.

'Zen's full of surprises,' I probed. 'What happened to the band?'

'Loosh lipsh shink ships,' she slurred. 'Besht let him tell you himshelf, but let's just shay, there's only one thing that can come between a musician and hish band and that's love.'

'Love? Tell me more...' I asked, intrigued, but my question fell on deaf ears as Aurora began to snore gently.

CHAPTER 29

I woke early after hardly sleeping a wink, Aurora snoring gently beside me. It was time to message the gang, otherwise my brain might have exploded right there on the expensive 300 thread count cotton duvet set.

Aidan becoming a bit of a sexy pest. He's great fun, and I do like him, but more as a friend, even though he is fit! I can't stop thinking about Zen. I'm just so confused. Island still blocked from mainland. Love you all, xxxxxx

I got an immediate reply from Stanislaw – selling coffee was an occupation for early risers.

Why not have fun and sexy time with Mr Blue Eyes the sexy pest and then marry Mr Coffee Guy so I can get a discount. That is my advice to my beautiful Ellie x

By the time I got up, Zen had gone, leaving a little note saying *Thank you for your hospitality x.*

A kiss, it had a kiss! One kiss was exactly right. Anymore and they would have cancelled each other out.

Far from having the hangover from hell I had

imagined, Aurora seemed as fresh as a daisy as she pulled on her clothes, gulped down a coffee and looked out of the window, jumping up and down in excitement.

'Jack just messaged me. Boats will be able to come into the island harbour later today. Whoop! Whoop!' She threw her arms around me. 'It's all systems go.'

The opportunity to dig any deeper on the mysterious Zen didn't arise, and as I had lots of chores to get on with, we gave each other a hug and went our separate ways with a view to catching up later.

'I'd almost forgotten,' she yelled as I crossed the yard. 'It's the fishing club shindig later this afternoon, but I'll be far too busy cooking to go today. You should go if you get the chance. It's usually great fun and I think today will be especially lively as no-one has anything else to do – take Aidan.'

'I'll see how I get on, but I want to start getting the dining hall set up for you when I've finished work.'

It was barely gone nine when the cavalry arrived. Zen must have posted the news of the changes to the wedding plans on the village group chat, and Imogen from *Love Lindisfarne* gift shop was first to appear to offer her services, and the loan of any stock, to dress the hall.

'That's so kind, Imogen. I'm sure you know the room, but if I open it up for you now, perhaps you can pull together some ideas. I wish I could stay and help you, but I've got to get on here,' I said, as the dogs bounded about, reminding me it was time to feed them. I could hear Nanny McPhee bleating noisily from her stall.

'That's fine, Ellie, you just get on. I totally understand.'

I was just about to take Imogen around to the front of the castle when Don and the kids came into the yard.

'Thought we would come and help with the menagerie today,' said Don. 'These two were driving me mad asking if they could come over.'

'Imogen's just popped across to see if we can come up with some ideas on decorating the dining hall. I was about to go and open up for her, but I'll be back in a tick.'

'Ellie, you go, leave the morning chores to me and the kids. The wedding is top priority. We were all thrilled to hear about it being transferred to the castle and pray that the weather is on our side.'

'Can I come with you, Ellie, pleeease?' asked Amelia, clasping her arms tightly around my left leg. She was not about to let go until I agreed. 'I can help put decorations up. I'm good at that aren't I, Dad?'

'Is that okay with you, Ellie?'

'Absolutely, Don. Text me when you get up to the alpacas and I will send her round to help with Murray. Deal, Amelia?' I said, lifting my hand.

'Deal,' she agreed, giving me a high five.

Imogen and I were just about to leave when I heard what sounded like a tractor labouring its way up the bank at the side of the castle.

'It's Maurice and young Ethan,' shouted Don. 'Maurice said they were coming over this morning with some wood to have a go at mending the shelters. Don't worry, I'll sort them. Off you all go.'

The kindness of the islanders warmed my heart. They were all pulling together to help each other, despite their own plans going awry.

Imogen, Amelia and I walked through the gate in the wall and onto the terrace to open up the main castle doors. The wind was still extraordinarily strong, but less so than yesterday, and it was a bright, clear day. The view of the bay to Greater Reef beyond was as picturesque as ever. The pale lemon sun reflected off the sea, which looked like molten silver, and foamy white waves were jostling their way onto the shoreline. I totally understood what Bert meant about it never looking quite the same twice, and today was no exception.

'Look! Look!' squealed Amelia excitedly. 'I can see seals. Lots of them. Look at them bobbing about, Ellie. They are grey ones. Mrs Brown, my teacher, told us that in class. There are loads of them on the Farne Islands over there.' She pointed randomly out to sea, her arm waving up and down like a railway signal. 'And some of them come to the Reef Islands too.'

'I hope they're okay,' said Imogen, as the three of us stood mesmerised by the beautiful creatures bobbing like buoys in the choppy water. 'Storms can be devastating for seals, and this has been such a bad one. No doubt Mike and Simone are keeping check, but even they can't get out on the rescue boat at the moment.'

'The wind is dropping, so let's hope that by later today they can at least make sure they are okay,' I said. I knew nothing about seals other than they were extremely cute and seeing them in their natural habitat was such a joy – there weren't too many sights like that in Peckham. 'When do they give birth?' I asked, worried about whether there were any babies being thrown about in the sea.

'It's all dependent on the weather, Ellie. Usually about mid-September through to November here in Northumberland, but potentially, there may still be some giving birth now. They're monitored for three months over autumn by the Rangers. Between the birds and the mammals, they have their work cut out for them.'

We left Amelia watching the seals and went inside the castle, which wasn't a great deal warmer than it was outside. The entrance hall and dining room looked entirely different in the light of day. It was clear that they hadn't been in use for a couple of months, and the first job would be to clean them and get rid of the dust which had piled thickly on any surface it could cling to.

'It's such an interesting room, isn't it?' said Imogen, gazing round the dining hall. 'I've never been in here when it wasn't full of tourists and to see it properly like this, without people and cameras everywhere, is wonderful. Anyway, Ellie, now I've got the chance to ask you, how are you finding island life?'

'Imogen, it's every bit as great as you told me it would be that first time when I met you in your shop.'

On that visit, I had noticed straight away that Imogen's accent wasn't local, and we ended up having a brief conversation about what led us to Lindisfarne. Imogen was originally from Oxford, and like me, had migrated to London, following a chosen career path in banking and had done very well out of it until she ended up burned out at thirty-eight.

'I knew you would settle in, Ellie. I could tell from the minute you bought the antler hat and were prepared to wear it without fear of ridicule! You are not the kind of career woman that both of us probably encountered more than we wanted to when living there – the ones that are more concerned about image, than actually being happy – and I can tell you are really embracing village life here on the island.'

'So how difficult was it for you to make the leap here?' I asked curiously.

'The usual story, Ellie. Like I told you in the shop, I thought I was in love, and I thought she loved me, but it was a relationship built on quicksand. She was my boss and was married, but I naively assumed that our big, big love would override everything else. I thought she would leave her husband and we would live happily ever after in a mews cottage with roses around the door. Stupidly, I should have seen the signs. She said she needed to stay in her *loveless marriage* – her words – for a while longer, and that while longer ended up being three years. We kept our relationship a secret as she said that having an affair with a colleague would affect her standing at work, so I agreed. She had worked hard to get to her position. Despite the progress we are making as women, we still find it extra difficult to break through the triple reinforced glass ceiling, especially in the male dominated world of banking. The end came when she got promoted and she needed a husband on her arm. Having a woman next to her at functions was not going to cut it – in her warped view – so she dumped me, unceremoniously, and told me that if I opened my mouth, I would be out of a job and never work in banking again.'

'Oh my God, Imogen, I'm so sorry. That must have hurt to your core. Did you not just want to expose her for the cow she was, regardless of the consequences?'

'Yes, of course I did. I would lie awake for hours plotting, but·Ellie, I was burned out both by her, and by the demands of the job, and when push came to shove, I really didn't have the energy to fight back. When I saw the shop advertised on the internet, something in me said go for it, so I did, and here we are. I've been here nearly eighteen months now, and I'm happy, healthy and really do enjoy getting up in the morning and being my own boss. I'm proud of the changes I've made to my little shop.

I've totally revamped it and turned it into the craft hub it is now, which has brought me into contact with so many gifted people, both on the island and from wider Northumberland, who can now make a little extra income from our joint venture. I rarely think of Antonia these days at all. Then I met someone special. Really special. Who would have thought I would come to a tiny island heartbroken and meet the woman I hope I spend the rest of my life with?'

'Oh Imogen, that's wonderful,' I replied, intrigued as to who the woman was, but that was secondary to hearing how Imogen came to the island and met her potential soulmate. So, it would appear it was possible!

'It's Harriet, by the way, my girlfriend. I don't think you two have met yet.'

'Ah Harriet. No, we haven't met yet. I was really looking forward to a trip to her farm and meeting her, but that will have to wait in the circumstances.'

'You must go and see the farm, Ellie. I was absolutely blown away by its isolation the first time I went, and I don't think I could ever take the view from there for granted. I have never ever been to someone's house that no matter which direction you look in, you can't see another property, save for a few animal barns. Just miles and miles of moorland and a never-ending sky, which on a clear night is unbelievable. There are stars on top of stars, they're so packed in!'

'It sounds amazing. Not sure I could live somewhere so remote; I'm just getting used to Lindisfarne, which, as you know, is such a huge contrast to London. Incidentally, Imogen, talking of stars, can I ask, did you think about the universe and things like that, when you were in London?'

'Ellie, I hardly even had time to notice the sky.' She roared laughing. 'Other than if I needed an umbrella, but that was it. No time for contemplating anything deep and meaningful. Most of my thoughts centred around Antonia or work, so the mystical or spiritual never got a look in, but the minute I got on this island, I felt a sense of peace, of calm, and I opened my eyes to what part the universe was playing in all of that. Okay, so our old colleagues in London might think we've gone ga-ga, but they're not here to feel it and I'm telling you, this place has healed me, put me back together in a better shape than I was before.'

'I feel it, Imogen, and know exactly what you mean. I'm so pleased things have worked out for you. Thanks for sharing it with me because you've helped me more than you probably realise. I've got much to consider about my own future and hearing your story has made me think.'

'You're a strong woman, Ellie, and you will come through even stronger. We have both been through similar situations in that we clearly had no taste at that time in our lives and ended up with a pair of users.'

'I felt so stupid afterwards,' I said quietly.

'So embarrassed and hurt, but mainly scared that I managed to get something so wrong. I'm terrified I'll make the same mistake again. How can I trust my judgement?'

'I was too initially Ellie but look at me now. It really was all for the best, and you and I have both learned from our bitter experiences. I reckon neither of us will allow things like that to happen to us again and, hand on heart, I know Harriet would never do that to me. Anyway Ellie, enjoy your time on the Island. Find the time to allow it to do its work and help you to heal. Maybe it will call out to you and tell you to stay – it called me. I knew almost immediately, even before I met Harriet, that this place would be home for a long time. I hope it calls you too Ellie – just follow your dreams. Now then,' she said, changing the subject, 'do you have ideas on decoration in mind?'

'Not really, and we need to run everything past Aurora first, but I was thinking keep it simple and tasteful, capitalise on the Christmas theme, let the history of the room shine through...'

'Cooee, is there anyone here?' shouted a voice from the hallway, interrupting us.

'The Crafty Lindisfarners,' announced Amelia, skipping in and introducing the visitors like she was presenting them at court.

'At your disposal, young lady,' said Dora, the butcher's wife, grinning at Amelia. 'We've spoken to Meg on the phone, and she suggested we come across and see what needs doing, so we're going to bottom this place. Once we've done that, we can have a tea break and you can let us know how we can help with making anything, like decorations or whatever.'

'It's got a bottom?' asked Amelia, giggling.

'You know what? I'm not too sure!' I winked.

'Now then, is there any chance of hot water, and maybe some heating before we all catch hypothermia?' asked Linda, the landlady from the *Crab*. She wrapped her scarf more tightly around her neck.

'Just you all wait there. I'll go and get Aidan. He should know what to do.'

Aidan opened his door wearing only a smile and a kilt. I had to admit, he looked so sexy, so tempting. But he was so bloody wrong for me.

'Err, what's that you're wearing?' I gawped, his taut golden skin still damp from the shower, an aroma of fresh citrusy shower gel teasing my senses, his bright blue eyes twinkling.

No! Stop! Don't even think it! Friend-zone – remember!

I remonstrated with both myself, and my overactive hormones, which, quite frankly, had stopped listening to me and just did their own thing anyway.

'Now, Ellie, I know you are from the south, but even you must have seen a kilt before. It's Uncle James' Northumbrian tartan. Thought I'd try it on as I might wear it for the wedding. What do you think?' He struck a pose in the black and white checked kilt that would definitely have got a lot of hits on Insta. 'Would you like to know what we Northumbrian's wear underneath?' He winked. 'I'll even let you stroke my sporran if you're very, very good. Anyway, Ellie, tomorrow has arrived and I'm eager to pick up where we left off last night,' he said, pulling me into the apartment. 'You might have come dressed slightly more appropriately for our, erm, *tryst,*' he said, laughing. 'Jeez, listen to me, like I'm straight out of the pages of some bodice ripper.' He grinned. 'Nice thought though. I don't suppose you're wearing a bodice of any sort under that ensemble that I can rip off with my teeth?' he questioned, looking me up and down, taking in my working gear. 'Ellie, do you not possess anything miniscule, wispy and made of silk? No matter, I'll soon get you out of that lot,' he said, as he whipped off my hat and twirled it round like he was a participant in the Highland Games throwing the hammer.

'Aidan, I need you...' *partially true, my hormones needed him, I did not, other than for practical purposes.*

'I knew that you would come around to my way of thinking. I need you too, Ellie Elf, right now, out of those goddamn ridiculous clothes, butt naked as nature intended and lying on that rug in front of the fire. Oh God! I'm ready and more than willing...'

'I don't mean for sex, Aidan,' I replied bluntly. 'I need you to come and sort out the boiler downstairs.'

His face was a picture. Just like "The Scream".

'You what? God above, Ellie! I don't think I've ever met anyone quite like you. You are giving up the chance of an almighty good seeing to from a very sexy man in a kilt, in favour of me stoking a bloody boiler like the hired help?'

'Erm, yes, that just about sums it up. It's all hands to the pump today. I've got the Crafty Lindisfarners down there who are also ready and more than willing... to clean... and we need to heat the place up so it's not like a flipping fridge and get some hot water on the go.'

'Crafty Lindisfarners? I've no idea what you are talking about, but have we not got time for a quickie? You can even keep the coat on...' he conceded, with a slight tinge of humour to his voice.

'Nope, no time at all. So, can you come and sort this out please?'

'If I must,' he said belligerently. 'I'm not happy about it, but the day is still young, so later, Ellie, make sure you clear your bloody diary.'

I didn't have time to begin to explain his demotion into the friend-zone.

'Thank you, thank you, thank you. Oh, and do you think you might lose the kilt in favour of a boiler suit or something more befitting the task? The Crafty Lindisfarners seem the type to find out what's under it, and I don't want them distracted!'

CHAPTER 30

Ten minutes later, Aidan made his entrance into the dining hall, all wax jacket and moleskin trousers, looking every inch the lord of the manor, which, technically speaking, he was, in the absence of his uncle. He had raided James' wardrobe and was wearing all the things he had said he despised.

'Will I do, Ellie Elf?' he whispered. 'I thought I would dress to impress your Crafty Lindisfarners.' He glanced around the room at the group of older women, who stared at him as if he was royalty, mouths flapping open like starving seagulls.

'I've not seen you since you were knee high to a grasshopper, Aidan,' said Dora. 'My, how you have turned into a handsome young man – the double of your dad. There's no mistaking the Bamburgh blues, as we call them,' she gushed.

'Eeh, you have that pet,' agreed Mabel, owner of one of the guest houses. 'You look like an actor – can't remember his name – but he's very sexy, quite dashing, and when he comes on the telly, I have to hide behind my knitting so that our George doesn't see me tongue hang out and me face go all red.'

'Mabel!' tweeted a chorus of faux shocked

crafters, howling with laughter.

'Right ladies.' Aidan smiled, fully immersed in his role and playing his audience like a well-worn fiddle, lapping up the compliments at the same time. 'Let me see if I can do something to warm you all up.' And the women cackled in delight.

'I'd warm you up anytime my pet,' grinned Ethel, patting her steel grey hair suggestively. Ethel was eighty if she was a day.

'I bet you would, you saucy little devil,' he said, winking at her, before strolling off in search of the boiler.

He soon returned with a big grin on his face. 'Right, that's sorted. Although, I do believe the heating system is not that efficient, so I shall light both open fires in here, and the one in the hall, and ensure that there's plenty of logs stacked to keep them going for the next few days.'

'You start on that, pet, then come and have a cup of tea with us. We've got flasks and have all brought homemade treats,' said Dora.

'It's a date.' He winked. 'I can't resist ladies that bake good cakes!'

Aidan was such a charmer; he had the crafters eating out of his hand like he was bloody Prince Charming.

It was gone 2 p.m. by the time we stopped for the day. The place was spotless. Dora had arranged for the tables and chairs to be delivered from the village hall, and we had a list of ideas to present to Aurora. To give Aidan his dues, he had worked extremely hard, bringing logs from the store in the yard and stacking them. I don't suppose he'd ever really done manual labour in his life, but he never complained, and the ladies all loved him, plying him with copious cups of tea and cakes.

'I think a chap deserves a well-earned pint after that. I'm drier than a meno...' He stopped abruptly, maybe realising the average age of his audience.

'Come on,' said Ethel, offering him the crook of her arm. 'You can help me across to the village, or as far as the fishing club, if you are going there? You can buy me a glass of their home-made brew – top secret recipe, you know, handed down through the generations of fishermen on this island. It's delicious,' she guffawed raucously.

'Ah, of course, it's the fishing club shindig today. It had totally slipped my mind. The chaps were telling me about it the other night. Yes, I will make an appearance at the hut, and as my date, I would be delighted to buy you a glass, or two, of whatever tipple takes your fancy.' He grinned. 'I'm keen to see what the old reprobates get up to. I hear it can be jolly good fun.'

'Don't let her have more than one glass of the home-brew Aidan, or seriously, you will live to regret it. I've seen Ethel under the influence of it before, and believe you me, it's not pretty!' warned Linda, laughing.

I knew that would be the last I saw of Aidan that day. If he participated in the home brewed hooch, then he wouldn't be trying to tempt me into bed later. He wouldn't be able to see straight, never mind seduce anyone. It was a weight off my mind.

After we locked up, I collected Nacho and made a fuss of the other dogs, promising to take them out for a walk in a while – even though they had spent the entire morning running around with Don and William – and went up to the apartment to check my messages.

So, old blue eyes is desperate to get his leg over? What's the matter with you, Ellie Nellie? He looked well fit in the photo. Go on, give yourself a Christmas treat! That said, I know you like I know myself, and you've totally fallen for him with the shiny hair, haven't you babe? You do what's best for you, Ellie. Tick tock and all of that... time is marching, and you'll be leaving your island before too long, and him too if you don't act soon. Love you stax, Sophie x

Hey miss. So, you are stuck on the island, which sounds about as fun as a day out at the Natural History Museum with Toby. Follow your heart, Ellie. Tell Prince Blue eyes if you aren't interested and tell Zen if you are... but...a casual encounter that you can happily leave behind on the island is one thing but leaving someone behind – that you don't want to be just a casual encounter – is something else entirely. Two more workdays to go before I get let out of this madhouse and put my Christmas pudding feet up. Spanna has worn her resting Grinch face throughout. Talk about bah humbug! That woman is about as festive as a brussel sprout in July. I only went and got her in the bloody Secret Santa, so do you have any idea where I can get her a personality?! Looking forward to our Christmas day catch up. Wear the silly hat. Love, Tara x

Come over about 6.30 p.m. if you aren't going to the shindig. I'll make pasta and you can sample the Christmas traybakes. Zen surpassed himself by coming up with some amazing flavours! I hear it's been busy over at the castle today. Can't thank you and the others enough. Hopefully see you later, Aurora x.

***

As I walked over to the village later that evening, taking Nacho and Robson with me, I passed the fishing club on the way, and the small hut looked packed. People had spilled outside onto the grass, and despite the chill in the air, were dancing and singing Christmas songs. Fairy lights were strung out around the boat, and the tables and chairs were set up, a small Christmas tree twinkling outside of the door. The place looked very festive.

'Ellie, over here,' shouted Maurice, waving at me. 'Come and join us. Have a glass of the, shhh you know what, our secret brew.'

'Thanks, Maurice, but I'll pass. I'm on my way to Aurora's and need to keep a clear head.'

'Probably best pet, this stuff teks nee prisoners. It's already got yon lad in there. He's swapped his posh togs with Jack's brother for some fisherman's dungarees and waders. He said it was for later, to impress you. I'd not heard of that meself mind. That kind of dressing up doesn't seem right to me. What's wrang with a baby doll nightie? He winked.

At that, a man staggered out of the hut wearing the wax jacket, pink trousers and tweed cap on his head backwards, like he was some posh boy rapper. I could only imagine what Aidan looked like dressed up as Captain Birdseye, because there was no chance of me going in to find out.

'No way!' Aurora laughed when I told her. 'I might try that on our honeymoon, although Jack will just think he's at work. That hooch is lethal. I hope Aidan doesn't overdo it, but if he has to be taken by boat to have his stomach pumped, at least he's wearing the right gear. I can't tell you how relieved I am that boats can now get into the harbour. Jack's dad and brothers are already at the shindig. They sailed straight across from Seahouses. Thankfully, Jack has more sense, well this time anyway. Zen's gone down to keep an eye on them. They're staying with him tonight; they'll be in no fit state to sail later.'

'That's the best news, Aurora. What's happening with your honeymoon?'

'I meant to tell you, but everything has been so busy. We've cancelled until later. The boat we were borrowing would have been coming up from Hull, so it's postponed for now, but we've managed to find a hotel in the Scottish Borders for a mini break, as long as we can get to Seahouses and Jack's car that is.'

As we ate a fabulous carbonara, I went through the list of suggestions that we had come up with earlier that day, and Aurora beamed.

'It sounds wonderful. I love the simplicity of it all. I like Christmas colours and reds and greens will look great in that room. Did the crafters say they could manage all the table drapes and chair ties?'

'Yes, apparently there's some old red velvet curtains at the back of the village hall which weren't affected by the storm, and they are going to see what else they can salvage.' I showed her a sketch of the room layout.

'That looks great,' she said, eyes shining.

'Imogen and the crafters are going to make table and room decorations using winter foliage that they'll collect from around the island. We can't use candles – no naked flames in case we burn the castle down – but the vicar's wife said they have plenty of battery tealights in the church, and we can borrow what they aren't using. Even Amelia got in on the act. She is organising her dad to bring all those small potted Christmas trees dotted around the village, and line them either side of the door with lights, to make a grand entrance pathway. The guys are bringing the big Christmas tree over from the *Crab* to put in the corner of the dining hall. The hotel offered the use of their tree, but there's nothing simple about that. Isla decorated it, so I guessed it might not be to your taste! All you need to do is tell me when you want the food collected and I will get Aidan to come in the Landy and take it over. The kitchen, as you know, is basic, but the ancient cooker will warm things up, and there's enough crockery from when they hold the charitable events. Dora is making a rota of helpers, so we all know what we are doing on the day – and you aren't on it.'

'I'm not going to cry... again.' Aurora smiled. 'My heart is bursting with love for everyone who is helping with mine and Jack's day. When the road thing happened, I was devastated, then the damage to the Village Hall roof ruining most of the stuff I had collected was just the icing on the bloody wedding cake, but every cloud and all of that. Right, how about we sample Christmas traybakes for dessert? I'll make us a pot of Zen's finest coffee. You go and sit in front of the fire and relax. You've had a busy day. We can catch up on anything other than my wedding and give my poor old brain a break!'

We settled down on the sofa, mugs of delicious coffee in our hands, and both sat for a couple of minutes, immersed in our own thoughts, mesmerised by the flames dancing in the hearth.

'Bert and Meg will be back in the morning, I hope. Jack's bringing them across first thing, along with Harriet,' said Aurora, between bites of a chocolate and mint traybake. We slumped in companionable silence and my eyes wandered around the room. It really was a lovely spacious flat with big square rooms, high ceilings and the same long Georgian sash windows as downstairs in the café. The room was full of colour, filled with cushions, throws, and bright artwork adorning the walls. There were loads of books in an ancient solid wood bookcase, which looked original to the house and took up almost one entire wall, and in front of one of the windows was a table with an angle poise lamp, packets of stones and chains, and a soldering iron. I guessed it was where she made her jewellery.

'It's a fabulous flat, Aurora,' I said, breaking the silence.

'Thanks, I love it. It was the first ever big space of my own, to do with what I wanted. I was born in miniscule Ravi; although I was too young to remember that really. Then we moved into the tiny cottage on Greater Reef, or I would be staying in the bunk bed cupboard at Meg's, so this place felt huge to me. What are you going to do after your time here comes to an end, Ellie? You seem to really enjoy island life and you have slotted in so well. Any chance of you staying on? There are always jobs going at the castle in the spring, and to be honest, I could do with a helping hand in the café every now and again until I get into a new routine. After the wedding, Jack and I will be splitting our time between here and Seahouses.'

'Lovely as it sounds Aurora, I'm not sure. I do love the island, and I can't bear the idea of leaving after only a few weeks, not to mention having to leave Nacho behind as I can't take him back to London.'

And of course, Zen. The idea of leaving him behind was not one I wanted to contemplate either.

'Thing is Aurora, would I be able to afford to live here on the island? I've got no savings.' I sighed, a vision of Matt popping up in my head, and I could feel anger and resentment bubbling inside me. The sensible thing would be to go back to London and at least try to get some of my inheritance back, and then I could do whatever I wanted.

'I don't know Ellie. I think if you could manage financially until the holiday season really kicks off, you'd be fine, so don't discount it, please. Let's just see what happens – if it's in the stars, they will tell us,' she smiled warmly.

'Okay, let me think about it – if I ever get the time.' I laughed.

***

By the time I got back to the castle, my head was whirring. Stay, go, stay, go... Ping. Aurora had sent a photo message. The picture was of Aidan, resplendent in banana yellow fisherman's gear, sou'wester on his head, flat out on the floor, alongside a few other men. They were all out for the count.

I know he's not your responsibility, but he's here, at Zen's, just in case you were wondering. Keep this photo. You never know when it might come in useful. We can do an Isla and bribe him! Please, please think about staying. See you at the nativity tomorrow xx

CHAPTER 31

After yet another sleepless night, this time tossing and turning, weighing up the pros and cons of staying or going, even I could see that the benefits of going back to London were looking rather scant. Apart from my wonderful close friends, what was there really to go back for? I had enjoyed my time in the city, thrived on the excitement and the buzz, and had seen everything I wanted to see. It had taken coming to Holy Island to realise that I still had a lot of living to do, just in a very different way. My thoughts, of course, had centred around Zen. I could not detach him from the equation, but I acknowledged that having Zen in my life as 'just' a friend, was better than a life without him in it at all. I was going to stay, and maybe those stars would work their magic eventually.

'Ellie pet, come here and give me a hug,' shouted Meg from the cottage door as I went to start my morning rounds.

'Meg! You're back,' I said, running over and hugging her tightly.

'You look tired pet. Sorry that you were left in the lurch. We came on the boat at first light with

Jack and Harriet. What a nightmare, but everything looks ship-shape here and I can see how hard you've worked. Ah, it's so good to be back home. What a thing to happen. Bert and I never go too far these days, and to be off the island was just bad luck. It was choppy on that boat mind, and cold, but worth every minute to get back in time for the Nativity and the wedding.'

'It's great to have you both back, Meg.'

'You go and say hello to Bert and fill him in on what he's missed with the animals, and then come back here and have a cuppa with me, because I want to hear *everything* that's gone on! You're off yard duties this morning. Maurice is coming to help Bert, and it will give you time to help in the castle.'

'Okay Meg, see you shortly,' I said, going in search of Bert.

'Ellie lass, you've done a reet grand job,' said Bert when I found him in the donkeys' stable. 'Thanks pet, we would be lost without you, you've fitted in so well and both of us missed you when we were stuck on the mainland.' He grimaced as if he'd been confined in a maximum-security prison. 'How was *his lordship?* I hope he behaved himself and got stuck in to help, the lazy article that he is. He's nothing like Lance, his brother. Now there's a lad who knows about family responsibility. Just as well they were born in the order they were,' he joked.

'Don't be too hard on him Bert. He has kind of behaved himself,' I said, laughing, 'and he has been helpful. I was pleased to have someone else around the castle, otherwise it might have felt scary being here all on my own. Are you taking the brood back down to the paddocks today?' I asked, changing the subject.

'Aye pet. It's a lovely day, and they need to run. Been cooped up long enough. Not the alpacas though. They are on duty at the Nativity later and Meg and the kids will be titivating them for their starring role!'

'Then there's one thing I would like to do this morning Bert. I want to lead the horses down myself. Is that okay?'

'It's more than okay, lass. Take them one by one, and just remember to keep your feet clear of Stout. Keep a short rein as they'll be excited to get back outside, and I'll stand at the top in case you need me.'

I led Stout down first. She really was a gentle giant and she sedately walked down the bank, whinnying all the way. I shut the gate, gave her some carrots and went to collect Hannibal, dreading how he might behave.

'Okay, you little devil,' I said, going in to the stable. 'You are going out, and I'm taking you, so be grateful. I don't want any nonsense, and when we get to the bottom, you can have lots of carrots, if you are good. No biting, or kicking, you hear me?' His ears were forward, and I could see he was eager to get out of the stable. He made no protest as I clipped on the lead rein and meekly followed me. When we passed Bert, he was astonished.

'Well, I'd go to the top of wor stairs, if we had any. You've got that wee beast literally eating out of your hand. Well done lass. I think you have passed your induction with flying colours.'

I got back to the cottage and found Meg laughing.

'Eeh pet, I've just seen Aidan come back from wherever he went after the Shindig last night. Between you and me, I'm so pleased that Bert couldn't go. Aidan looks like death warmed up, and why is he wearing fishing gear? Do you know? I've told him that he needs to sober up and get himself presentable for the Nativity at 2 p.m. His uncle and aunt always attend, and it's down to him to represent them today and I'm not taking no for an answer. I'm surprised he's still on the island. Thought he would have organised a rescue helicopter, like James' blooming Bond. Something must be holding his interest here. Has that Isla Thompson been hanging around by any chance?'

'Err, she has called a few times, but as far as I know, Aidan hasn't even met her... yet. I'll check on him when I go over and remind him of his commitments,' I promised, laughing. 'Now, let me tell you what you missed...'

***

Aidan was suited and booted in one of his uncle's Savile Row specials when I knocked on his door to make sure he was ready.

'You look smart,' I said. 'Better than your

fishing outfit!'

'Oh, don't Ellie,' he groaned. 'I might look okay, but I seriously feel like shit. What the hell do they put in that stuff? The last I can remember was sitting in a boat on the ground trying to row, while singing "What Do They Do With A Drunken Sailor", or at least that's what I think I was singing. Then I woke up on Zen's floor with three other equally inebriated fellows, all relatives of the groom, I do believe, and I was wearing waders covered in fish guts and a sou'wester. I hope I can track down James' clothes. I'm running up quite a tally of replacements, aren't I?'

'You are that!' I laughed. 'Come on, let's get across to the church and you can pray for all your sins.'

'I might be there a while then.' He smiled. 'Please Ellie, drive us over. I don't think I have the walk in me. My legs no longer hold me up very well.'

We parked up near the village green where the Nativity was due to start from. It had been transformed into Nazareth from where the procession would head to Bethlehem, which had been created in the nave of the church. There were a few small sheep in one pen, and Pacino and Murray, who made rather interesting camels, with padded humps strapped to their backs, were in another, along with the three wise men. Wise was perhaps a misnomer, as they were being portrayed by Maurice, Ethan and Dean, all of whom looked green around the gills and were propping each other up, wobbling about next to cardboard palm trees. As there were only six pupils currently attending the village school, and because of the road closure, the children from the mainland who usually took part couldn't get on to the island, so to make the Nativity happen, there had been some very last-minute additions to the cast, and pickings were slim. Ethel was the Angel Gabriel (probably about the same age), Ian and Linda from the *Crab* were typecast as the innkeeper and his wife. Jack's dad and brothers had stepped in to be the shepherds, and, like the wise men, looked the colour of sheep, all grey faced and in need of a shave. A totally recovered Wilma was ready for her journey, being led by Amelia as Mary, and William was Joseph. The other island children, who were all under-fives, looked wonderfully cute tucked inside big golden stars, with a hole cut out for their huge unblinking eyes to peep through. Meg handed the 'baby' to Amelia, and I did a double take, as there was Nacho, swaddled in a blanket and wearing an adorable bonnet.

'Hope you don't mind lass,' she whispered to me, 'but we've got no babies on the island this year!'

The motley procession, led by the vicar, who was narrating, set off from Nazareth, across the village green, to their destination of Bethlehem. Aidan and I followed and took our seats to watch. Talk about laugh and cry at the same time. The adults had no clue and were just making things up as they went along, and the kids all looked adorable, gazing around in confused wonderment. We had just reached the bit where Mary was about to give birth to baby Nacho Jesus, when the sound of a donkey braying loudly was heard from outside.

'What the bloody hell is that racket?' cackled Ethel. 'It's my bit and no one can hear me.'

'Ethel! I don't think the Angel Gabriel would swear. Think of the kids,' hissed Imogen.

Suddenly, Wonky rushed in and trotted noisily down the aisle on a mission, pushing everyone aside so he could finally get to his beloved Wilma. Wilma responded, equally pleased to see Wonky, and nothing could be heard over the loud eeyores of greetings, the pair showing their affection by way of nuzzling each other. The two 'camels', who had been patiently standing in the nave, saw their chance of escape and hot footed it out of the church, their humps swaying. The place was in chaos.

'Love, as you can see demonstrated before us, is the true meaning of Christmas,' shouted the vicar above the noise of the donkeys, trying to rescue the situation.

'You didn't tell me this would be as much fun,' said Aidan, creased up laughing, and looking much better than he had earlier.

'And this is precisely how Joseph felt about Mary...' the vicar bravely continued, gesticulating at Wilma and Wonky.

'Quick Ellie, go and follow the alpacas,' shouted Meg. 'I'll sort out the donkeys. Bert must have left the gate open when he put them out.

Just wait until I get my hands on him,' she fumed, proving that even true love had its glitches.

'And so, the baby Jesus was born...' shouted the vicar over the chaos, mopping his brow with a hankie and bringing the Nativity to a speedy conclusion. 'Happy Christmas everyone and we shall see you all tomorrow for the wedding.'

'Hair of the cod chaps?' yelled Aidan to the wise men and shepherds, and without any second bidding, they formed a line behind Ian the innkeeper and headed towards the *Crab*, which was just left of Nazareth on the village green.

I ran down the aisle in chase of Pacino and Murray, Mary and Joseph running behind me, followed by a tiny dog dressed up as a baby, bonnet bobbing and swaddling clothes trailing on the ground.

'Try the garden at the cafe,' shouted Aurora, doubled up laughing. 'They'll be after carrots.'

'I'll make sure the sheep are penned in until Ethan gets back,' said the woman sitting next to Aurora, smiling at me as I ran past. 'I'm Harriet, nice to meet you, Ellie. See you very soon.'

True to form, Pacino and Murray were found in the garden at the café, unaffected by their adventure, and after removing the humps and giving them treats, baby Nacho and I led them back to their paddock.

***

I went straight around to the castle, where everyone

was meeting, to put the finishing touches to the room – it was all systems go. The place looked beautiful. Zen was busy making a temporary stage out of pallets in the corner of the room, his hair tied back as he worked, giving me full view of his amazing cheekbones. He looked so handsome, and I stood mesmerised, as usual, hardly able to take my eyes off him.

'How did the Nativity go Ellie?' he shouted, looking up and breaking into a broad grin, as I eventually managed to co-ordinate myself to walk towards him.

'Don't ask.' I laughed. 'Organised chaos, but highly entertaining!'

'Wish I'd been there to see it. I knew that last-minute replacements had been drafted in. I did wonder if the vicar knew what he was doing when he agreed to the guys standing in. They couldn't even accomplish the standing bit when I swept them up off my floor this morning.' He laughed. His mobile began ringing in his pocket. As he answered, I saw the expression on his face change, and he spoke quickly, nodding and putting down his hammer before hanging up.

'Everything okay?'

'That was Pa. They've got an emergency over on Greater Reef and he needs me to go across and look at an injured seal,' he said, pulling on his coat and hat.

'You go pet,' said Meg. 'Leave this to Bert. He'll finish it for you. It can be his punishment for letting

Wonky out.'

'Zen, can I come with you? I would love to see Greater Reef.' The words were out of my mouth before I had time to think about it.

'Yeh sure. The crossing might be a bit rough, but it's only ten minutes. Think you can manage it? Get togged up. It'll be freezing. I'll meet you at the harbour as soon as you're ready. I'm just popping home to collect some gear.'

He smiled at me, his face lighting up. And even if he had asked me to swim across, I would have gone in a heartbeat. My stomach was already in knots at the thought of spending time alone with Zen, so I doubted being tossed around on the waves for ten minutes was going to make it any worse.

'Don't forget our girls' get-together for Aurora tonight. She never got her official hen party, so this is just a wee celebration. I hope you get back in time.'

'Only got to help Pa get the seal onboard Meg, give Ellie a quick tour of the island, and we'll be back before you know it.'

I rushed off to get ready humming "My Heart Will Go On"!

CHAPTER 32

'You can't be serious. We are not going over there in that, surely?' I said, pointing across to the island with one arm, and to the bright blue boat with the other. I wasn't too sure what I had imagined the craft would be like, but this was little more than a rowing boat, with a small outboard engine at the back. It didn't look like it could cross Hyde Park lake, let alone the stretch of choppy ocean ahead of us. Zen smiled at me from beneath his swaddling of coats and scarves, and I peeped back at him through my layers of everything I could wear and still actually move.

'Here, put this on,' he said, handing me a life jacket, which I regarded curiously, having no clue what to do with it. He wrapped his arms around me to strap me in, and my heart did its flippity-flippity thing. Our cheeks were side by side, and I could feel his warm breath on my face as he leaned around my back to cross the ties, and even if I was currently the girth of a whale – thanks to all the clothing – I felt in seventh heaven being so close to him.

'So, how long have you been driving, err, sailing, this boat?' I stuttered.

'Only since I was about seven, Ellie. You are in safe hands, and look, if it makes you feel better, she even has oars in case we break down! She's only ever used for the crossing to and from Greater Reef. She's not meant for long distances, so don't worry. I'm not going to sail us off to Holland over there. Have you heard of Grace Darling?'

'Err, vaguely,' I replied.

'She's a local heroine. She rescued nine people from a shipwreck in 1838 in a coble, which is a small rowing boat, and she was only twenty-two years old. I wish we could go to the museum in Bamburgh so you could find out more about her. Perhaps next time.' He smiled.

'I'd like that.'

The sea looked a bit rough, but hey, it was ten minutes, and surely even I could manage that. I settled down on the bench seat and gripped onto the sides of the rocking boat.

'Trust me, Ellie,' he said, as he pulled the motor cord, and the little boat spluttered into life. 'This old girl has taken us back and forth to the island since we were kids. She is very dear to me. Her name is Lady Eleanor.'

'No way! That's my full name, Eleanor, although no one ever calls me it these days. Only my mum when she's annoyed at me about something.'

'Lady Eleanor is special around these parts. Have you never heard the song?' he asked, looking at me curiously.

'No, should I? Who sang it?'

'Oh, way before our time, but what a classic – one of my favourite songs. Ma and Pa named the boat after the song. The band who sang it were proper Geordies and were called Lindisfarne; talk about full circle.' He smiled. 'If we were looking for signs…' he whispered, trailing off, but I had heard him loud and clear, like he had shouted it from the top of the lighthouse.

My heart missed a beat, and it wasn't the rocking of the boat, which I had hardly noticed. I was so engrossed in what he was saying. *Looking for signs*. Well, I had been looking for a sign, and this was surely it, all my earlier doubts about what I overheard him say forgotten.

'Tell me about the song.'

'Well, it's a love song of sorts, but not in the way that maybe you would want it to be. It's dark, but hauntingly powerful and open to interpretation. To my way of thinking, Eleanor is an extremely beautiful woman, a formidable force, adept at getting what she wants, in this world and the next.'

'I need to hear it,' I said, entranced.

'Do me a favour,' he said. 'Wait until after the wedding, because if you hear the unsurpassable original, mine will pale into insignificance.'

'I'm sure it won't.' I laughed. 'Okay, it's on hold, and I'll look forward to hearing both versions. I wish I could join up the circle by saying I was named after the song too, but I wasn't. It was after my great-grandmother on my dad's side.'

'That would have been too freaky,' said Zen.

'Look, we're nearly coming into the harbour. Doesn't time fly when you are having fun? And I've told you nothing about the coastline; but not to worry, when we climb up to the top of the lighthouse, you can get a much better view than from the boat,' he said, pointing to the red and white striped building, which was looming right above us.

He was right about the time passing. Listening to Zen, I hadn't even noticed the boat bouncing about and, quite frankly, I could have sailed on to Australia, as long as I was with him.

'Well done, Ellie.' He laughed. 'Your inaugural trip to Greater Reef on your namesake concluded without so much as a hint of seasickness!'

Zen's dad was waiting for us at the harbour. They seemed alike, sharing the same sparkly coffee bean eyes, which was about the only feature I could see clearly, as Mike was as bundled up as we were.

'Pa, this is Ellie, or Eleanor.'

'Eleanor?' Mike smiled. 'Same as our little boat? Now there's a coincidence. Lovely to meet you, Eleanor, or Ellie! Aurora has told us all about you and how much you have done to help with the wedding. Sorry we haven't got more time to chat, and I know that Simone is looking forward to meeting you too, but we really need to push on and get this seal sorted. We can all catch up tomorrow at the wedding.'

'Yes, of course, no problem,' I said, following them up the steep path that led from the harbour to the cottage, lighthouse, and various outbuildings.

They were all built on a flat piece of land from where you could see across most of the small island. A woman appeared at the door to the cottage. She was dressed in waterproofs, a long grey plait dangling down the side of her bobble hat. She looked like an older version of Aurora, the same smiley face and twinkling eyes.

'Ellie, welcome to Greater Reef.' She walked towards me smiling, gathered me into her arms and gave me a big hug. 'Thank you so much for everything you have done for Aurora. I felt so helpless the day after the storm when she needed me and I couldn't get across and Meg being away on the mainland, but you helped her more than you might realise, and we are so grateful. We're not going to get much chance to talk properly today, so I hope that we can put that right tomorrow. Okay, let's go and sort this seal out.'

'He's in here,' said Mike as we went into the first building. Inside were open tanks, like big baths, and in one, lay an adorable seal; I could see a sore patch on his side. Zen crouched down and took a careful look at the injury.

'I agree Pa. He definitely needs to go down to the rescue centre. I'll help you load him up.'

'He's quite large for his age,' said Mike to Zen. 'I'm thinking about thirty-five kilos. I haven't weighed him as I wanted to spare his distress, and they'll do that at the centre, but he's around two to three weeks old, I should think.'

'How can you tell?' I asked, as they collected

the gear that they'd need to transport him.

'See the colour of his coat?' said Mike. 'See how white he is? That tells us his age. They change colour as they get older. This little chap should still be on land, feeding from his mother, but the storm has blown him off course – from the Farnes, I suspect.'

'Where are you taking him?'

'To the Marine Rescue Centre further down the coast. They have the facilities to look after him there. If all goes well, he'll be with them for about six weeks, then released back into the sea to fend for himself.'

'Oh, I do hope so, little one,' I said, looking at the seal's huge liquid brown eyes, his small face covered in black splodges and thick inky whiskers contrasting against his white fur.

'Right, let's get him into the bag, Zen, and down to the boat.'

I watched them work together to put the animal into a special type of seal carry bag. They were both so gentle with the creature, I could feel a lump forming in my throat as I watched them. I followed them back down to the harbour as they carried the precious cargo and loaded him into a 'proper' boat.

'Make sure you give Eleanor a grand tour of our island,' he said, as Zen untied the rescue boat.

'And make her some coffee,' shouted Simone.

'I will. Safe trip. Hope the weather holds out. Speak later, and text me as soon as you get to the centre.'

We waved goodbye and watched as the boat, which travelled much faster than Lady Eleanor, sped out to sea.

'So, ready for the grand tour?'

'Looking forward to it!'

'Right, we'll have a walkabout. This place isn't much bigger than a couple of football fields, so it's not going to take long. There's only this bit that's flat. The rest runs down in a slope towards the edge of the island and the cliffs. That's where the birds nest. Most people want to see puffins, but you are a shade too early. There's plenty of terns, gulls and cormorants though. Just watch where you walk – although it's probably impossible to avoid – this many birds means lots of bird poo everywhere!'

'Bert told me a little about the birds and how many there are. How do your mum and dad get any sleep?'

'Earplugs – and you do get accustomed to it, kind of. It's far worse in breeding season, and at that point, you have to wear protective headgear because they dive bomb you.'

'Oh my God, it sounds like that Hitchcock film *The Birds.*

'It can be just like that.'

'I may give it a miss.'

'Coward!' He laughed.

We walked on, and the view of the mainland changed as we went. You could see Bamburgh Castle standing proudly in the distance and the other Reef islands, which were even smaller than this one. You really got the full experience of being on an island because it was so small – you could literally see the sea all around you.

'I'm not sure I could live on here,' I said honestly. 'It's beautiful but feels quite isolated. Your mum and dad must be so in tune with each other to spend all day every day without any other people around.'

'They are, which is something I aspire to one day...' he trailed off. 'But I know what you mean about Greater Reef. I loved it as a kid, but I doubt I could do what Ma and Pa have done and stay on here permanently. They aren't here on their own all year though. They get help from temporary volunteer wardens in breeding season. They sleep in one of the outbuildings, and Ma and Pa look forward to the company. Lindisfarne is a better proposition for me entirely. You still get the island feel, but with a sense of community and easy access to the mainland.'

'I agree. I've really settled on the island. I didn't have a clue where I was even coming to initially, other than Northumberland, but I'm so pleased it turned out to be here. I've made some good friends and have been busier than I ever was in London recently. And happier too,' I confessed quietly.

'I'm pleased to hear it.' He smiled that smile, the one that lit up his entire face, and my heart at the same time. 'Coffee? Let's go in out of the cold, thaw out, and you can tell me more about London.'

CHAPTER 33

The cottage was a bijou version of Aurora's flat. The sitting room was packed with books, craft materials, paintings of birds and the island, all decorating the whitewashed walls. No television was to be seen, but there was an old-style record deck, with hundreds of vinyl albums piled up next to it. There were also a couple of guitars propped up against the wall. I could see where Zen had got his musical abilities. An open fire was throwing out much-needed heat, and the place exuded cosiness, somewhere to thaw out and relax after battling the elements on the island. Zen went into a tiny galley kitchen and made a cafetiere of coffee, his own blend no doubt.

'So, this is it,' he said, handing me a mug and gesticulating around the room. 'There's a bathroom off the kitchen, and two small bedrooms up that wooden ladder into the eaves. When I got older, and Aurora and I needed our own space, I moved into the outbuilding where the casuals now stay.'

'It's charming, Zen, and so warm and cosy. I could stay here for ages, but it'll be dusk soon. Are we going back across before it gets too…'

I was interrupted by his phone ringing.

'Okay Pa, will do.' He turned to me. 'Apparently, there's a squall coming right for us.'

'A squall?'

'A narrow band of severe weather. A storm, most likely. Anyway, it's heading this way and Pa says to ride it out here rather than risk getting caught up on the way back.'

'Oh okay, sounds sensible. What about him and your mum?'

'They're fine. It's going nowhere near them, so don't worry. Anyway, it will give me a chance to show you the lighthouse, and we can watch the storm as it rolls across. Here, carry these,' he said, shoving a packet of chocolate biscuits in my hand. 'I'll take milk. There's a kettle in case we want another drink. There are 137 steps up to the top, which puts the spiral stairwell in the castle to shame, but at least it's well-lit this time!'

I was gasping for breath by the time we reached the top of the lighthouse.

'I bet you never ever get an unfit lighthouse keeper having to do that day in and day out.'

'Probably not,' he said, laughing. 'The lighthouse is decommissioned now. Advances in satellite marine technology means it plays a much bigger role in navigation, and there isn't always a need for a lighthouse, so it was taken out of service. Shame in many ways. It has been here since 1898 but went out of service in the late eighties. Now only the chosen few get to even see it, so you are incredibly lucky.'

I gazed around the circular room, windows looking out in full 360 degrees. There were a couple of garden loungers positioned to look out directly towards the open sea, a pile of throws and cushions on each. A small table held a mini kettle and mugs, bottled water, coffee, tea bags and a biscuit tin. There was also a small camping heater.

'Ma and Pa like nothing better than escaping up here and watching the weather, the sky and the stars.'

'No wonder they don't need a television. How fabulous is this?' I said, settling down to weather watch. It was getting quite dark outside now, and I did wonder how much we would be able to see, but it was matter less. I was here with Zen, all warm and cosy, and the stars would be out in force soon. We sat side by side, and as it darkened and the wind whipped up, we began to talk properly for the first time.

'Have you enjoyed your island experience, Ellie? I realise the causeway situation has got in the way, but in general?'

'I've loved every minute. Well, apart from my scary arrival.' I smiled.

'It was a bit of a nightmare,' replied Zen, 'but it all worked out in the end, fortunately.'

'I love working with the animals, even Hannibal, although Lulu is still a little witch. Bert and Meg are such a joy to be around, and I've met some of the warmest people I've ever met on your island.' *And you, of course,* I wanted to say.

'What will you do when you go back to London?' he asked quietly.

'I'm trying not to think about it. I really can't see me living in London. I packed in my job and have no desire to go back into big agency PR. For the first time in my life, I'm free of ties.' *Apart from the small matter of being absolutely broke of course.* 'I might try to find something in an animal rescue.'

'Have you considered staying on the island?'

'Of course. It's crossed my mind. Aurora asked me the same thing, and I've been thinking about it. It feels right here, Zen, but even though I said I was free, I still have to earn a living.'

I couldn't bear telling Zen about my stupidity in giving away most of my savings to Matt, and I felt a shiver run up my spine. I was trying hard to forget about it all, but it needed to be confronted, and soon.

'I would need to make sure I could afford to stay on the island. Oh, and not to mention finding somewhere to live. I'll be leaving the apartment when James and Grace return, and I can't live in Bert and Meg's cupboard forever.'

'Ellie,' he said seriously, 'I do hope you decide to stay.'

'Do you really?' I said quietly.

'Of course, why wouldn't I?'

Suddenly there was a flash of lightning, which lit up the lighthouse and gave me such a shock that I screamed. It was followed by the loudest rumble of thunder that I'd ever heard.

'Oh, my goodness, it must be right over our

heads. I feel like I'm in the middle of the eye of the storm up here. Is this place safe?'

'I would say so, Ellie.' He laughed. 'Just roll with it. Don't be scared. We'll be fine.'

Darkness seemed to have engulfed us and, as I sat huddled in the recliner, I watched, fascinated, as the lightning forked its way spectacularly across the sky. It threw light on Zen's iridescent face with every bolt. Our conversation about what I was going to do was temporarily halted as we watched what was happening before us. At another huge crash of thunder, I jumped, and Zen held out his hand until it found mine, and I clasped it tightly.

'Hold on to me,' he said gently. And so, we sat, hand in hand, in companionable silence, drinking in every flash and crash, until the storm moved further away, and the thunderclaps became less threatening.

'Wow, that was spectacular! I think you have just helped me get over my fear of storms. I do love the island,' I said, once we could hear each other speak again, 'even in weather like that. Tell me about your time away from here, Zen. I'm curious as to why anyone would want to leave. It's such a special place.'

From the glow of the lanterns dotted around the room, I could make out his serious face in the dusk. He looked so lost in thought. He dropped my hand and gripped on to his silver coffee bean.

'I left to go to university in St Andrews in Scotland to study Marine Biology. I never did the gap year thing before I went, so when I finished the course and got my degree, I decided to see some of that big world out there.' He gesticulated towards the vast sky in front of us. 'There were four of us travelling together, all members of the band Aurora mentioned. We'd formed at uni and had already begun to gain a following. It was music that helped keep us on the road. We picked up gigs for food and places to stay. Not much money involved, but it was fun, and sadly, the marine biology quickly took a back seat. I had wanderlust, Ellie, like Ma and Pa before me, and I embraced it all: the cultures, the food, the freedom. We travelled around for a couple of years, predictably doing the usual student route through Asia, ending up in Thailand. It was there at a beach bar that I met Bethania.'

My heart missed a beat; I almost forgot to breathe as I waited for him to continue.

'Bethania was Brazilian. It was an instant attraction and we fell in love very quickly. We stayed together in Thailand for a while, and when it was time for her to go back home, she asked me to go with her. By that time, we'd met a record producer who was on holiday and had attended one of our acoustic beach gigs. He wanted us to go back to London to record a demo, but I chose Bethania, left the band, and went to Brazil. My band mates were far from happy. Anyway, we got to Bethania's parents' coffee plantation, and that's where I discovered my love of coffee. It's such a fascinating product. Don't get me started on that though. I'm an official bore on the subject, but suffice to say, I started working for her dad, learning all about beans and roasting and what makes the perfect cup. We were so happy. Beth was one of the most vibrant people I had ever met. She was a force of nature and I idolised her. I suppose you might say we were opposites – me the introspective Geordie and her a Latin firecracker – but it seemed to work and, shortly after we got to Brazil, we got engaged.'

I sat listening to him intently, hanging onto every word.

'All seemed to be going well. I continued learning about the business, and Beth was wrapped up in planning our wedding. It wasn't going to be as low key as Aurora's and Jack's. Tell you the truth, the prospect of a huge affair with every bow and whistle scared me, but it was Beth's dream, so I just went along with it. Guests started arriving for the big day and my old bandmates came – we'd put our differences aside by that point. They'd found a replacement for me and had done okay; although they hadn't made it to the level we had all dreamed about. Two nights before the wedding, I'd worked all day, but got back to our annexe earlier than expected. I found Beth and Lee, one of my bandmates, having sex in our bed.'

I gasped.

'I was devastated and felt so let down by both of them. Lee bolted straight back to the airport, and as for Beth, well, she was unrepentant. I think my obsession with her must have clouded my judgement of her personality, because she said it was just sex, and if I thought that because we would be married, that she wouldn't sleep with anyone else again, that I was deluded. It transpired that Lee was far from the first. I can still remember her standing in front of me with her hands on her hips saying, "I'm a woman with red hot blood, and I have big sex needs," in her fabulous accent. To be quite honest, I think I might have found it funny if it wasn't so tragic. But it marked the end, because seriously, that is not the kind of relationship that I want, so I cancelled the wedding. I travelled straight home with Ma, Pa and Aurora to lick my wounds. I stayed here on Greater Reef at first. I was a mess, but in true Lindisfarne tradition, the familiarity and kindness shown to me helped so much. And of course, I had Ravi, and when the going got too tough, I would go off on my own, take photos and recharge. After a while, Aurora and I took on the café building; and the rest, as they say, is history. I started my coffee business, and it gave me focus. Being able to throw myself into something that took up all my time was the best kind of therapy.'

I gently touched his arm in reassurance and was interrupted by my phone ringing.

'It's Meg,' I croaked. 'Better answer it. She'll be worried.'

'Ellie, where are you? The girls are all here and we're waiting for you.'

'I'm so sorry, Meg. I should have rung you sooner, but we're stuck on Greater Reef. The weather has held us up. Anyway, don't worry. Zen is here. Everything is fine and we'll get back when we can. Tell Aurora to have a great night. I'll text her later but will see her tomorrow for her big day.'

'Okay my pet. I won't worry knowing you're with Zen.'

I hung up and turned my attention back to him.

'Telling you how sorry I'm sounds so meaningless, Zen, but I am, truly. Having been through the pain and embarrassment of being cheated on myself, I totally understand. You know I've recently split up with someone and that he'd been seeing a work colleague behind my back, but naïve me, oblivious to it all, went ahead with that stupid plan to ask him to marry me in front of all our colleagues. It was like trying to stick a band aid on a broken leg. Our relationship was in tatters already, and I was desperately trying to fix it without a hope in hell. It seemed that most of my colleagues knew all about the affair already. I felt so embarrassed, but mostly stupid. I still do, I suppose. What I didn't mention the other night was that he got officially engaged to her the day after that happened and plastered it all over social media – that is the kind of man I was trying to keep.' I looked down at the floor, unable to meet his eye, and I could feel myself beginning to shake.

Zen's arms reached out, gathered me in to his chest and held me tight, telling me everything was going to be okay. I found my arms wrapping around his back and we clung on to each other like we were holding on to life itself.

'Ellie,' he said, pulling back to look me straight in the eye, 'you can't spoil the rest of your life being controlled by something that happened but is now nothing more than history—' He stopped mid-sentence and let out a huge chuckle. 'Listen to me. A case of pot calling kettle black if there ever was one. I'm guilty of that myself, but it's true. I'm trying to move forward and so should you. Don't let the past stand in the way of your future.'

'The thing is, Zen, there is someone on Lindisfarne that from the very moment I met him, made me realise that I didn't want the past to get in the way.'

I took a deep breath. Bert had taught me a Geordie saying, "Shy Bairns Get Nowt", and if there was ever a time to put that into practice, it was now.

'He's gorgeous, brave and makes the best—' *Coffee*, I was about to say coffee, but the expression that descended on Zen's face stopped me dead in my tracks. He looked like the wounded seal, so sad and vulnerable.

'Aidan, I assume,' he said quietly, dropping his arms and shuffling back in his chair, putting distance between us.

'No! Not Aidan. He's great fun, a complete charmer, but he's not for me, and I'm not really for him. I hope we will stay friends though, as I do like him. This guy is kind, rescues humans and animals, and he's got the most beautiful soul of anyone I've ever met. Oh, and he makes great coffee.'

I couldn't quite believe I'd actually plucked up the courage to say what I was really feeling for once. Maybe the universe was doing its thing and instilling me with a newfound confidence. As I looked at Zen, the range of expressions on his face went from confusion to incredulity, to absolute joy.

'Zen, I heard you talking to Isla outside the *Crab* on the night of the gansey party. I apologise for eavesdropping, but I hold my hands up, I couldn't stop listening. Anyway, I get what you were saying, especially now I know what you've been through. You don't want a quick fling, and you're scared of entering another long-term relationship, especially with someone like me, who might just be passing through the island, and who you don't really know. But I like you Zen, I mean really like you.'

'And I like you too, Ellie. From the moment I saw you, soaked to the skin and peeping out at me terrified on the causeway, something weird – no that's not right – something *magical* happened. It was like the stars were in the process of aligning, and I was struck with a force drawing me to you. I felt an instant attraction and, whilst it thrilled me, it also scared me, because I didn't think I was ready for another relationship. I'd felt so betrayed by Bethania that it's taken me ages to settle back down into a new routine, and I was scared to jeopardise that. I knew you were only coming to the island on a short stay and I'm not into brief encounters, or one-night stands, or bunk ups or whatever you want to call them. I knew that something like that with you was not an option, because it would never be enough, so I tried to keep my distance. But that was tough. The more I met you, saw how kind you are, how you are with Bert and Meg and Amelia, and especially hearing you talking to the animals and looking so cute in your hats and giant coat—'

'Yes, very elegant,' I interrupted, smiling.

'—the idea of losing you to London got even harder to contemplate.

'So, what are we going to do?' I whispered.

'Do? This is what we do.' And he leaned forward to face me, put a hand on each of my shoulders and gently drew me towards him. Our faces were nose to nose. I could smell his signature scent of espresso and pine, and I thought I might just drown in his gorgeous eyes as he stared at me so intently. I wrapped my arms around his back, his long curls tickling my arms, and suddenly our lips found each other, and we kissed. A perfect, short but incredibly passionate kiss, where time seemed to stand still, and an inexplicable feeling washed over me; this was a moment I had been waiting for my entire life. When we drew back and smiled shyly at each other, judging by the expression on his face, I reckoned that Zen was feeling exactly the same as me.

CHAPTER 34

We sat in the dusk, motionless, holding on to each other's hands, our eyes fixed firmly on each other's face.

'Zen, I can't promise that I can stay on the island, and there's over 300 miles between Lindisfarne and London, if that's where I end up.'

'Ellie, I can't do a long-distance relationship, not with anyone, but especially not with you, not yet. We've just met, and we are both wary, scared of being hurt, so we need to take this slowly and together, not with hundreds of miles between us. I want to date you Ellie, get to know every last thing about you. I want to show you my Northumberland and watch your face as you see its beauty for the first time. I want to hug you every day, kiss you every day and eventually...' He tailed off, but I got the message, loud and clear. 'Does that all sound so very wrong?'

'No, of course not. I would like the same, but I've got to be realistic. Zen, I've got money troubles. I'm not going into it now as it would spoil this wonderful moment, but sadly the real world, outside of us cocooned in this lighthouse on a tiny island, still exists and...'

He leant in and kissed me again stopping me mid speech. The kiss was longer this time, deeper, more urgent and once again, perfect.

'Just one question, Ellie,' he said, pulling back. 'If there is a way that makes it possible for you to stay on the island, will you? I can't give up my coffee business yet, so there's no way I can go anywhere at the moment, otherwise I would consider it, if it meant we could give this a go.'

'Just one answer to your one question then. Yes, whey aye man! If it's possible to stay on the island, then of course I will,' I shouted, hoping I'd got the context right.

'Well, that's okay then!' His face broke into a broad grin, the coffee bean eyes twinkling with joy. 'No more trying to work out the logistics and what we are going to do; that can wait. We've got a wedding to attend, and then afterwards, we have a lot of things to do.'

I felt my insides doing cartwheels at the very prospect of doing anything with Zen!

'Come on.' He jumped up and pulled me out of the chair. 'I'll race you down the stairs, and if you're lucky, I might even let you steer the boat back!'

After a long lingering kiss when we got to the harbour on Lindisfarne, I just about floated back up the hill to the castle to get ready for the wedding. I was desperate to ring Sophie, but it would have to wait, so Nacho got it chapter and verse instead. His feathery tail never stopped wagging, so I took that as a firm seal of approval!

***

'You both look lovely,' I said, gazing at Bert and Meg as I called over to the cottage to show Meg my choice of wedding outfit.

'You don't scrub up too badly yourself, pet. I don't think we've ever seen you look so glamorous, but are you okay Ellie, pet? You seem like you're in a daze.'

'Sorry Meg, miles away, yes thanks. I'm okay. In fact, I'm more than okay.'

I was longing to tell her about me and Zen, but maybe that was best done when we were together.

'Do you like my outfit?' I held out my foot, laughing. I'd brought a couple of dresses with me that hadn't seen the light of day since my arrival and had chosen a soft blue wrap-over for the wedding. The footwear had been more of a problem. It was either wellies, horsey boots, elf shoes minus the bells or Converse; so, the Converse won. After all, Aurora had said that she just wanted people to wear exactly what they felt comfortable in.

'You look reet bonnie lass,' said Bert. 'A rhapsody in blue.'

'And what about my plus one?' I scooped up Nacho, who was wearing a cute bow tie, made especially for the occasion from one of Amelia's old doll's dresses.

'Smart as a dart.' Meg smiled.

'Sorry I missed the hen do last night; we didn't get back across until first light.'

'That's okay, pet. We understand all about the way the weather dictates things around here.'

'Right, I'm just popping back for my bag, and I'll see you at the gate in ten minutes.'

I made my way back up to the apartment to find Aidan coming out of his door, resplendent in his black and white tartan kilt and a black fitted jacket with shiny silver buttons. His hair was groomed to perfection, his bright blue eyes twinkling – he looked so handsome.

'Ellie Elf, look at you! You're absolutely stunning!' His eyes travelled up and down the length of my body before coming to rest on my chest, where they lingered maybe just a smidge too long. The expensive push up bra that I hadn't worn since arriving on Lindisfarne was obviously doing what it promised on the advert!

'Thanks, you don't look too shabby yourself,' I replied. Aidan moved in for a hug. He was wearing a different aftershave and smelled like a forest after a spring rainfall. 'And you smell gorgeous too,' I said, taking in a deep breath as I hugged him back.

'Uncle's most expensive. Never ever tell him I've used it. I'm surprised he hasn't got it under lock and key.'

Aidan looked into my eyes, and I could feel the sexual tension. His, not mine.

'I don't suppose we have time to conclude our unfinished business?' he murmured, as he attempted to nibble my neck. 'If I were a betting man, I'd say that there's only flimsy, sexy garments under your dress instead of the usual layers of thermals and workwear...'

I still hadn't got around to friend-zoning Aidan, but now wasn't the time, and I promised myself to have a quiet word with him at the party.

'Aidan,' I said, gently pushing him away, 'I need to talk to you, but there's no time now, so later.'

'It's not talking that I've got on my mind, Ellie!'

'We need to go,' I said firmly. 'We've got to get across to the church. Meg and Bert will be waiting for us at the gate.'

The wedding service was perfect. The small church was dressed in an abundance of winter foliage collected from the gardens and hedgerows of the island yet looked every bit as impressive as if they had come from a top florist. As Mrs Brown struck up the notes of the Bridal Chorus on the church organ, Aurora floated down the aisle on the arm of her father, looking beautiful in a simple cream slip dress, a soft alpaca shrug draped over her shoulders. She carried a small posy that matched the foliage in the church and was wearing the most exquisite head-dress I'd ever seen. It was made from sea-glass intertwined with iridescent shells on a silver band. I'd seen nothing like it before. I knew she must have made it herself. It was dazzling yet delicate, and so fitting for Holy Island.

Jack, who stood at the front, nervously stepping from one foot to the other, waiting for his bride, was as handsome as I had imagined. Tall, broad and fair haired like his dad and brothers, they all shared the same rosy complexions from their constant exposure to the elements at sea.

Aurora's dad, Mike, proudly walked her up the aisle. Now I could see him properly, minus the winter sailing gear, the similarity between him and Zen was clear. Mike had the wayward curls, although greying, and the same aura of calm surrounding him. He beamed at everyone in the pews as he passed, his smile so bright it would light up the night sky.

Harriet looked great in a dark green velvet trouser suit, her brown hair pulled into an updo, as she followed Aurora to the front of the church. I glanced at Imogen, whose attention was focused on Harriet. There was no mistaking the look of love on her face. I heard giggling coming from the pew opposite me and Amelia was hiding behind a hymn book and peeping out at me, a mischievous expression on her cute face. She looked gorgeous in a red velvet dress and matching beret. Meg and Bert were in the front pew, their rightful place as grandparents. They may not have been blood relatives to Aurora and Zen, but they loved them every bit as much.

As I glanced around at the islanders waiting for the ceremony to begin, it seemed unbelievable that I'd only arrived here a matter of weeks ago. I had been accepted into this wonderful community and it made the idea of leaving even harder to contemplate. I looked at Zen's back as he faced the front of the church. He was head and shoulders above everyone else in the row, standing next to his mum. He looked so handsome in a crisp white fitted shirt and black jeans which hugged every muscle. The dark chocolate curls were tamed, except for a few strays that framed his translucent face. He spun around and scanned the church until he saw me, and our eyes locked. He broke into a huge smile before turning back and concentrating on his sister's big day. I forced myself to focus on the service, trying to shove my thoughts about Zen out of the way... for now! It was a truly joyous celebration, with lots of laughter and happy tears amongst the entire congregation when the bride and groom eventually said I DO.

***

The castle loomed above as the crocodile of guests made their way to the reception, slowly negotiating the steep hill. The entrance pathway at the top created by Amelia was so cute; the small twinkling Christmas trees were lined up on either side of a runner of red carpet. I had no idea how or where she got it, but it led people into the entrance hall, warm and welcoming from the roaring fire. Aidan had not let the side down and had made sure the place was heated. The dining hall looked amazing; the decorations were perfect. Everyone had worked so hard, and the finished result was really something to be proud of.

'I can't believe how lovely this is,' said Aurora,

coming across to give me a hug. 'Nice shoes, by the way.' She laughed, pointing to my feet, and lifted her wedding gown to show me her wedding shoes – red trainers! 'Now come and have that glass of champagne with me.' She took my arm as we headed for the drinks table.

'You look beautiful, Aurora, and Jack is so handsome. I can see the attraction.' I smiled.

'I'm so lucky.' She grinned. 'But one thing would make my day even more special. Have you decided if you can stay on the island yet?'

'Sorry, Aurora, not decided yet, but I will let you know soon; I promise.'

'That's okay, Ellie, I understand,' she said, handing me a glass of bubbly, which I downed in one.

'Ellie! I know you've not had a drink in a while, but that was impressive.' Aurora leaned forward with the bottle to top up my glass.

As I walked back across to my table, I passed Imogen and Harriet looking very relaxed in each other's company.

'Ellie, come and join us.'
I sat down and we all clinked glasses.

'To the happy couple!' Imogen smiled.

'That might be you two soon,' I quipped, and judging by the look that passed between them, I may not have been too far off the mark.

'Ellie, talking of, I've got something to put to you,' said Imogen. 'You know we were having that conversation about whether you might stay on the

Island? I'm going to be spending a lot of time up on the farm during the lambing season when Harriet's not able to get away much. So, I was wondering how you might feel about sharing my flat? In exchange for helping in the shop on the days I'm not here. Opening up when the tide doesn't play ball, that kind of thing. I can't pay you much, but it would be cheap board and you'd have the place to yourself most of the time – oh, and Nacho will be more than welcome.'

'Imogen, I need to have a final think, but thank you, I'm interested – very.' I replied excitedly.

If I could have retrieved some of my savings from Matt without the need to go back to London, I would have said yes on the spot.

'Ellie.' I turned to see Aidan. 'Come and dance with me.' He smiled. 'I promise I'll keep my hands to myself... for now.'

'You'd better.'

I needn't have worried because within seconds of being on the dance floor, I could see his attention wavering towards the door. Poison Isla had made her grand entrance. What the bloody hell was she wearing this time? Talk about an attempt to upstage the bride. She was sporting a spray on bright pink bodycon dress edged in feathers, with crystal covered skyscraper heels. If you'd have asked me, I'd have said she looked like a flipping pink flamingo, but whatever floated her boat. I tried to be charitable.

'Err, I'm still here.' I hissed at Aidan, poking

him in the ribs to regain his attention. 'And yes, that's the daughter from the hotel.'

'Oooer, she is rather, erm...'

'Tacky?' I offered, finishing his sentence for him.

The song ended and he smiled, kissing my cheek.

'I suppose I'd better go and get this over with and introduce myself,' he said nonchalantly. But his eyes were telling a whole other story.

The next couple of hours passed in a haze of dancing and listening to Zen perform. The rendition of my namesake song was simply haunting. As I watched him lean over the guitar, the words of the song filling the room in his crystal-clear voice, I was even more smitten than ever, and I felt my heart swell with pride. As he stepped down off the makeshift stage, I ran across and gave him a brief hug and a kiss on the cheek.

'That was amazing Zen, and I want you and me to listen to the original together. I really want to give you a proper kiss, but now isn't quite the right time. We're not going to hijack Aurora's wedding with a PDA in front of the whole island!'

'You're right,' he smiled. 'We're going to be the talk of the island soon enough. Besides which, we need to tell Meg first, or she will kill us both. Oh, and Ellie, you look absolutely beautiful, by the way.'

I squeezed his hand.

'Thank you, you don't look too shabby yourself. I just need to pop upstairs a moment, got something to do, but I'll be back in a tick so get your dancing shoes on Rock Star!'

I ran up the stairs to find Aidan, who was nowhere to be seen in the dining hall. As I approached the top of the stairwell, I could hear noises. The door to the Lindisfarnes' apartment was open, and there in the corridor was Aidan, back to the wall, a look of pure ecstasy on his face. The red soles of a pair of diamante heels were on display. Caught in flagrante! I didn't think I'd actually need to friend-zone Aidan anymore; he had done it for me.

'Don't mind me,' I said in a loud voice. 'At least I now know what a Northumbrian has under his kilt!'

Aidan had the grace to look embarrassed, but true to form, there was no response from Isla. I went into my apartment, shutting the door behind me, and then laughed and laughed. So that was one bit of business taken care of without any effort at all.

I had time for a quick video call to Sophie.

'Hi Soph, haven't got long so just a quick one to see how it's going. Not many more days left in paradise, eh?'

She opened an eye and propped herself up in bed, squinting at me.

'Ellie, it's 1 a.m. here.'

'Oh sorry, totally forgot. I'm all over the place Sophie. Couldn't wait to tell you but I can call back tomorrow.'

'Don't you dare! Whatever it is, I want to hear it.'

'And so do I,' came Jake's sleepy voice from off camera.

'By the way babe, you look gorgeous! No fancy dress costume, there's a first since you got to that island. My Ellie is back in the building.' She smiled. 'You look beautiful in that blue dress, always liked it on you, shows off every curve you lucky witch! So, who is it for?'

'For? No-one, me, err, Aurora's wedding, or err, maybe Zen.'

'The hippie? Oh my God, are you joining a cult or running off in his campervan?' she snorted.

'No, not in this dress anyway, but listen, we got stuck on an island...'

'You are already stuck on an island.'

'No, I mean another island. Oh, don't worry about the detail, but we got the chance to talk, and we like each other, Sophie. I mean REALLY like each other. He wants me to stay here on Lindisfarne and make a go of things, slowly and properly, no rushing in, taking our time to get to know each other.'

'That's wonderful babe. I'm really happy for you, but not happy that I might be so far away from my bestie.'

'Well, it won't be happening immediately Soph. I need to come back to London. I was too ashamed to tell anyone, even you, but, and please be gentle with me because I know how stupid I've been. I gave, lent, call it what you will, most of my inheritance and savings to Matt over the years. He promised to pay me back but he hasn't given me any of it, including his share of the holiday. I've got nothing to support me until the season here on the island picks up, when I might be able to find enough work. Even if I could afford to stay, which I can't, I really need to confront Matt and get this sorted.'

By that point, Jake had appeared on the screen.

'The thieving bastard. Ellie girl, you get yourself back down here pronto once we get home, and we can try to recover what's rightfully yours – you'd be best doing that face to face. If that fails, I'll take a contract out on him.'

I wasn't sure if he was joking.

'It might take months, but I've thought about that and have decided that if he drags his feet, I could get agency work down there for a couple of months and build up a little money to come back with. I really don't want to leave Zen, or Nacho, or the island though...'

'Ellie babe, you must. You can't let him get away with this. If this thing with Zen is the real deal, then he'll understand and wait for you, and from what I've seen, Nacho will be well looked after by Bert and Meg.'

Deep down, I knew she was right, so I said goodnight and made my way back to the party to speak to Imogen about whether our timescales were compatible and, if so, I would accept her wonderful offer. I would then drag Zen off to a dark corner in the castle and get further acquainted with him!

CHAPTER 35

The morning after the wedding, I woke up and luxuriated in bed, thinking happy thoughts of snogging Zen in the castle pantry the night before. Then, the image of Aidan and Isla flooded into my head, and I found myself laughing out loud. I suspected that Aidan wouldn't hang around for long once the initial thrill in the bedroom department had abated, but Isla was hard to get rid of, and he might have just met his match. There was no doubt they made an extremely good-looking couple, and I could see the pair of them gracing the covers of the glossies with their impossibly gorgeous children.

It was Christmas morning, and I forced myself out of my nice warm bed, tucked my thoughts of Zen to one side – for now – and got ready to start the daily routine – the animals didn't suddenly look after themselves just because it was Christmas Day.

It was freezing cold and crisp. Sadly, not a white Christmas, but there had been a thick frost, which gave the impression of a sparkling winter wonderland. I went over to see to the dogs first, but Bert had got there just ahead of me, and had opened up the kennel door. They came bounding out, full of joyous enthusiasm, and off they went, skidding around the yard. I was slightly concerned about Tri, wondering if his three legs were up to the job of a skating rink, but like Bambi on ice, he had a few wobbly starts and then he was off! Nacho joined in with his friends and came sliding towards me, demanding to be picked up by pawing my foot with his, so I scooped him up and he snuggled into the yellow coat, his bright hazel eyes looking at me with such love and devotion that I was momentarily overcome.

'Nacho, you are just the best Christmas gift ever,' I said, planting a kiss on his spikey head.

'Happy Christmas, lass,' shouted Bert, his head buried in the feed sack. 'Meg said to remind you we're all going to the jetty to wave goodbye to the newlyweds, then back for lunch at 1.30 p.m. prompt, and you know my Meg – on the dot. I love turkey,' he said, licking his lips. 'But Meg does a smashing nut-roast for the others if you like that kind of thing. Only fit for squirrels if you ask me!'

I glanced over towards the bird houses. Thankfully, Sage and Onion were still there, waiting to be let out. I'd become rather fond of the 'brainless birds', as Bert called them. Maybe it would be nut-roast for me today.

'Mike, Simone, and Zen are coming. It'll be a grand day and we'll give all the animals their Christmas treats after lunch. They're part of this family too.'

After sorting the menagerie, I ran back

upstairs to quickly change before going down to the jetty. There was a card propped up against the door. I ripped it open – it was from Aidan.

'Happy Christmas, Ellie Elf. What can I say other than sorry? I was led by my sporran, so to speak, and, quite frankly, that Ivy is very persuasive – there was no escape—'

I couldn't help but laugh at him calling her Ivy. She wouldn't find that amusing, but Poison Ivy actually suited her so much better!

'—I do like you Ellie, and maybe we can still be friends and meet up in London when we both eventually get back there? I'm sailing across to Bamburgh for the day, but will be back later, weather permitting—'

No prizes for guessing why.

'—so hopefully no hard feelings. You are the most gorgeous elf I've ever met. Love, Aidan x'

I would meet up with Aidan, in London or Northumberland, and despite how magnetic he was, there would be no more steamy clinches. I'd leave that all to *Poison Ivy!*

***

There was quite a crowd standing on the jetty by the time I got there. Amelia ran towards me and gave me a huge hug.

'Happy Christmas, Ellie. What did Santa bring you?' she squeaked, excitedly speaking at a hundred miles an hour. 'He brought me loads. Will you come tomorrow and help me make a bracelet for my mam? Pleeeease! I got a lovely box with beads and everything in.'

'That sounds like fun. I can't wait. I'll see you then.'

A faint scowl passed across her cute little face.

'I did ask Santa for an extra special present. Well, not a present but a thing, but I'm not allowed to tell otherwise it might not come true. He said he would do everything he could to make it happen and I don't know if it has. What shall I do? Will I write him another letter, or does he go off on his holidays after Christmas?'

I couldn't help but smile. I knew she meant me staying on the island.

'You know what, I think Santa will be having a holiday. It's been such a busy time for him, and he will be exhausted. Why not wait until after Christmas and see what happens? Then maybe you could send him the letter if the *thing* hasn't happened.'

She seemed happy with that and skipped off in search of her brother. I saw Zen waving at the newlyweds on board the boat as it puttered out to sea. He turned and looked at me, and my heart did a gold medal standard backward flip. I didn't suppose that would ever stop; he just had that effect on me. Last night, when I had returned to the party, there had been far more exciting things to do than tell him of my decision to go back to London, hopefully temporarily. I needed to have that conversation with him today.

'Ellie, Happy Christmas! We've got exactly

twenty-three and a half minutes before lunch. Fancy a little stroll?' He winked suggestively.

'Is that a euphemism?' I laughed. 'Happy Christmas to you too. Yes, let's go down to the headland bench overlooking Greater Reef. I need to talk to you.'

'Sounds ominous.'

'Meg!' I shouted. 'We know, twenty-two minutes and counting, but promise we'll be back in time.'

'Make sure you are, pets.' She laughed, linking arms with Bert for the walk back to the cottage.

We walked to the bench in silence and sat down. The sun had appeared and was reflecting off the choppy sea, the little island ahead with its red and white striped lighthouse catching the pale winter light. The birds were circling above, mewing at each other, and Bamburgh Castle looked particularly impressive in the distance, perched on top of its hill, and wrapped in a scarf of silver sand. I would never ever forget the view; it was truly spectacular. I cleared my throat, my eyes focussed on a shell which was lying at my feet.

'What did you want to speak to me about, Ellie?'

A pause followed as I looked up to see Zen staring at me, desolation clouding the coffee bean eyes, clearly worried about what I might say.

'Zen, I want to stay here on Lindisfarne. I want everything that you want...'

'There's a but coming Ellie, I can feel it,' he

almost whispered.

'There is. It's only a little but, not a big one though, so don't worry. I do need to go back to London to sort some things out. I can't leave everything to Sophie, and there are some loose ends that need tying up that only I can do myself.'

Stringing up more like, but I wasn't going to divulge my financial history with Matt to Zen. There really wasn't any need for him to know about my stupidity.

'So, I'm going to go as soon as I know Grace is on her way home, and I promise, I will be back as soon as I can, but I really can't say how long it will take as I don't even know myself.'

'Ellie, are you sure? You're not just saying you will be back and once you get to London, to the bright lights and the buzz, you won't change your mind?'

I could see the uncertainty in Zen's eyes. I felt his anxiety. It was palpable. This was a man who had trust issues, as did I, and this was just the kind of situation I knew he was trying to avoid when he hadn't wanted to get into a relationship with me.

'Zen, you are going to have to trust me on this. I do need to go, but I will be coming back to the island as soon as I can. Try stopping me. Imogen has offered me a room in her flat in exchange for me helping in the shop, and I said yes.'

I wrapped my arms around him and drew him towards me, looking directly into his beautiful eyes. Sometimes there was no need for words to reassure someone, and this was one of those moments. I was just about to kiss his gorgeous lips when…

Dong!

We both jumped off the bench quicker than Usain Bolt leaving the starting blocks.

'Oh my God, it's 1.30 p.m. Meg will kill us!' I shrieked, hearing the village church clock strike the half hour in the distance.

'Can you run in those wellingtons, Ellie? I reckon we can get there in four minutes if we hurry.'

Hand in hand, rocking with laughter that lifted the mood, we ran towards the castle.

'Ellie, I'm going to kiss you before this day is out. That's a promise,' gasped Zen as we laboured up the hill.

'Don't you worry,' I replied. 'I know exactly where Bert has pinned the mistletoe and it's a very big bunch!'

CHAPTER 36

My first Christmas on Lindisfarne was magical. Meg's Christmas lunch was the best I'd ever tasted, the company was excellent, and secretly holding hands and brushing my fingers against Zen's taut thighs under the table was the most exciting party game I'd ever played. We had decided not to tell anyone about us getting together until I got back from London. So, for now, it was our very own delicious secret, and we were both enjoying the subterfuge. Before it got dark, we all walked round the yard and down to the paddocks, giving each of the animals their Christmas treat. Even Lulu, the devil cat, seemed to have called a Christmas truce! Zen and his ma and pa left for the short boat crossing back to Greater Reef, and I spent an enjoyable evening with Meg and Bert playing board games, all four dogs piled in front of the fire in a cosy heap.

'I spoke to Grace earlier,' said Meg, whilst shaking the dice holder. 'They're setting off in a couple of days and will be back by the end of·the week, in time for New Year, so I hope the causeway has opened by then.'

'It should have, pet,' replied Bert. 'Two days' time all being well.'

Whilst that was great news, it kind of sealed my fate. I would make plans to return to London at the weekend.

'Meg, go directly to jail, don't pass go!' I laughed.

'Can I buy my way out with chocolates?' She winked, and as I looked at her and Bert, I realised just how fond I had become of the pair of them, and how much I would miss them when I went back, even for a short time. I worried about Bert, and without a shadow of a doubt, when I got back to Lindisfarne, I would prioritise helping him as much as I could.

As Nacho and I snuggled up in bed later that evening, and I listened to the rhythmic lapping of the sea against the shore below, I reflected on how my life had spun around in such a brief time. Coming to Northumberland really had been the best thing ever, and I had truly regained my Christmas spirit. I'd had the most fabulous day.

At 10 p.m. my tablet buzzed for the group call with the gang. Once we got the Christmas greetings out of the way, and the oohs and aahs over Nacho looking deliciously cute in his wobbly reindeer antlers had settled down, I could see that Sophie was bursting to say something. She pulled Jake into view and began waving her left hand about in front of the screen. We all began to shriek.

'Sophie, Jake, congratulations!' I yelled, looking at the gorgeous diamond ring.

'Oh, it was so romantic,' she gushed. 'Jake had arranged for me to find a beautiful pink clam shell on the beach and, when I prised it open, the ring was inside! I can't wait to show you, Ellie. We're coming home to London in a couple of days, and you'll be back soon too. I'm so looking forward to seeing my bestie, and the rest of you all, of course!' She laughed.

'Err, Stanislaw, why are you and Aleksy standing freezing outside of *Boycie's Bargains* on Christmas day in the dark?' I asked curiously.

'We have news too. Big news.' They both grinned at the screen like Cheshire cats. 'We now own *Boycie's*. It is ours!'

'You're going to run a second-hand furniture shop?' I asked, confused.

'No, Ellie. Boycie, well Ernie, is retiring, and the shop was up for lease, so Aleksy and I have taken over. We are changing it into a coffee shop. No more freezing my big balls off outside all day! Aleksy is giving up his job at the gym and will be running front of house, while I will be busy on the distribution side, hopefully for the best coffee I have ever tasted, from your coffee guy in the north place.'

'You mean Zen?' I asked, even more perplexed.

'We have been talking to your coffee man, Zen, online since you sent us samples. I'm going to distribute in south for him once we have come to your island and learned more about the business.'

I was flabbergasted. The dark horses – including Zen.

'So, Tara, top those if you can. What have you and Toby been up to?' I asked jokingly.

'Oh, I think we might just be able to do that,' she said, smiling beatifically as she produced an ultrasound image and held it up to the screen.

'Meet baby Butler Dunne...'

'History in the making,' said Toby proudly.

Once again, the screeches grew to eardrum bursting proportions, and we all shouted over each other, yelling congratulations.

'And you Ellie? Maybe time to widen your news.'

'Erm, yes, you're right Sophie. I'm coming back to London to collect some things and tie up loose ends. I'm not sure how long that will take, but eventually, I'll be moving to Lindisfarne and seeing where life takes me, *and Zen*, here in Northumberland.' I beamed.

'You mean you and the gorgeous rock god?' squealed Tara.

'Great.' said Stanislaw. 'Does that mean we get bigger discount on coffee?'

'Oh, Ellie Nellie, we're all going to miss you, especially me, and I can't wait to meet Zen. We can see how much happier you've been in the frozen north. Don't you dare forget us – or else,' croaked Sophie, wiping away the tears that were rolling down her face.

'Not a chance. And I'll be coming back to wrap things up down there at the weekend, so we can all get together.'

'Excellent,' said Stan. 'So, me and Aleksy will travel back to the island with you on your return, for our induction.'

'Err, hold on a minute. There's not a chance in hell that you two are going up there first without me and Ja... I mean my fiancée,' said Sophie.

'Or us three,' added Tara, patting her stomach. 'Toby is desperate to get to the island and learn more about the Vikings, like he doesn't know enough already.'

'Well, perhaps we can hire a mini-bus and we'll all go for a holiday, not to live permanently, of course.' Sophie laughed.

'I would live there,' said Toby. 'Did you know that in AD...'

'Okay Toby,' said Tara, cutting him off. 'Tell us later, and don't you go getting ideas about moving to Lindisfarne.' She smiled. 'Although what a perfect place to bring up a child...'

The next couple of days raced by. I told Bert and Meg that I was heading back to London, but that I would be returning and moving in with Imogen. They were delighted.

'You know you are welcome to the broom cupboard any time,' said Meg, giving me a hug.

'Thanks Meg, and you will be seeing plenty of me as I intend to come over to help Bert as much as I can, and that means Nacho can see his friends and Hannibal won't forget me!'

'I hope you're going to find plenty to keep you occupied, pet. All work and no play and that kind of thing. The island can be a little dull for young people, especially single ones.'

'Oh, don't you worry about me in that direction Meg. I'm sure I'll find plenty to keep me occupied.' And I knew exactly what that would entail and, quite frankly, couldn't wait!

Aidan had returned to Lindisfarne and hadn't been seen for two days, being locked in his apartment with Isla. It didn't take a genius to work out what was going on behind closed doors. Good luck to him. Maybe she would change her ways for a catch like him. Or maybe not. I suspected that particular leopard would never let go of her spots.

I hadn't managed to see much of Zen, who had been over on Greater Reef for a few days helping his dad. He was due back the day before I was leaving, and the excitement of seeing him was helping me get through all the jobs on my list with energy to spare.

***

The causeway re-opened and normal service on the island resumed. I booked my ticket to London for the day before New Year's Eve. Doing the rounds of my last afternoon of bedding down the animals was quite emotional. I'd become attached to them all, even Sage and Onion the turkeys who gave nothing much back at all, but they had their own quirky little ways which were quite endearing. Nacho trotted at my heels as I went around saying my goodbyes. Stout and Hannibal whinnied gently as I entered their stable, and the cute devil pony actually looked pleased to see me.

'I'll miss you two.' I gave Han a carrot. 'Best behaviour until I get back mind.'

I went down to the paddocks. Pacino and Murray came rushing across to the gate demanding treats, and I scratched their long woolly necks and looked into their deep, soulful eyes.

'You two will be okay, Amelia and William will be making sure of that, and we'll be doing lots of walks to the village when I get back.'

I walked on towards the donkeys. There, in the corner, were Wonky and Wilma, together at last, side by side and not at all interested in me; eyes only for each other. Jenny was currently sharing a stall with Nanny and the arrangement seemed to be working well, until new additions could be found to keep each of them company.

I breathed in the late December afternoon air. It was a pleasant day, with little wind. The island felt serene, bathed in a haze of pale winter hues. I really hoped I wasn't going to be away too long. I wanted to experience Lindisfarne in all seasons and couldn't wait to see what Spring would be like, as the island began to come to life with new growth and lots of visitors.

'Ah, there you are lass,' said Bert, making his way across the paddock towards me. 'Taking a moment, eh?'

'I am Bert. I remember you telling me when I first arrived that no two days are the same on

Lindisfarne, and I get that now. I really wish I didn't have to go back but I do, unfortunately.'

'Well lass, you will be missed, and we want you back as soon as possible. My Meg is going to miss her little chats with you.'

I wiped away a stray tear that bounced down my cheek.

'Now don't go getting maudlin. You'll be back before you know it. I've come to tell you that you need to get yourself over to the *Crab* tonight. We're having a little celebration of the causeway reopening, and it will give you a chance to see everyone before you go. Try and get Lord Muck out of that apartment. He's been in there long enough, and he'll be going back to London soon too, what with Grace and James coming home. Mind, I'm not interested in him bringing that trollop with him tonight. Time she went back to the hotel where she belongs if you ask me!'

I linked arms with Bert, and we made our way back up the cinder path towards the yard. He stopped and turned to me.

'And Ellie...'

'Yes Bert?'

'You don't need to worry about the wee scamp.' He pointed at Nacho, who was sniffing his way up the hill, his feathery tail wagging enthusiastically from side to side like windscreen wipers on full speed. 'Meg and I have decided he will live indoors with us and Flo until you get back.'

'Thanks Bert.' I squeezed his arm. 'I won't

worry because I know he's in the best hands ever!'

CHAPTER 37

I walked over to the *Crab* later that evening with Aidan, who I had managed to extract from the apartment. Isla had gone back to the hotel to stir her cauldron, or whatever it was witches like her do.

'So, how is it going with *Ivy*?'

'Erm, a gentleman never tells, Ellie Elf, but just let's say I'm exhausted, in the best possible way. Ivy is very forthright and knows exactly what she wants.'

Hmm, I could imagine – and he was still calling her Ivy!

'She is very beautiful, don't you think?'

'If you like that kind of beauty,' I replied noncommittedly.

'Downside is her terribly snobbish parents, who I'm having drinks with later this evening at the hotel.'

I could think of far worse downsides than her parents, but hey, Aidan was a man about town and was more than capable of making his own decisions.

'I've only got one more thing to say on the subject Aidan, and I say it as a very wise elf – prenup!'

The pub was busy with locals, and most

importantly, Zen, looking more handsome than ever despite him still wearing his sailing gear. Not seeing him for a couple of days had managed to increase my longing for him, and I had a sudden spine-tingling moment imagining peeling off his layers to find what lay beneath!

'Hey you.' I looked into the coffee bean eyes, my voice seemingly deciding to audition for a triple X movie by dropping to a husky rasp.

'Hey you too, Lady Eleanor. I've missed you.' He smiled, kissing me ever so delicately on the cheek.

'And me you.' I smiled back, secretly squeezing his hand. 'Maybe it's time we went and told Bert and Meg, because I can't wait much longer to be able to throw my arms around your salopettes!'

'Good plan. I'll just get a pint, then let's go and find them.'

The atmosphere in the pub was jovial, everyone happy about the causeway re-opening. I knew that Bert and Meg would be even happier when we told them our news, but before we had the chance, alerts started pinging on lots of pagers and mobiles across the room. The lifeboat volunteers all immediately abandoned their soft drinks, and ran out to the lifeboat station, followed by several locals, including Zen and Aidan.

'Bloody hell!' shouted Bert. 'It's the first tide since the causeway has re-opened, and it seems some daft bloody tourist has gone and got stuck and is in the rescue box.'

The atmosphere in the pub immediately took a nosedive. I'd learned in my brief time on the island that the locals held little sympathy with those that tried and failed to beat the tide. The rescue costs and dangers it put people in was something that was just not tolerated.

'No doubt it'll be a daft bloody Southerner,' cackled Maurice, who seemed to put the North/South divide line at Alnwick where even Geordies from Newcastle were southerners to him!

The chatter picked up again, but everyone was keeping an eye on their phones, waiting for news. Eventually, the door opened, and Zen and Aidan came into the pub, flanking a very damp, sheepish looking... Matt!

Oh My God, this couldn't be happening. I felt sick to the pit of my stomach. What the hell was he doing here? I looked at him, a pathetic, bedraggled figure stood between the two gorgeous men at his side. Zen was all dark, brooding good looks and Aidan, a testament to his blonde Viking heritage. What on earth had I ever seen in Matt? The atmosphere in the pub was suddenly colder than an arctic ice hotel. A stony silence had descended, and all eyes were fixed on the cause of so much unnecessary trouble. At least my own arrival hadn't got as far as an all-out rescue. Plus, I was sure Matt's highly proficient sat nav would have informed him that Lindisfarne was an island. Everyone in the room continued to glare at Matt, and the angriest face of all belonged to Zen.

'What have you brought him here for?' I gulped. 'Maybe it would have been better to take him to the hotel out of everyone's way.'

'That was the plan, Ellie Elf,' said Aidan, 'but chappie here insisted. Said he had come on a very important mission and that he needed to see you immediately.'

'I was all for sending him direct to Seahouses,' muttered Zen, looking mutinous.

'Can someone get me a brandy?' squeaked Matt. 'I'm probably dying of hypothermia here.'

'He's not, unfortunately,' growled Zen. 'He's been checked out; he was only in the rescue box briefly.'

'My car, it's ruined,' wailed Matt. 'And all my clothes were in it.'

'Tough,' said Bert. 'There's so many warning signs and you chose to ignore them. What was your bloody hurry? What was it that was so important that it couldn't wait?'

Matt glared at the older man, and then suddenly dramatically dropped down onto bended knee.

'This was what was important – luckily it was in my pocket,' he said, retrieving a ring and waving it about in front of the crowd.

I thought I might just pass out on the spot.

'Ellie, I've been so stupid.'

'You can say that again,' I muttered.

'You are the Yin to my Yang, the star to my moon, the Miss Bennet to my Mr Darcy.'

He was word perfect, damn it!

'Erm, just three words Matt, Karen the Cougar?'

'She was only after my money, it would seem...'

At that point, I just about fell to the floor in hysterics. *His* money? He meant my money surely, and he had spent most of it on that diamond he was waving about like a flipping fairy wand.

'Anyway, she's gone, and I promise I will never look at another woman ever again. Ellie Montague, will you do me the honour of becoming my wife?'

I felt the intake of breath in the room. The silence was deafening, and everyone's eyes were fixed on us – it took me back to that awful hotel when I had proposed to him. My cheeks were burning, and I felt quite sick, but I knew what I had to do. I held out the palm of my hand and gave Matt a sickly smile.

'Ring please,' was all I said, and Matt, obviously still in shock, placed it on my palm without question.

I glanced towards the back of the room and looked at Zen, who was as white as a ghost, his eyes glazed over with a red mist of anger, and he turned on his heels and almost ran out of the door. Meg came across and took me by the shoulders.

'Ellie pet, you don't have to do this. Give him the ring back and let's go home and talk about this over a nice cup of tea.'

'Thanks Meg, but I'm not quite finished yet.' I looked down at Matt, who was still kneeling on the floor. 'Matt, I wouldn't marry you if the future of civilisation depended on it.'

Another big gasp filled the void in the room.

'You are the worst kind of human being. You are greedy, unkind, and devoid of any feelings for anything or anybody but yourself. You basically robbed me of all my savings, including my inheritance from Granny Joan, which was meant to be the deposit on a house. So no, I won't marry you, but I will keep this ring. I will sell it and if it makes more than you owe me, I will give you back the difference.'

'He doesn't deserve that,' shouted Ethel. 'Don't give the creep a penny!'

Matt slowly got to his feet.

'You've got no right to keep that ring. It's mine. Give it back immediately,' he spat.

At that, Aidan stepped in. He towered over Matt and glared down at him.

'If Ellie says the ring will pay off *your* debts to her, then that's the end of the matter. We trust Ellie and every last one of us believes she is telling the truth.'

A hum of agreement went around the pub like a Mexican wave.

'In the brief time she's been on this island, Ellie has shown kindness towards people who were little more than strangers to her, but who are now friends. If you aren't happy with her keeping what is rightfully hers, maybe a night in the castle dungeon will give you time to think and reassess the

situation? You will be amongst friends, what with all the other rats down there.'
Matt looked defeated and not inclined to argue with the very muscular and authoritative Aidan.

'Keep it, Ellie. I wouldn't want to marry you either now that you have embarrassed me, but maybe you could pay for a night in the hotel out of the balance up front? My credit cards are in the car, which is currently floating in the sea.'
Cheeky grasping Matt to the end, but it would be worth it to get rid of him.

'One-night, cheapest room, no room service or fancy food, take it or leave it? It's more than you deserve.'

'I'm going there myself, so will deposit him, and make sure the Thompsons know the score,' said Aidan.

'Just before you both go; I've got an announcement to make and might as well tell you all when we're together. Bert, Meg, we wanted to tell you first but there's no time like the present.' I searched around the room. Zen wasn't there, but I was on a roll so continued. 'Zen and I are together, and I'm going to be staying on the island and sharing Imogen's flat above *Love Lindisfarne* and I, er, we, couldn't be happier.'

'I knew it!' said Meg. 'Didn't I say that to you Bert? You two couldn't keep your eyes off each other on Christmas Day. Ellie pet, we are delighted.' She threw her arms around me and gave me a big Meg hug.

'Our Amelia is going to burst with excitement,' smiled Don.

'Just make sure you remind her that Santa keeps his promises.' Aidan winked at Don as he steered Matt out of the door.

The atmosphere defrosted, the rescue crew returned safe and sound, and normal service resumed in the *Crab and Oyster*. Everyone wanted to buy me a drink, which I politely declined, because I needed to find Zen. I hoped my burst of bravado in telling everyone about us wasn't going to bounce back and hit me slap bang in the face.

CHAPTER 38

I left the pub. I knew that Zen had to be on the island as the tide was in, so I ran across to the café and looked up at his flat, but the place was in darkness and there was no answer when I rang the bell. I considered texting him but then suddenly had an overwhelming feeling that he would be down by the harbour, on the bench, looking over to Greater Reef. He had mentioned that he liked to go there sometimes when he needed to think, so I set off at a pace past the upturned boats, onto the shore and there he was. I slid onto the bench next to him. He didn't even acknowledge me – it was as if he were made of stone. I held out my hand and touched his arm, and he flinched.

'Zen, that wasn't what it looked like,' I whispered.

After a momentary silence, he turned towards me, his face clouded with an equal measure of anger and sadness.

'It looked pretty clear from where I was standing, Ellie. How could you? Apart from anything else, that man is a complete and utter wanker, and I'm not at all sorry for saying that.'

'I agree with you.'

'You do?'

'Yes, I've called him far worse myself.'

'So, why did you accept his proposal?'

'I didn't. I accepted the ring. There is a world of difference, and if you had stayed around, you would have heard the rest. Zen, we both have trust issues and it's not going to all be plain sailing for you and me, especially until we get to know each other better. What I can promise you, is that what I did in the pub was to prevent the need to stay in London very long, so that I could get back to Lindisfarne far sooner than I otherwise might have done. I want to be with you. I want to get to know you, and I want that now, not in however many months I might have had to stay away.'

It was time to just tell him the truth.

'I've been incredibly stupid. Matt owes me money, a lot, and I needed to try and get some of it back so that I can support myself on the island until the season gets going, when hopefully I'll find enough work to pay my way. You've just met him; you can see what he's like...'

'A slimeball just about covers it.'

'Yes, it does. Anyway, I assumed he was still with Karen, maybe even thinking of getting a place with her which would require money, and that it would be easier to get blood out of a stone than get back what was rightfully mine. It may have taken ages, but then this opportunity just presented itself and I grabbed it. I'm going to sell that bloody ring and hopefully, it will cover his debt, but even if it doesn't, that's the end of the matter. I don't want any more contact with him, ever.'

'Ellie, I could have helped. You could have done some work for me.'

'What as?'

'A coffee roaster, or grinder maybe.'

'You've just invented a non-existent job! Thanks, but it's far too soon for that kind of thing between us. I will accept the odd free coffee though, as long as I don't have to roast or grind it myself.' I smiled.

His phone pinged.

'Aren't you going to look at that message?'

'No, it can wait.'

'It might be important.'

He pressed the screen.

'It's from Aidan. Listen to this Ellie,' he said, suddenly rocking with laughter.

'Chambers, what a dark horse, you bloody hippie! Ellie is my favourite elf in all the world, and if you mess her about, you will have me to deal with. I've just limbered up my right hook by decking that weasel of an ex. He was coming on to Ivy. Can you believe the gall of the chap? He's retired to his small room, with a fat lip and his tail between his legs, the rat that he is. I'm escorting him off the island myself as soon as the tide is in.'

'I don't think we will see any more of Matt, do you?' I smiled.

'How does Aidan know about us?' Zen raised an eyebrow.

'Err, well, I might have just mentioned it to the whole pub. I've told you, I'm serious about us. You're not mad that I didn't wait for you to be there, are you? I think it was adrenalin that made me just blurt it out.'

'No, I'm not mad at all, Ellie. Actually, I feel a bit of a prat rushing off like that.'

'You'll get over it. Anyway, I have a proposition for you.'

'The answer is yes!'

'You don't know what I'm going to ask you yet.'

'I can but hope.' He winked.

'Let's go to London in Ravi. Now. I mean as soon as the causeway is open. We can collect what I need, say hello to my friends who are all going to love you, and be back here in time to spend our first New Year together on Lindisfarne.'

'Maybe not quite the proposition I hoped for, but okay. The sooner we go, the sooner we can get back.'

'Oh, and one other thing.'

'Yes?' He raised an eyebrow.

'You will need to share me with Nacho because he's the other man in my life.'

'I think I can manage that!'

'Glad to hear it, sharing is caring. It's freezing tonight.' I shivered.

Zen shuffled along the bench and wrapped his

arms around me. I could smell the espresso and pine as I buried my face into his dark curls.

'That's because it's a clear night. Look up at the sky. The stars are really out in force.'

I gazed upwards. The sky was filled with millions of twinkling stars, all jostling for position. It was then that I noticed *my* stars, the two brightest of all, side by side, as if they were holding on to each other. Suddenly, they appeared to merge into one big bright star.

'Oh, my goodness! I can't quite believe what I've just seen.' I blinked. 'Did you see that Zen? I think our stars have just aligned.'

'I think you could be right.' He smiled, drawing me in for the most romantic kiss I'd ever had.

'See all those stars Ellie? Think of each one as a kiss.'

I gently clutched his chocolate curls and drew his face towards mine, staring into the beautiful coffee bean eyes.

'Wow, that's a lot of kisses to get through. Perhaps we'd better make a start.'

'That might just have to wait.'

'What? Why?'

'Because look, Ellie!' He said excitedly, pointing upwards. 'Look!'

It started with a pale green band of light in the dark night sky, which deepened to a vivid lime, then moved fluidly across the horizon as it merged upwards into shades of blues, pinks and purples.

The sky danced, swirled and shape-shifted in an explosion of colours. What looked like shafts from spotlights dropped down vertically, cutting through the colours, and then bounced back up to the inky blue sky. It was truly mesmerising.

'Zen, pinch me because I can't believe I'm seeing this,' I gasped. 'It doesn't seem real.'

'Ellie.' He grasped my hand tightly. 'I've seen the aurora many times, but never quite like this – it's mind-blowing. This depth of display is so rare outside of the Arctic Circle. We'll probably never see it like this again in Northumberland.'

'We'll never forget it, and it seems so special seeing it with you,' I murmured, without taking my eyes off the sky.

And then, the brightest of shooting stars shot through the colours at speed in a perfect arc, leaving its silvery light trail behind it, as the colours in the sky began to fade and disappear into the darkness.

'I think the universe has just given us its blessing in spades, Zen.'

'I think you could be right and who are we to disappoint it?' He checked the time. 'We've got a little while until the tide turns and we're safe to cross the causeway, so let's make a start on those kisses right now.'

'Sounds good to me,' I murmured. And as I drew him towards me for the first of a million kisses, I silently thanked the universe for bringing me to Lindisfarne, the most magical of islands which I looked forward to calling my home.

AFTERWORD

I hope you have enjoyed your time in Northumberland via the pages of Love Lindisfarne - the story and characters of course are fiction; however, the setting is most definitely real.

Whilst there are no Lords of Lindisfarne or Bamburgh, the castles exist and are as stunning in the real world as in the book. The good news is that you can visit them both.

Lindisfarne Castle is looked after by the National Trust:

www.nationaltrust.org.uk/visit/north-east/lindisfarne-castle

Bamburgh Castle is open to the public too:

www.bamburghcastle.com

And of course, Alnwick Castle, which is mentioned and is owned by the Duke of Northumberland. You can visit both the ancient castle and the spectacular gardens and water features (but no hemlock please!)

www.alnwickcastle.com

Whilst there are no Reef Islands, you can visit the Farne Islands where you will find all the birds and wildlife mentioned:

www.nationaltrust.org.uk/visit/north-east/farne-islands

Or pop to the harbour in Seahouses to explore several options on sailing.

The Heritage Centre is a must to find out more about the amazing Lindisfarne Gospels and the history of the island:

www.lindisfarnecentre.org

You can find out more about visiting fabulous Northumberland from:

www.visitnorthumberland.com

I can't promise you will find any alpacas on Lindisfarne, but I can promise a beautiful location and some warm northern hospitality in the various hotels, pubs, cafes, and shops on the island. Lindisfarne is a unique, special place. Whether you visit for the spectacular views, the abundant wildlife, the rich history, or some time to quietly reflect and recharge, then you won't be disappointed. Finally, the tides and the causeway are most definitely real and if you visit Lindisfarne, please do check the crossing times, and don't end up in the rescue box like hapless Matt!

ACKNOWLEDGEMENT

It would be impossible to personally name every individual who has played a part in getting me this far in my writing endeavours. I'll start with a big general thank you to each and every one of my friends and family who have supported me on what can be a long and lonely journey to write a book – love you all!

To everyone at Northumbrian Writers Group – you have all been so instrumental in helping me progress, listening to my whacky ideas and throwing some of your own in the mix too. To Claire, our ever-positive tutor who keeps us right, corrects our commas and pushes us to write in genres we don't think we have in us (poetry!) Without this group my writing career would not have taken off.

To Kerri, my writing class buddy. Meeting you has inspired me beyond words. Kerri writes as Holly A Harvey and has become my friend, my mentor and has always been there with sage advice and words of wisdom. I wish her well in her own writing endeavours.

To Helen, my editor, who has turned my musings into a readable format and been so kind and supportive on the way. If you have a book to edit you can find her at:

helenhawkinseditorial.co.uk

To Sarah, the artist of the most fabulous cover that I had dreamed of since the beginning. It was important to me to work with other Northumberland creatives and Sarah was the perfect choice. I'm sure you will agree the cover is stunning.

sarahfarooqi.co.uk

To Rachel, another Northumbrian from remote Redesdale, who completed the cover with her wizard-like graphic design skills which finished off the book to its final stages.

And finally, to the writing tribe on social media platforms from where I have learned so much and have had immeasurable support from total strangers who are now writing friends. I wish you all well with your own writing journeys, no matter what stage you're at. Thanks too to the advance readers who freely spent time giving me their helpful views and suggestions – you are all shining stars!

ABOUT THE AUTHOR

Kimberley Adams

Kimberley Adams was born in Corbridge in Northumberland, and still lives in this gorgeous corner of the world. Passionate about the area, Kim usually sets her work in the northeast, and no matter how hard she tries to change location, it keeps returning like a homing pigeon!

Kim wrote her first published work (on an ancient thing called a typewriter) when she was a teenager writing happy ever after stories for teen magazines. Then as a poor student she progressed to writing short stories for women. Life and work then got in the way until the last few years, when Kim found a re-ignited love for writing, and this time from a laptop.

Love Lindisfarne is Kim's debut full novel. It started off its journey being shortlisted in a Penguin Michael Joseph Christmas Novel Competition, which gave Kim the impetus to carry on and finish it. Kim hopes that you have enjoyed escaping to

Northumberland via the pages, and perhaps will visit in person in the not-too-distant future – you won't be disappointed!

Say hello to Kim on Social Media...

Twitter X: @kim_adamsWriter

Facebook: Kimberley Adams-Writer

Instagram: love_lindisfarne

PRAISE FOR AUTHOR

'Ellie's voice is so warm and funny and cheeky and is just cheering me up on a cold, grey day...' *Literary Agent*

'We really enjoyed the humorous nature of the characters and they felt very relatable throughout. The opening scene is brilliant for this genre and the voice of the protagonist shines through...' *Book Publishers*

'What a setting – I obviously had to google it as I was so intrigued by the beauty and treachery of the landscape in the story, and obviously you weren't exaggerating. Amazing!' *Literary Agent*

'It's a lovely story and I hope at least some of it is true. The hard work, love and care you have put into it obvious.' *Beta Reader*

'I was sorry to leave Lindisfarne when it ended! It's got all the major elements, that for readers like me, make an ideal romantic comedy.' *Beta Reader*

BOOKS BY THIS AUTHOR

The Book Of Witty Women

Kim was shortlisted for the Comedy Women in Print Prize Short Story Competition earlier this year, and as a result you can find another of her stories, Go Your Own Way, about a Newcastle nana and her granddaughter, in The Book of Witty Women published by Farrago, September 2023.